A. STAUFER

HORSESHOE CURVE

Grif Teller

PENNSY POWER

STEAM AND ELECTRIC LOCOMOTIVES OF THE PENNSYLVANIA RAILROAD 1900-1957

BY ALVIN F. STAUFER

text writing by **BERT PENNYPACKER**   research by **MARTIN FLATTLEY**

copyright 1962 by Alvin F. Staufer

printed in the United States

first printing

Library of Congress Catalog No, 62-20878

Printed by The Standard Printing & Publishing Co., Carrollton, Ohio

FOREWORD

To know and understand the Pennsylvania Railroad is to grasp the significance of countless superlatives that literally become monotonous in their description of this Colossus among rail transportation plants. The uncanny genius and know-how of gifted men, stretching through the years since 1846, have effected the amalgamation of many railroad companies into the gigantic Pennsy— AMERICA'S LARGEST RAILROAD. Its 1946 Centennial Year statistics speak for themselves: 10,690 main track miles; 26,109 total miles located in thirteen states; $1,670,000,000 total financial capitalization; $2,981,000,000 total property investment; 4,848 locomotives (in 1924 there were 7556, and in 1910 the total was 6600); 240,293 freight cars; 7299 passenger cars; $983,800,000 total operating revenues; 63,812,000,000 gross freight ton miles; and 14,920,000,000 gross passenger train miles. The foregoing figures represent a late year of almost total steam-electric operation, with very few diesels.

And so it goes. Besides sheer overall size, PRR operations remain astronomical in scope, even when its coagulated segments are broken down and considered separately. Greatest main line traffic density in the World rolls over the four-tracked New York Division. Its fleet of tuscan red, Blue Ribbon Limiteds (and lesser trains) haul more passengers than any other railroad. Famed Enola Yard, near Harrisburg, with 145 miles of tracks and total car capacity of 9,900, clears 16,000 cars on a busy day. Ultra-modern and larger (12,000 car capacity) Conway Yard, just north of Pittsburgh, cost Pennsy $35 million and was opened in 1957 at the close of the steam era. All-time locomotive roster of nearly 25,000 engines tops all other railroads. So do electrification totals which include (1947 figures listing) 671 route miles, 2,248 total miles, 272 locomotives, and 432 electric multiple-unit passenger cars. No other railroad ever had 3,335 locomotives of just one wheel arrangement on its roster at one time— that was Pennsy's almost unbelievable 2-8-0 total back in 1924. Most other types were used by the hundreds, such as 601 Atlantics, 579 Mikados, nearly 700 Pacifics, 598 Decapods, and so on.

Successful bigness wasn't achieved without surmounting obstacles just as big, and to Pennsy men this meant standardization of everything from locomotive steam guages to entire boilers. The slogan was "DO IT YOURSELF", and it was done to the tune of ten thousand home-built engines planned and constructed at the World's largest railroad shops, Altoona, under the capable direction of men like Vogt, Gibbs, Wallis, and Kiesel. Compared to many railroads, Keystone methods spelled unconformity in capital letters. A retired special duty man who worked in the motive power department for many years, put it this way: "Our engines weren't very fancy, but they did a darn good job out on the road", and that sums it up very well.

Pros and cons regarding the railroad's methods and policies aren't hard to find. "The Standard Railroad of the World" (Pennsy) has often been stamped with an "ultra-conservative" brand name which doesn't exactly hold water. True, it is a highly unusual road with its own ways, but no other rail carrier had to plan for traffic volumes produced by the fabulous industrial and residential complexes served by Pennsy. The word "conservative" becomes a

Pennsylvania Railroad

myth when the record is bared: first steel passenger cars, outstanding electric locomotive development, pioneer in cab signals and trainphone, user of heaviest rail (152 lbs. per yard), inventor of hundreds of locomotive improvements and designs, first to scoop water on the fly, pioneer in position light signaling, classification hump yards and many other innovations throughout the years.

Regarding locomotive specifications quoted herein, the weights and tractive efforts are representative figures in every case, since it is impossible to record all minor changes that occurred through the years.

In preparing this volume we fully realize the magnitude of our task and the limitations imposed by a 320-page book. Our purpose is to preserve a living image of the glamor and excitement that was Keystone-heralded steam and electric railroading, together with a high degree of factual information.

This is by no means a technical manual, nor is it our purpose to editorialize or pass judgement upon operating successes or failures of various designs. It would of course be ridiculous to assume there were no lemons among nearly 25,000 locomotives, and where information scources pointed to shortcomings, the issue is faced squarely.

The years 1900 through 1957 were selected as our coverage span because they represented the Golden Years of Steam Railroading; the years that most of the well-remembered locomotives were built. The cut-off year of 1957 was steam power's last year of service, although electrics remain and will probably continue for many years. In this respect, some electric data has been included (in brief form) to bring that section to the current year of 1962. More importantly, steam memories and nostalgia are preserved herein, and may they live long in the hearts of those who knew and thrilled to stack music and steam whistles.

Alvin F. Staufer
Martin Flattley
Bert Pennypacker

Jim Shaughnessy

CONTENTS

Pennsylvania Railroad

PENNSY MEN

J. M. Symes

Chairman of the Board

A. J. Greenough

President

Axel S. Vogt

Mechanical Engineer from March 1887 to retirement in February 1919. He served as an advisor to Baldwin till his death, November 11, 1921.

One of the greatest factors directing the course of the Pennsylvania Railroad is that PENNSY MEN have always been RAILROAD MEN. While other railroads have had their share of stock manipulators, financiers, and politicians (with varying degrees of success), the Pennsy has had an unbroken line of management succession that was "up from the ranks". Greatest representation has been from the Engineering, Motive Power and Transportation depts.

STANDARDIZATION would not have reached such completeness or the Railroad such greatness had it not been for great presidents like W. W. Atterbury and Alexander J. Cassett. (both former motive power men).

In addition to the present President and Chairman of the Board, we have pictured here the five men most referred to in this volume. Three others who must be mentioned even though they served most of their time in the 19th Century are: John P. Laird, Master Mechanic 1862 - 1866, developed the balloon stack and Laird Guide; Theodore N. Ely, Chief of Motive Power 1893 - 1911 who put Science into locomotive development; and F. D. Casanave, Supt. of Motive Power Lines East from 1893 - 1901, who supervised the design of the famous D16 and other classes.

Enthusiasts of locomotives tend to look upon them as if they were living, self-created objects; this is not so. They are the product of MAN.

Thousands are responsible for the development of any given class of motive power but these are the ten leaders most responsible for Pennsy Power: W. W. Atterbury, John P. Laird, Alexander J. Cassett, Theodore N. Ely, F. D. Casanave, Axel S. Vogt, Alfred W. Gibbs, James T. Wallis, William F. Kiesel Jr., and J. V. B. Duer.

Pennsylvania Railroad

6

Alfred W. Gibbs

He succeeded W. W. Atterbury as General Superintendent of Motive Power for Lines East on January 1, 1903. Appointed Chief Mechanical Engineer July 1, 1911. Died in service May 19, 1922.

James T. Wallis

Born June 11, 1868 and entered service in 1891. Rose through the ranks from machinist to Chief of Motive Power (1920) and Ass't V.P. —Operations (1927). Died in service November 7, 1930.

William F. Kiesel Jr.

Born September 1, 1866 and entered service April 1888. Began as a draftsman and became Mechanical Engineer February 1, 1919. Served until retirement October 1, 1936 and died May 24, 1954.

J. V. B. Duer

Electrical Engineer 1920-1935. Chief Electrical Engineer 1935-1941. Assistant to Vice President of Operations 1941-1947.

Dec. 3, 1932, K4s' waiting to leave Washington, D. C. with Army-Navy football crowd.

Pennsylvania Railroad

Passenger engines at Altoona, 1916. The famous K29s is in the front of the second row.

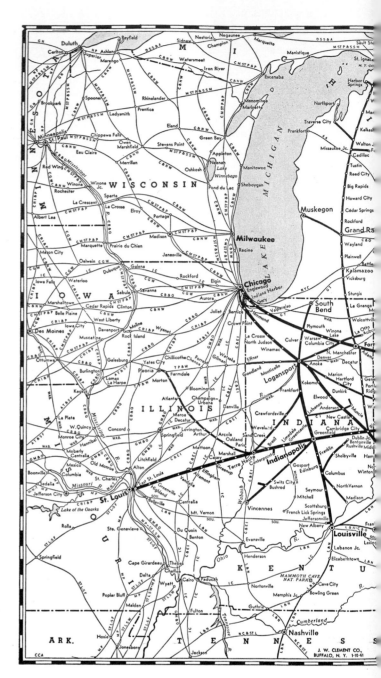

PENNSYLVANIA

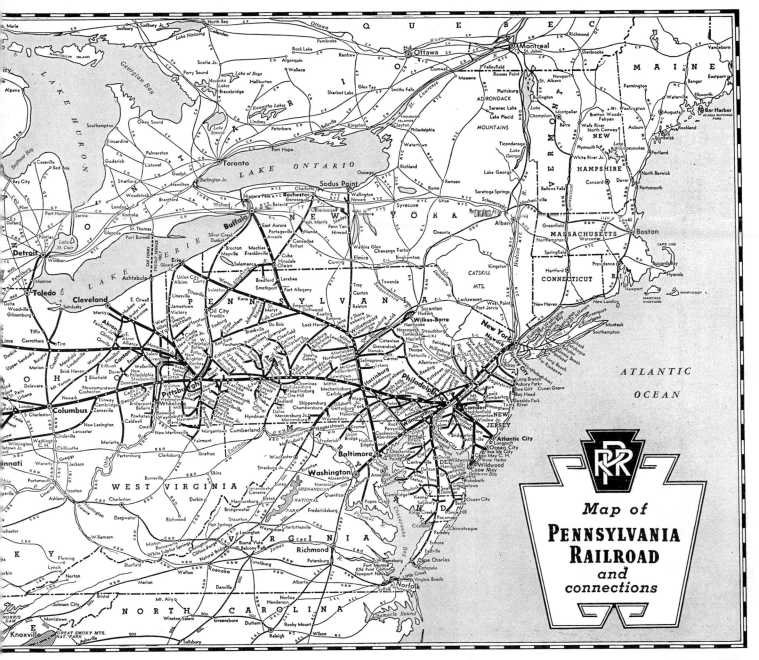

Map of **PENNSYLVANIA RAILROAD** and connections

RAILROAD

From upper left - N.Y. division signal bridge; Uniontown, Pa., Station; Penn Station, N.Y.; Conway Yards, Pa.; Zoo, W. Philadelphia; Mainline electric line; old 32nd st. enginehouse, Philadelphia.

ALTOONA SHOPS

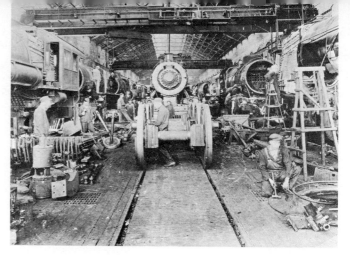

Juniata 1913, building Consolidations.

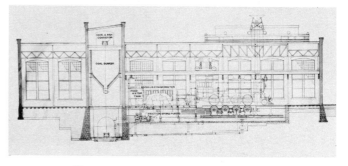

Testing plant with H8b shown.

ALTOONA— a magic word denoting the location of the World's largest and most famous railroad shop complex of all time. This fabulous home of standardized locomotives and cars had its beginning in 1850 when fledgling PRR was being projected westward across rugged Allegheny Mountain territory. Constant growth for more than one hundred years produced a labrynth of shops, foundries, and other facilities employing 13,000.

The three-mile long shop installation included four units— Twelfth Street Car Shop, Altoona Car Shop (2nd Street), Juniata Shops, and South Altoona Foundries. Shop yards covered an area of 218 acres, while 122 shop buildings contained 37 acres of floor space. There were 4500 machine tools and 94 overhead traveling cranes. One day's output included heavy class repairs on six locomotives, sixteen new box cars, ten new gondolas, and two cabin cars. Two new electric locomotives and two steam tenders were completed each week in addition to others being built, repaired and renovated.

Extensive and exhaustive testing facilities tried out everything from bolts to entire locomotives. The unique loco test plant was designed by Axel Vogt and operated as an exhibit at the Louisiana Purchase Exposition in St. Louis back in 1904. After removal to Altoona, it pointed the way toward successful motive power planning.

Two Altoona shops built new power and, for a time, they operated simultaneously. The original shop operated until 1904 and affixed badge plates to 2289 new engines. Newer Juniata Shops went into operation in 1889 and turned out 4584 new engines. Its final builder's plate went into T-1 number 5524 in the year 1946. The name "Juniata" was discarded in 1928 in favor of ALTOONA WORKS which included all facilities. Pennsy built ten thousand engines at Altoona and several other smaller shops. Including home-built locomotives, plus those bought from commercial builders, the grand total approached 25,000.

Juniata Shops and Altoona Works, about 1920.

HORSESHOE CURVE

Pennsylvania's multiple-tracked, east slope ascent of the Alleghany Mountains is still considered a brilliant engineering triumph, even though original construction dates back to the early 1850's. Westward from Altoona, the route staked out by J. Edgar Thomson and Herman Haupt, climbs 1,015 feet in eleven miles to burrow through a trio of adjacent tunnels at Gallitzin summit. Average gradient is nearly 1.8 percent.

Five miles west of Altoona, main line progress seems to be solidly blocked by towering mountains. The high shelf at Kittanning Point is rounded, revealing the spectacular sweep of the Horseshoe. The right of way is carried upon a high fill as it swings gracefully through the mountain-hugging curve to gain altitude. The Horseshoe is termed a nine degree curve, extending over a distance embracing 220 degrees. At a point two thousand feet on either side of curve center, it is 1400 feet across. From the northern calk (Kittanning

Point), tracks rise 122 feet as they traverse the entire curve and reach the extreme southern calk. Without the imagination to create a mammoth U-shoe, Thomson's efforts would have ended in failure. The only alternative would have been an impossible 8½-percent grade.

The scenic Curve has long been a big attraction for train passengers and ground level tourists. Rugged mountain beauty is further enhanced by Altoona's water reservoirs and park below the Horseshoe. At trackside, there's another park containing a K-4s locomotive. Multiple combinations of locomotives have always pulled and-or pushed trains upgrade. Coal dust laid thick along the tracks in steam days. Back around 1940, late-night Curve action was tremendous. Between 10:42 PM and 3:41 AM, twenty-eight famous Blue Ribbon passenger trains rounded the Horseshoe in both directions. Add to this the ever flowing freight trains and it became a show beyond equal.

BELPAIRE BOILER

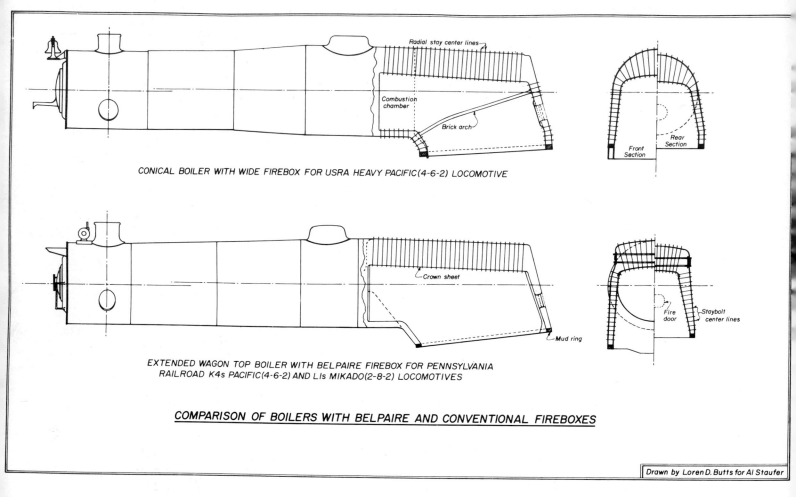

CONICAL BOILER WITH WIDE FIREBOX FOR USRA HEAVY PACIFIC (4-6-2) LOCOMOTIVE

EXTENDED WAGON TOP BOILER WITH BELPAIRE FIREBOX FOR PENNSYLVANIA
RAILROAD K4s PACIFIC (4-6-2) AND L1s MIKADO (2-8-2) LOCOMOTIVES

COMPARISON OF BOILERS WITH BELPAIRE AND CONVENTIONAL FIREBOXES

Drawn by Loren D. Butts for Al Staufer

Pennsy's most obvious trademark and deviation from the norm, was the Belpaire Firebox. Only one other large American railroad (Great Northern) used them to any extent. Though its popularity was limited in the U.S.A. it was certainly a favorite throughout the world.

It first appeared on a little H3 Consolidation in 1885. First passenger application was on a D class in 1889. The advantages of the Belpaire are its increased steaming and water capacity in a given grate area. Its construction, with firebox and boiler plates normal (parallel) to each other, makes "staying" (radial stay bolts) a simple proposition.

We do know that the Belpaire Firebox was more expensive to build, but we have no information as to its maintenance and servicing requirements.

An example of its increased capacity was when the N2s (of USRA design) was converted to N2sa by replacing the conventional firebox with a Belpaire. The total heating area was increased 252 sq. ft. while the grate area (fire size) remained the same.

The "hump-back" wagon-top boiler teamed up with the Belpaire Firebox to establish Pennsy's unique, yet handsome "look".

Pennsylvania Railroad

Line up of K4s waiting to return the throng from Bowie Racetrack.

Is there a lover of steam who wouldn't give plenty to wander through this display of new equipment, including the first M1, 4700. It's 1923, and the place — Philadelphia's 32nd St. Yards.

above—A Million Dollars a Dozen! awaiting the call to duty. below—Ready track at Meadows Enginehouse in 1927. Some have keystones—some not.

Yard goats were numerous and varied while Mallets barely got a toehold.

Dieselization was complete by the end of 1957. The last steam locomotives had pulled their final trains on Middle and Susquehanna Divisions and in New Jersey. Yet there remained one Belpaire boiler in steam – 0-6-0 switcher Number 5244 was leased to 14-mile long Union Transportation at New Egypt, N.J. That stalwart little B 6sb class holdout lasted until July of 1959, when she chuffed sedately into Camden terminal and was subsequently relayed across Delair Bridge to West Philly enginehouse on her final run. When 5244's fire was dropped, a 113-year steam power history that embraced nearly twenty-five thousand locomotives was at an end. PRR's last operational steamer was accorded a significant honor prior to being towed away to Modena, Pa., for scrapping in March of 1960. Her Juniata builder's oval was carefully removed, cleaned, and placed upon a wall in the railroad's Philadelphia headquarters building. Fate had decreed a plodding, six-coupled switcher of 1916 vintage to far outlast ultra-modern, high-horsepowered machines built during the 1940's.

Sizable herds of shifter classes (PRR men rarely called them "switchers") emulated standard designs and vast assortments were found throughout the motive power roster. For example, back in the month of July, 1924, there were 953 switchers in existence; twenty-three years later, in 1947, that total had dropped to 591 engines. Strongest emphasis was placed upon six-coupled locomotives, while 0-4-0 and 0-8-0 types were used less extensively. There were one or two classes of saddle tankers in use at all times, employed primarily as roundhouse goats, to move dead engines.

Although car assorting machines had been on the roster since about 1860, the first standard design wasn't built until 1869. The Altoona product was class F (later B 1), a neat looking 0-6-0T with squared, completely enclosed cab, a feature that prevailed through several early standard classes. Aside from ever-present Belpaire fireboxes and uncluttered neatness of look-alike planning, switchers quickly assumed eye-catching trademarks that remained practically unchanged for many years. Tenders had long, sloping after decks to allow better rear vision from cabs. Of course, this cut water supply, and, where increased water carrying capacity was needed, square tenders were used. Air reservoir tanks hung beneath cabs. Piston valve cylinders slanted inward at the top and outward toward the bottom until 1923. Classes A 5s and B 6sb built from that year on had re-designed cylinders featuring the opposite slant.

0-4-0's were generally considered an archaic shifter type used in modern steam years by private industrial plants and replaced almost everywhere by six-coupled power. This status quo didn't prevail on PRR where diminutive four wheelers had a definite place until diesels came. Class A 5s was actually built at Juniata, right along with heavy 0-6-0's, until 1924. A 5s was a junior edition of mammoth road power, having modern appliances and machinery details never associated with anyone else's 0-4-0's. PRR's mighty little quadrupet-drivered midgets were the most powerful human

interest magnets of the shifter family. Their stonghold was always around Philadelphia, where they wobbled up and down Delaware Avenue, while negotiating sharply curved industrial sidings and wharf tracks. They also sauntered confidently out of Frankford Junction terminal and shepherded cars along narrow streets and around corners where no other switchers dared tread. Although Philly Terminal Division was the 0-4-0's principal habitat, she also resided, in much smaller numbers, on New York, Maryland, and Philadelphia Divisions, plus the Central Region. A latter year A 5s outpost was Fort Wayne where engine number 730 was sent for roundhouse goat duties. Many 0-4-0's built prior to A 5s experienced relatively short life spans; in many cases they averaged about ten years per engine. Classes A 3, A 4, and A 5s were developed at approximately ten year intervals; many new engines received numbers of scrapped ones they replaced. Apparently, neither long-lasting construction and or usage was considered important for small, limited-service power—at least until deluxe edition A 5s engines were built. A brief run-down of Twentieth Century four-coupled shifters follows:

Class A 3 (originally class U). 84 engines built by Altoona and Juniata Shops from 1895 to 1905. First one was PW&B number 6, shop number (J)331, date 1-1895. Starting in 1901, some were built with saddle tanks and classed A 3a. Both classes had radial stay fireboxes, slide valve cylinders, Stephenson link motion, and used saturated steam. In 1929 there were still three A 3a's in existence.

History Center—Schenectady

Class A 4. 64 engines built by Juniata Shops from 1906 to 1913. First one was number 502, shop number 1584, date 10-1906. A 4 had Belpaire fireboxes, slide valve cylinders, Stephenson link motion, and used saturated steam.

Class A 5s. Largest of the 0-4-0's, 47 engines built by Juniata Shops as follows: 1916 - nine units; 1917 - 32 units; 1924 - six units. First one was number 511, shop number 3166, date 12-1916. A 5s had Belpaire fireboxes, piston valve cylinders, Walschaert valve gear, superheaters. The final six (road numbers 3890-3895) had re-designed cylinder slant and power reverse. In later years all A 5s received power reverse; many carried a reel of fire hose in a square metal box. Class 60-S-66 tenders held 5700 gallons and seven tons. Locomotive number 94 has been preserved at Northumberland enginehouse.

*6s 4035 switches P.R.S.L. R. D. C. cars at
amden, N. J.*

Philip R. Hastings

Pennsylvania Railroad

Cylinders	20"x 24"
Driver Diameter	50"
Steam Pressure	185 lbs.

New A5s working at Delaware Ave., Philadelphia.

Grate Area	38.3 sq. ft.
Engine Weight	131,750 lbs.
Tractive Force	30,190 lbs.

At this century's beginning, class B 4a (formerly class M) was Altoona's standard built 0-6-0. 96 were constructed from 1893 to 1904, and a few had saddle tanks as class B 4b. Improved six-wheelers replaced many B 4a's in years following 1900; whereupon secondhand dealers resold quite a few. None were thought to be in existence at this late date; however, the 1961 demolition of Phoenix Steel's Harrisburg plant provided a surprising revelation in the form of an old and rusted B 4a carcass, tucked away in a dark corner. Williams Grove Steam Engine Association was equal to the task of securing and preserving the B 4a relic.

Six coupled power was quite varied, with a wide assortment of classes, both standard and non-standard.. B 6 and B 8 class groups emerged as those acquired in greatest numbers and used the longest; however the B 6 family proved most successful. Although class B 4a was built until 1904, the year 1902 saw Juniata put together a new, big 0-6-0, class B 6, for Lines West. She was number 8026, shop number 942, the first PRR engine to have piston valve cylinders with inside steam passages—outside steam delivery pipes didn't appear on 0-6-0's until 1913. This was the prototype for over 350 shifters which were considered the standard heavy 0-6-0's of the system. Baldwin, Lima, and Juniata turned out 79 B 6 engines from 1902 to 1913; all were for Lines West. All but eleven were subsequently superheated to become B 6 s. They had Stephenson link motion, later received power reverse.

While class B 6 was a'building, Lines East's conservative-minded mechanical department planned a smaller and relatively simple 0-6-0, the B 8. A grand total of 247 were built by Baldwin, Juniata, and Lima from 1903 to 1913, first for Lines East only, then for both sections of the system. Lima's share was only three engines, road numbers 9565, 9566, and 9567, for GR&I. First B 8 engine was number 44, shop number (J)1162, date 5-1903. In the mid-1920's, as A 3a's were retired, a total of twenty-four B 8's were made into roundhouse goats by substitution of saddle tanks for tenders; this created class B 8a. Both classes had Belpaire fireboxes, slide valve cylinders, Stephenson link motion, and used saturated steam. Power reverse was added in later years, but they never got superheaters. Class 50-S-66 tenders held 5500 gallons and six tons. By 1947, there were still forty-four B 8 engines and twenty B 8a's on the roster. B 8a number 3131, assigned to East Altoona enginehouse, carried a keystone number plate on her smokebox front. It seems a minor mystery why so many were built; they were poor steamers, not modern, and light in weight. A plausible explanation is that B 8 was an economy engine, for countless light jobs where muscle and brawn were required.

Juniata Shops upgraded the highly successful B 6 blueprints in 1911 and turned out its initial ten B 6a class engines for Washington Terminal Company, in which PRR and B&O own half interests. In 1913 and 1914, Juniata built

A5s, refurbished by P.R.R. at Northumberland, Pa.   Don Wood

B 6sb, JUNIATA 1916, - 1940 with Futura Lettering

Cylinders	22"x 24"		Grate Area	61.6 sq. ft.
Driver Diameter	56"		Engine Weight	180,300 lbs.
Steam Pressure	205 lbs.		Tractive Force	36,140 lbs

fifty-five more B 6sa's which were the superheated version of B 6a's. The first B 6a was WT number 20, shop number 2284, date 8-1911. Major changes from B 6 included radial stay fireboxes with nearly twenty additional feet of grate area, and Walschaert valve gear. Outside steam delivery pipes were another innovation.

Class B 6sa was merely a prelude to its nearly identical blood-typed relative, the B 6sb, which came along in 1916 and was built to the tune of 238 engines. Juniata Shops worked on the project for ten years. First one was number 1652, shop number 3018, date 1-1916. Basic structural changes included Belpaire fireboxes, which added only five square feet of heating surface over that of B 6sa with radial stayed. The final 97 B 6sb's, built from 1923 to 1926, had power reverse and re-designed cylinder slant, as mentioned previously. All B 6sa-b's eventually got power reverse. Factor of adhesion was a very commendable 4.98. Class 60-S-66A tenders held 6350 sloping gallons and 6½ tons. B 6sa-b stayed pretty much east of Pittsburgh although some got west of that point after a few years. Five B 6sb's went to P-RSL as numbers 6076, and 6095 to 6098. B 6 classes were, by far, the best steam switchers Pennsy ever had. Engine number 1670 (B 6sb) has been saved at Northumberland.

Other 0-6-0 classes included a varied assortment, principally on Lines West. Most were old fashioned clunkers using saturated steam in slide valve cylinders and were retired by early 1930's. One exception was USRA class B 28 s

B 5 and B 5a - about 30 engines, converted from 2-8-0 classes I (H 1) and H 2a.

B 7 and B 7a - (Lines East) about 25 engines, converted from 2-8-0 classes H 3, H 3a, and H 3b. Out by 1914.

B 21 - ex-Vandalia, road numbers 8795 and 8796, built be Pittsburgh, 1893.

B 22 - ex-Vandalia, road numbers 8783 to 8793, built by Baldwin and Alco (Schenectady), 1899 to 1902.

B 23 - ex-Vandalia, road numbers 8770 to 8782, built by Alco (Schenectady), 1903 to 1907. Some were sold to Norfolk & Portsmouth Belt Line where they lasted until late 1940's.

B 28 s - USRA design, 30 built by Alco, 1918 and 1919. Radial stay fireboxes, piston valve cylinders, Baker valve gear, power reverse, superheated. Lasted until early 1950's. Many were sent East in late years, some to Wilmington, where they saw little service.

B 29 - 115 built by Alco, 20 built by Lima between 1903 and 1913. First engine number 7369, Alco (Schenectady), date 1-1903. This was probably Lines West version of the B 8. Class B 29 had two sand domes, radial stay fireboxes, slide valve cylinders, Stephenson link motion, used saturated steam, never got power reverse, and was completely gone by early 1930's.

There were also a few odds and ends classified B 31 to B 35.

Eight-coupled switching locomotives didn't quite achieve ladder-track prominence that was usually associated with this wheel type elsewhere. The principal class numbered only 90 units and failed to produce expected operating benefits. As a result, many 0-8-0's spent considerable leisure time on the sidelines while more dependable 2-8-0's handled the work (Decapods also did much hump shoving). The Kiesel-planned C 1 class was a handsome and well-proportioned example of standard design as it was practiced in the 1920's. Among 0-8-0's, C 1 was a pachyderm-sized example of its breed, the largest two-cylinder engine of her type anywhere. Juniata Shops built all ninety. Road numbers 6550 to 6599 were out-shopped in 1925 while numbers 6600 to 6639 were added in 1927. Three others were built for Washington

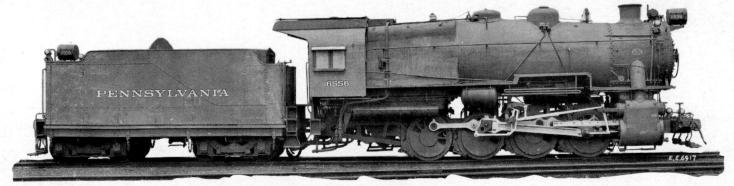

C 1 0-8-0 SWITCHER, JUNIATA 1925

Cylinders	27"x 30"		Grate Area	61.75 sq. ft.
Driver Diameter	56"		Engine Weight	278,000 lbs.
Steam Pressure	250 lbs.		Tractive Force	78,107 lbs.

HH 1 MALLET ARTICULATED, AMERICAN LOCOMOTIVE CO., MAY, 1911.

Cylinders	27"x 28"	Weight on Drivers	437,500
Drivers	56"	Weight of Engine	482,500
Steam Pressure	160 lbs.	Tractive Force	99,144

CC 1s MALLET ARTICULATED COMPOUND, BALDWIN 1912

Cylinders	25 & 39x30"	Weight on Drivers	408,700 lbs.
Drivers	56"	Weight of Engine	408,700 lbs.
Steam Pressure	205 lbs.	Tractive Force	82,716 lbs.

HC 1s MALLET ARTICULATED SIMPLE LOCOMOTIVE, JUNIATA 1919

Cylinders	30½ x 32"	Weight on Drivers	553,000 lbs.
Drivers	62"	Weight of Engine	586,500 lbs.
Steam Pressure	205 lbs.	Tractive Force	147,640 lbs.

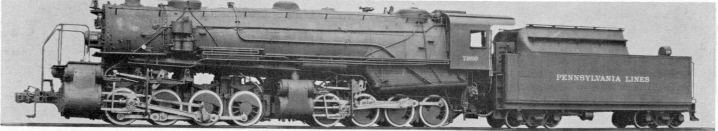

CC 2s MALLET ARTICULATED COMPOUND, BALDWIN 1919

Cylinders	26 & 40x28"	Weight on Drivers	458,150 lbs.
Drivers	51"	Weight of Engine	458,150 lbs.
Steam Pressure	225 lbs.	Tractive Force	99,792 lbs.

Terminal Company. Grate area and driver size were similar to those on B-6sb although about everything else was greatly expanded; many dimensions equalled those found on road power. Class 70-S-66 square tenders held 7300 gallons and 15½ tons. In line with changed classification policy of the time, small letter "s" was omitted from this class, since superheaters had long been standard equipment. Unsatisfactory design features turned up in the form of rigid frame and axle construction. These permitted very low speeds, even causing frequent derailments on wavy yard tracks.

Rigidity was also considered a contributing factor to firebox staybolt failures which raised maintenance costs. Short cut-off of 62½ percent was another drawback; however this was later adjusted. C 1 engines were scattered all over the system, usually at large freight yards. Enginehouse foremen were usually reluctant to fire them up unless business was extremely good and no other power, such as Consolidations, was available. All ninety C 1's were in existence by 1947, and most lasted until diesels came.

There were a very few old 0-8-0's on Lines West many years ago. Class C 29 was converted from 2-8-0's of H 1, H 2, and H 2a classes. C 30 engine number 8434 was a saddle tanker built at Columbus shops in 1895; C 31 engine number 8542, another 0-8-0T, was a Baldwin product of 1892.

In the year, 1947, switcher classes looked like this: A 5s 46; B 6 9; B 6s 69; B 6sa 50; B 6sb 233; B 8 44; B 8a 20; B 28s 30; C 1 90.

Rough and tough Central Region topography spoke loudly for training-lugging merits incorporated into mallet-type engines. However, after experiments with a handful of four-cylindered power, they went into obscurity and Pennsy trains labored uphill without the aid of four cylinders per boiler. Mallets were as follows:

CC 1s - 0-8-8-0 engine number 3397, Baldwin 1912, Lines East.

HH 1s - 2-8-8-2, engine number 3396, Alco, 1911, Lines East.

HC 1s - 2-8-8-0, engine number 3700, Juniata Shops, 1919, Lines East

CC 2s - 0-8-8-0, engine numbers 7250 7332 7335 7649 7693 8158 8183 9357 9358 9359, Baldwin, 1919, Lines West.

All except HC 1s were planned as pushers. The two Lines East pushers operated principally out of Altoona on the Big Hill; number 3397 ended its days on the hump at Pitcairn Yard. CC 2s pushed on Cleveland & Pittsburgh, Erie & Ashtabula, and Panhandle Divisions. It wound up around Columbus where all ten CC 2s lasted until the late 1940's, hauling transfer drags across town and also working hump assignments.

HC 1s was one of the most unusual experimental loco-

8342 A3s, was rebuilt from A3 (originally built as C & P 426, Juniata 1895). She is shown here outside Logansport, Ind. enginehouse.

above—A3 was built at Altoona in May 1896. Note the oil light on the tender.

below—A5s 3895, one of the latest of this class, stands in Philadelphia. Some were equipped with firehoses.

motives PRR ever had. When built it was billed as the largest engine in the World and was packed off to Atlantic City, as an exhibit at a Master Mechanic's convention. Number 3700 was intended for head-end work over Pittsburgh and Eastern Divisions; but its tremendous drawbar heave-ho was simply too much for many freight cars of the day with older styles of draft gear. It wound up in pusher work and, along with CC 1s and HH 1s, was gone by the early 1930's. Although HC 1s possessed many outstanding features that were later used on modern articulateds built elsewhere, she wasn't too successful. The steam distribution was figured wrong, plus high cylinder maintenance costs. This added up to a costly operation which the railroad didn't like. Although most railroads turned to articulateds for similar mountain climbing work, PRR's trials apparently showed the lumbering, two-cylindered I 1s Decapod's power close enough to desired levels, at reduced operating costs. All of which explains why 598 I 1s engines were built and four-cylindered ones forgotten. Had HC 1s been a big success, the PRR would probably have had a large fleet of articulateds such as B&O, N&W, and C&O. It's interesting to think about.

During World War II, power-hungry Pennsy bought six Y 3 class 2-8-8-2's from Norfolk & Western. These became PRR numbers 373 to 378, class HH 1. One or two operated on transfer and hump assignments out of Enola; all ended up at Columbus, not far from their former owner's property.

7834 class B29, built at the Pittsburgh Work of the American Locomotive Co. 6-1906. All of this class were gone by 1931.

This B6 had 56" drivers and rolled out of Lima in 1913.

B6sa sports new lettering in this 1940 pose. She is one of the few Pennsy built (Juniata 1913) engines that lacked the Belpaire Firebox.

B6sb tender, rebuilt for the burning of fuel oil while working in the Baltimore area, 1939.

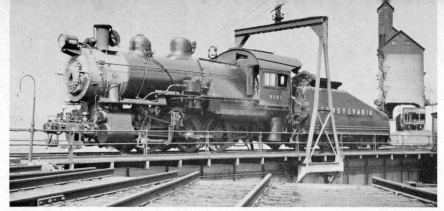

The hostler of this finely polished B6sa alights to turn the table towards the ready track for the afternoon crew to take charge. Chester, Pa., 1941.

B28s, 9215 is one of the few "non Pennsy" engines owned by the Railroad Built by Alco, she is of USRA design.

B8 at West Philadelphia about 1910. Note the oil head light, flangless (blind) main-driver and clerestory cab roof vent.

H9 & B6sb combine talents to pull small "DRAG" from Camden yard to Broadway Station. 3597 couldn't quite make it alone.

B6 switching near P R S L engine terminal, Camden, N. J. Note the Reading loco, smoking in the background.

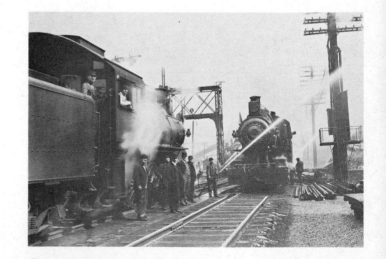

left, 0-6-0 "goat" looks alive in steam.
right, A group of B8's show off their fire equipment.

B8 15 on the "table" about 1912. Note the outside steam pipe forward at the cylinder saddle.

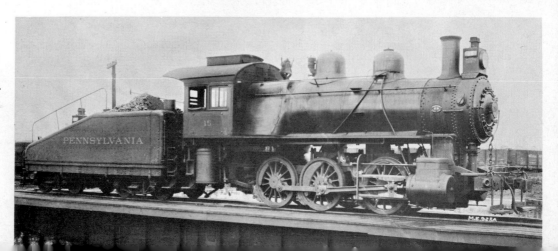

Pennsylvania Railroad

B8a 2788 "tank" was built by Baldwin in 1905 as class B8. She is shown here, freshly converted, and assigned to Altoona Shops.

right, B6sb *is backing towards the Camden coal chutes.*

below, Easy *firing, good tracking and snug cabs made the B6sb's favorite of the crews. They were seldom run fast as they rode like "bouncing corks."*

Don Wood

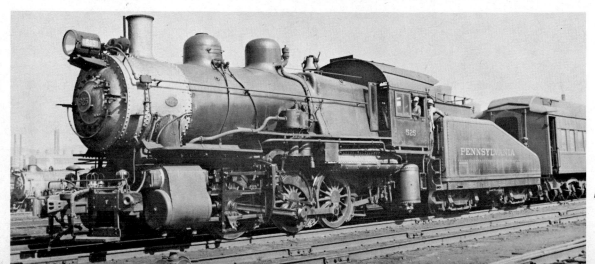

Milton A. Davis

Harrisburg, Pa. about 1922. B6sb 2382 is making up a passenger train.

A picture wasn't a picture in the good o'l days unless a few of the boys got in. The setting is Chicago in 1926. The yardmaster comes out and poses with the crew of their newly acquired "transfer" engine C 1,6551.

No. 18 is one of the three C-1's built by Juniata for jointly owned (PRR&B&O) Washington Terminal. Slope back tenders were the only noticable difference.

Brute strength and rugged beauty were the only virtues of these mammoth switchers. The 0-8-0 type was a nationwide favorite, but on the Pennsy they were disliked. Sheer size (as large as road engines) contributed to their undoing.

It was a common Pennsy practice to paint the rods, valve gear, and marker lights a flat white on new power for official portraits. They were also left a soft gray and the shiney black was not applied till later. 6556 is "so" painted.

Norfolk & Western Y3 class, before and after being purchased by the Pennsylvania. May 1943.

After ten years of sluggish business, Pennsy was hit by World War II traffic with a vengeance. Her desperate need of power created a flurry of building and buying. Pennsy's relationship to the N&W was more than slight (40% stock ownership to this day) so it was natural to turn to her for power. N&W could spare but six old 1919 circa Mallets. They worked hump and transfer chores at Enola before being sent west to Columbus, Ohio.

Pennsylvania Railroad

Rail Photo Service, G. Grabill Jr.

CC2s 7649 moves a coal transfer in Columbus, Ohio, 1933. The built up coal bunkers were sloped in for visibility purposes.

26

Like everybody else, Pennsy had their fling with mallets, but after the smoke and dust had cleared away it was the good ol' two cylinder power that did the chores. The railroad's reasoning was that their topography was simply too rugged for any single unit, so why have costly four cylinder engines when double heading was inevitable anyway. All Pennsy's Mallets except one, HC 1s 3700, were planned as pushers. It is interesting to contemplate what would have resulted if the Road had gone all-out on articulateds.

right, The fearful face of CC1s, 3397.

Pennsylvania Railroad

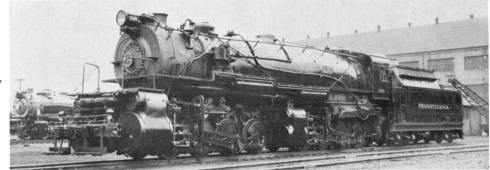

CC2s on display at Columbus, Ohio for a fan trip.

Milton A. Davis

CC2s at Columbus, Ohio

Jack Pearson Collection

Alco's lone contribution to Pennsy's articulated fleet. She is shown here at Altoona.

Smithsonian Institute

F CLASS 2-6-0 MOGULS

Fast freight moved behind big 2-6-0's at the turn of the Century

Christmas day, 1912, found Charles Chaney down trackside preserving this scene for posterity. F3c 5163 is hustling a typical freight of that period.

Most early Moguls (2-6-0 Type) were a wide and varied assortment of non-standard designs inherited from subsidiary railroads which Pennsy acquired. It wasn't until the year 1895 that the railroad's own mechanical engineers inked 2-6-0 specifications on their drawing boards. The succeeding ten years brought forth 305 Moguls, in six different classes, to burnish Keystone rails. They turned out to be unusual and ambidextrous during their many faceted lifetime of service.

On the average railroad you'd normally expect the 2-8-0 Type to succeed the smaller Mogul, but such was not the case here. Class F 1 Moguls were built to out-pull and out-run H 3 class Consolidations. The 2-6-0 went forward from its fast freight hauling duties to later become a heavy suburban passenger job. Of course its later life was confined to the usual hum-drum chores of local freight peddler. This locomotive type was just about extinct by the late 1920's. It was one of the earliest wheel arrangements to become non-existant and probably one of the least known and remembered.

The line-up of class "F" engines was as follows:

Class F 1 - 33 built by Juniata, 1895 to 1897
Class F 1a - 89 built by Altoona and Juniata, 1897 to 1901

Class F 2 - 4 built by Juniata, 1895-96
Classes F 3, F-3b, and F 3c - 179 built by Altoona, Juniata, and Baldwin, 1901 to 1905.

Prior to 1895 there had been little or no basic improvements in freight power designs. Ten year old class R (later H 3 and sub-classes) formed the backbone of heavy main line tonnage toters. Naturally something bigger was in order, but this was one time the mechanical slight-of-handers at Altoona did the unexpected. Instead of unfurling a larger Consolidation blueprint from a tophat, they had a mammoth new 2-6-0 design tucked up their garter-banded shirtsleeves. The F 1 Mogul class had just about bigger everything — cylinders, driving wheels, steam pressure, weight, and pulling power. Its large Belpaire boiler was somewhat similar to the ones used on class D 16b Americans, consistent with development of high-powered boilers of the day. Tractive effort of 28,400 pounds was sixteen percent greater than that of H 3b Consols, and steam pressure of 185 pounds was up a healthy thirty-five pounds. Driver size of sixty-two inches was a whole foot larger, and was eventually to set the standard in 1907 with class H 8, for driver size on hundreds and hundreds of freight engines.

A further Consol-Mogul comparison reveals that 2-6-0's 127,000-pound weight on the six drivers was ten percent

28

above the H 3b's weight on eight. Classes F 1 and F 1a were good steamers and speedy runners. They quickly took over much of the fast freight work, leaving slow drag assignments to smaller-drivered 2-8-0's. Where grades were favorable, particularly along fairly level Eastern divisions, the Moguls could handle up to 2700 tons, which was considered excellent for their day.

Class F 2 consisted of just four Juniata-built, two-cylinder experimental compounds having 20 & 29x28" cylinders. 205 pounds boiler pressure and 35,847 pounds tractive effort. Each engine featured a different steam distribution system, designed by Von Borries, Golsdorf, Richmond Locomotive Works, and Pittsburg Locomotive Works. These "super moguls" were actually planned at about the same time as class F 1, and as might be expected, they were flops. This led to normal, single expansion cylinders used on F 1a engines.

During the five-year period of F 1 and F 1a construction, development proceeded rapidly upon much heavier drag freight Consolidations which far surpassed Moguls in power. PRR operating men however wanted to continue using higher-drivered Moguls to haul the fast freights. Toward this end, the year 1901 saw souped-up, bigger-boilered 2-6-0's having 205 pounds boiler pressure and greater pulling power. Three classes were included in this category, each having differing fireboxes, as follows:

    Class F 3 — narrow Belpaire
    Class F 3b — wide, radial stay
    Class F 3c — wide, Belpaire

At least two F 3c engines got superheaters in later years making them class F 3sc. All Moguls had square-topped slide valve cylinders and Stephenson link motion. The 62-inch driving wheel and 205 pound steam pressure were carried forth to become standard on hundreds of larger Pennsy engines that followed the next twenty years.

Some Moguls assumed a spit-and-polish character when various members of their clan were gold-striped and equipped for passenger service. They had the guts and speed to outperform Americans on certain heavy local runs, where

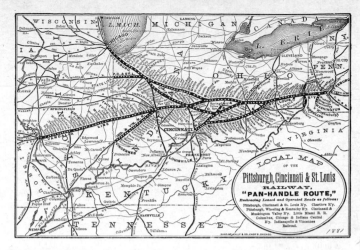

frequent stops and fast schedules prevailed. Such runs operated out of points like Philadelphia, Baltimore, Harrisburg, and Pittsburgh.

Practically all 2-6-0's were built for service along Lines East routes, with only a few on Lines West. Grand Rapids & Indiana received six F 3c's. There were also a number of non-standard Moguls which formed the principal freight power of Vandalia, which later became the St. Louis Division. These 2-6-0's were built during the early years of the Twentieth Century by various Alco plants, and were classified F 24, F 25, and F 27, some later being superheated. By July of 1924 there were still 232 Moguls on the roster, most of them in F 3 class groups. None were assigned to passenger work, fifteen were listed as switching engines, and the balance were used in local freight service. Moguls didn't last long after that; they bowed out of existence during the late 1920's. Pennsy's roster of December, 1929, showed none.

A brief postscript to the above concerns Waynesburg & Washington narrow gage 2-6-0 locomotive 9687, which has been saved for more than twenty years as a historical relic. For many years it was located in Canton, Ohio, later brought to Northumberland, Pa., and then sent to Waynesburg, Pa., for display.

F3c, with plow, during a blizzard.

Pennsylvania Railroad

F 1a 2-6-0 FREIGHT LOCOMOTIVE, ALTOONA 1898

Cylinders	20x28"	Weight on Drivers	127,000 lbs.
Drivers	62"	Weight of Engine	145,000 lbs.
Steam Pressure	185 lbs.	Tractive Force	28,406 lbs.

F1a prepares to leave Meadows, N. J. with a local freight. Mogul's were Kings of the "Turn of the Century" freight power.

F3b, Baldwin 1901, prepares to leave with an "extra" on the Philadelphia Division about 1904.

30

Dec. 11, 1923, Washington, Pa. 9685, odd F narrow gauge, waits with her consist of open-end coaches.

Martin Flattley Jr.

Paul W. Prescott

left, 8279 shows Lines West influence with centered headlight and automatic bell ringer. She was built by Juniata in 1898.

below, All coaled up and set to go, 923 poses on the icicle laden Harrisburg turntable.

Pennsylvania Railroad

31

H CLASS 2-8-0 CONSOLIDATIONS

In 1924 Pennsy had 3,335 "Consols" on the roster.

Hundredfold multiples of various standard-designed wheel arrangement types were literally dwarfed, numerically speaking, by thousandfold multiples of the Consolidation (2-8-0) Type. This overpowering emphasis upon the 2-8-0 occurred during rapid growth and booming business years, coincidental with times when "Consols" were the principal heavy freight haulers. During the early Twentieth Century years, new 2-8-0's for Pennsy rolled off erecting shop floors in numbers comparable to a much later-dated LaGrange, Illinois out-pouring of diesels for all railroads. Most of these engines were still on the roster by the year 1924, when the Consolidation head count was no less than 3,335. Not only did this represent forty-four percent of the entire motive power inventory numbering 7,556 units, but it probably exceeded the rosters of most other railroads at any given time. For example, just consider two of PRR's Consolidation classes, H 6a and H 6b, which embraced a total of 1,835.

Consolidation development ranged in size from the first standard design of 1875 (balloon-stacked class I, later H 1), which weighed nearly forty-six tons and developed 20,400 pounds tractive effort, to Belpaire-boilered H10s class of 1913 vintage, topping the scales at nearly 124 tons with a pulling power of 53,200 pounds. Although early versions of the type were real heavyweights among the species, modern day 2-8-0 classes didn't reach beyond the medium sized category. "Consols" performed work in all types of freight service through the years, not to mention occasional passenger train assignments. They were main line freight power for nearly fifty years; 2-8-0's actually did main line honors along some level routes until the latter 1920's. The type gradually became the prime light utility engine, working local freights, branches, work trains, or what have you. "Consols" also performed considerable switching and yard work, since PRR's efforts in the direction of a hefty 0-8-0 type weren't exactly successful.

Although the first 2-8-0 road engine having a separate tender is generally considered to have been assembled by Lehigh Valley Railroad's Master Mechanic, Alexander Mitchell, in the year 1866, PRR actually had a 2-8-0 tank engine as early as 1864. This was an Altoona-innovated rebuild for Allegheny Grade pusher work. Its boiler came from a ten year old (Baldwin-built) eight-wheeled monstrosity named "Bedford."

Aside from its famous keystone-shaped emblem, the squared-off Belpaire firebox on most Pennsy steam locomotives has been the railroad's familiar trademark of motive power recognition for many years. It all began way back in 1885, when the first Belpaire was lowered onto the underframes of a little class R (later H 3 and sub-classes) Consolidation. These squat, fifty-seven tonners were built in large numbers for more than ten years, and served very successfully all over the railroad.

They ranged from class H 3 to H 3e, all having 20" x 24" cylinders, dinner plate-sized drivers measuring just fifty inches, 140 to 150 pounds boiler pressure, and tractive efforts ranging from 22,848 pounds to 28,560 pounds. In April of 1892, PFW&C (Pittsburgh, Fort Wayne and Chicago) class H 3 locomotive Number 263 hauled a forty-car trainload of grain from Chicago to Girard Point, Philadelphia. Train tonnage was around two thousand, and helpers were used at several points east of Pittsburgh.

Years after all H 3 engines were supposedly out of existence, one was accidentally discovered, tucked away on the property of a stone quarrying company near Birdsboro, Penna., to whom it had been sold years ago. A search of records revealed the nondescript dirty straggler as the former Number 1187- a number held by an H 9s class engine at the time. PRR quickly bought the H 3 back, restored her at Altoona for historical purposes, and exhibited her, together with some much newer steam power at New York's Worlds Fair held during 1939 and 1940. The diminutive Consol remains intact, stored at Northumberland, Pa.

An H 3 replacement was long overdue by the late 1890's, when classes H 4, H 5, and H 6 were designed as more-or-less trial balloons. Built in small to moderate quantities, the type was assuming bigger proportions and familiar shapes which were destined to blossom forth into a post-1900 "Consol" population explosion that broke all records. Towering domes and stacks were sunken deep into fatter boilers (which were more than sixteen inches larger in diameter) and total engine length was nearly nine feet greater. Cylinders had grown to 22 x 28" (H 5 had 23½ x 28"), boiler pressure hit 205 pounds (H 5 had 185 pounds), and drivers had grown a full half foot over class H 3, to fifty-six inches. Tractive power soared to an average of 42,000 pounds with increased weight. The 2-8-0 was on its way in earnest. A brief, factual run-down of the three classes follows:

H-4 - Lines West design, built principally for PFW&C by Juniata Shops between 1897 and 1901. First engine Number 6, shop Number 441, date 9-1897. Radial stay, narrow firebox, slide valves, Stephenson gear.

H-5 - Heaviest of three classes, only a few built for pusher work. Juniata Shops, 1898. First engine Number 872, shop Number 485, date 4-1898. When built, they were too large for the turntable at Altoona. Radial stay, narrow firebox, slide valves, Stephenson gear.

H-6 - Lines East design, 101 built by Baldwin and Juniata Shops between 1899 and 1901. First engine Number 673, shop Number 560, date 1-1899. Belpaire, narrow firebox, slide valves, Stephenson gear. Some rebuilt with superheaters and wide Belpaires to class H-6s, cylinders 23" x 28", pressure 190 pounds.

Consolidations to class H 6, inclusive, had narrow fireboxes which became quite difficult to fire properly as locomotive size increased. Class L (D 16a) Americans had successfully inaugurated wide fireboxes on passenger engines back in 1895, but it wasn't until the year 1901 that freight power got them. Class H 6 was revamped to include the principal modification of a wide Belpaire firebox that straddled the rear drivers, increasing grate area by a generous forty-seven percent (33.3 versus 49 sq. ft.). This produced the wonderful steaming H 6a, THE freight engine of all freight engines of her day. So successful was this class that the railroad went whole hog with it during booming

Publicity photo of H9s 3526 with the Keystone painted in.

traffic years of the early Twentieth Century. It was built in fantastic quantities and used in every nook and cranny of the System. Between the years 1902 and 1905, Baldwin alone rolled 1,017 of them through its Hamilton Street erecting shop doors in the Quaker City.

In 1905, the design was again altered to include piston valve cylinders and Walschaert valve gear, making class H 6b. Except for the larger fireboxes on classes H 6a-b, major dimensions of class H 6 were retained throughout with only minor variances. Baldwin, Juniata Shops, and Alco forces put together a grand total of 1,835 H 6a and H 6b engines between 1901 and 1913, with Baldwin doing the lion's share. Road numbers were scattered, as usual, with the first engines being H 6a Number 1890 (BLW 5-1901) and H 6b Number 2811 (BLW 10-1905). A prominent feature on classes H 4 through H 6b were the air reservoir tanks mounted underneath roomy, double-windowed cabs. H 6a-b had vanished from the roster by 1934, although superheaters gave some a longer lease on life as classes H 6sa and H 6sb. The latter class was longest lasting of all, retained because newer engines were too heavy for certain light branchline assignments. H 6sb's chuffed along with local freights until the late 1940's (there were still 117 of them in July of 1947). The H 6sb as we remember it, was strictly a little modernized gem with power reverse, pilot-mounted air tank, and some had slightly larger cylinders measuring 23" x 28."

Two notable Alco experimentals, offering big boilered concepts, arrived on the scene in September of 1905. Classified H 28, locomotive Number 2762 was assigned to Lines East and Number 7748 was sent to Lines West for testing. Total heating surface was far above the accepted H 6a-b figure of 2844 square feet. H 28 boasted 3779 within the bulging contour of its fat boiler and radial stay firebox. It also had piston valves and Stephenson gear. Most other specifications were, of course, enlarged. H 28 was a companion to (more-or-less) similarly conceived big versions of passenger power delivered to Pennsy by American at the same time, (two Atlantics and two Prairies). These three couples played a part in subsequent development of larger power, leading, in this case, to the H 8 class.

Even though H 6b construction lasted until the year 1913, work had begun on larger main line freighters in 1907, when Juniata Shops built the first H 8 class engines. The initial Altoona-centered output included twenty-five H-8's for Lines East and twenty-seven nearly identical H 8a's assigned to Lines West. H 9 and H 10 class groups, designed and first built in 1913, represented the final, and largest, phase of Consolidation development. All three class groups shared nearly identical boilers, which were considered large enough to supply steam for use in cylinders featuring one-inch jumps in piston diameters between each succeeding numbered class grouping. Some common dimensions used throughout the series included 62-inch drivers, 205 pounds boiler pressure, and Belpaire fireboxes having 55.2 square feet of grate area. Alco, Baldwin, Juniata Shops, and Lima all shared in constructing a grand total of 1,206 H-8, H-9, and H 10 engines (Lima built class H 10's only) between 1907 and 1916. Most H 8 saturated classes were eventually converted to other classes at Altoona by additions of superheaters and-or larger cylinders.

Early models of Crawford and Street underfeed stokers were applied to some H 8sc and H 10s engines when built, but were later removed as unsatisfactory. A few H 10s again got efficient Standard stokers during World War II years. Although a few Consols sported power reverse during the late 1920's, this appliance didn't become standard equipment until the late 1930's. When out-shopped, 2-8-0's had pointed cowcatchers which were later exchanged for the usual footboards. H 10s, being of Lines West design, originally carried her headlights at smokebox center, and had the extra-high decked L.W. tender with raised-squared coal bunker. Most H 8 classes were constructed as saturated engines; superheaters became standard equipment in 1912, and Altoona entered upon a program of upgrading and conversions to include superheaters and-or larger cylinders. This was a madcap spree, wherein changes were made at a rapid rate. Definite records are incomplete and it's impossible to ascertain exact figures, however, below is a listing of all H 8 through H 10s classes, showing from whence they came:

H 8   Lines East, first engine Number 3193, Juniata Shops, 1907

H9s 3506, built by Juniata, 1913.

H 8s   Class H 8 superheated

H 8a   Lines West, first engine Number 9384, Juniata Shops, 1907

II 8sa   Class II 8a superheated

II 8b   Lines East, first engine Number 151, Juniata Shops, 1908

H 8sb   Class H 8b superheated

H 8c   Lines West, first engine Number 9900, Alco (Pittsburgh), 1910

H 8sc   Class H 8c superheated

H 9   Converted from H 8b, 25" x 28" cylinders applied

H 9s   Lines East, first engine Number 3470, Juniata Shops 1913

H 9sa   Converted from H 8a, superheater and 25" x 28" cylinders applied

H 9sc   Converted from H 8c, superheater and 25" x 28" cylinders applied

H 10s   Lines West, first engine Number 7001, Baldwin, 1913. Some also converted from H 8c and H 8sc superheater and-or 26" x 28" cylinders applied.

Bringing the above-listed class evolution through the years to late modern steam days, PRR's roster dated July of 1947 listed the following classes and number of engines in each class: H 8sa 27, H 8sb 22, H 8sc 54, H 9s 538, H 9sa 13, H 9sc 9, H 10s 369 (hand fired), H 10s 45 (stoker fired). This equaled a sub-total of 1,077 Consolidations, plus 117 small H 6sb's, brought the grand total to 1,194, still the largest single group having a given wheel arrangement. These figures include six H 10s on P-RSL, plus fifteen H 6sb's and nineteen H 10s engines on Long Island.

For those who were privileged to witness pairs of mighty Decapods and Texas Types canting boisterously to the uphill sweep of the Horseshoe, long past years of Consolidation-powered freights operating over the same heavy grades must seem really archaic by comparison. And yet, when first built, each class of power was the big main line engine of its day. Back in the times of "heavy" 2-8-0 type locomotives, iron men in wooden cabs hand-fired H 6a-b doubleheaders and tripleheaders across the Pittsburgh Division's zig-zag profile. Swarming teams of little "Consols" puffed lustily as they crawled around, between, and over Western Pennsylvania's rugged Alleghenies, pulling and pushing tonnage. They were eventually replaced by Mikados, Sante Fe's, and Decapods. In less severe topographic areas, such as the nearly level New York and Maryland

Divisions, H 9s, class 2-8-0's actually held topflight main line sway until the early 1920's, when Decapod-displaced Mikados came East.

Latter day "Consols" habitats included practically every engine terminal on the railroad. Their numerical superiority was indicative of their widespread use as a general light utility engine, particularly in local freight and work train categories. They also handled many jobs done by 0-8-0 switchers on other railroads, since PRR's one 0-8-0 class left plenty to be desired. Local freight was purveyed to lineside industries and along branches from innumerable small mid-division yards, staffed by capable 2-8-0's. For example; local yards on the Phidelphia Division were Thorndale, Lancaster, and Columbia. Middle Division yards were Lewistown and Huntingdon. At the last-named spot, a busy-body H 9s would see-saw back and forth across switches connecting all four main line tracks, switching Supplee milk tank cars dropped (or picked up) by passenger trains. Some diversified occupations of the H 9s included hump trimmers at Enola Yards, transfer engine for the heavier passenger cuts between Penn Coach Yards and Old Broad Street Station in Philadelphia, fast-stepping dashes between lineside yards while hauling the Paoli local freight (to clear many local and express passenger trains), and wire maintenance train hauler anywhere east of Harrisburg (after electrification). Consols participated in the unusual, upon occasion. They became seagoing voyagers, via carfloats across the mouth of Chesapeake Bay from Cape Charles to Little Creek, for use on Pennsy's Virginia mainland orphan beach head, connecting with Norfolk & Portsmouth Belt Line. P-RSL occasionally teamed up a highly unusual doubleheader to haul a sand and gravel train from Millville, N.J. This freight was sometimes headed by a PRR 2-8-0 and a Reading Company high-drivered camelback Atlantic.

Lines West H 10s engines, which usually remained in Central and Western Regions, made a sudden eastward hegira under pressure of World War II traffic demands. They remained in the East until the end of steam operations. A few even got trainphones, such as one that was used to haul (and anchor) the cable-propelled Brownhoist ballast cleaner. A highly interesting exchange of H 9s and stoker-fired H 10s occurred between Pennsy and P-RSL in June of 1945. The swapping of six engines from each class was made, with H 9s and H 10s engines merely trading numbers back and forth.

H6sb 1, built by Baldwin 1906, shown here at Altoona 1934.

H 3a, Altoona Shops, 1888.

Cylinders .... 20"x 24"
Drivers .... 50"
Steam Pressure .... 150 lbs.
Weight on Drivers .... 111,500 lbs.
Weight of Engine .... 126,500 lbs.
Tractive Force .... 24,480 lbs.

Pennsylvania Railroad

H 5, Juniata, 1898

Cylinders .... 23½"x 28"
Drivers .... 56"
Steam Pressure .... 185 lbs.
Grate Area .... 33.3 sq. ft.
Weight of Engine .... 196,500 lbs.
Tractive Force .... 43,400 lbs.

Pennsylvania Railroad

H 6, Juniata, 1899

Cylinders .... 22"x 28"
Drivers .... 56"
Steam Pressure .... 205 lbs.
Grate Area .... 33.3 sq. ft.
Weight of Engine .... 186,500 lbs.
Tractive Force .... 42,170 lbs.

Pennsylvania Railroad

H 28 Alco, Schenectady, 1905

Cylinders .... 23"x 32"
Drivers .... 63"
Steam Pressure .... 200 lbs.
Weight on Drivers .... 201,500 lbs.
Weight of Engine .... 221,500 lbs.
Tractive Force .... 45,679 lbs.

History Center—Schenectady

H 6b Alco, Pittsburgh, 1906

Cylinders .... 22"x 28"
Drivers .... 56"
Steam Pressure .... 205 lbs.
Grate Area .... 49 sq. ft.
Weight of Engine .... 200,700 lbs.
Tractive Force .... 42, 170 lbs.

History Center—Schenectady

History Center—Schenectady

H 8a Alco, Pittsburgh, 1910

Cylinders .... 24"x 28"
Drivers .... 62"
Steam Pressure .... 205 lbs.
Grate Area .... 55.2 sq. ft.
Weight of Engine .... 235,000 lbs.
Tractive Force .... 45,327 lbs.

H 8b Juniata, 1908

Cylinders .... 24"x 28"
Drivers .... 62"
Steam Pressure .... 205 lbs.
Grate Area .... 55.2 sq. ft.
Weight of Engine .... 240,700 lbs.
Tractive Force .... 45,327 lbs.

Pennsylvania Railroad

H 8sb Juniata, 1913

Cylinders .... 24"x 28"
Drivers .... 62"
Steam Pressure .... 205 lbs.
Grate Area .... 55.2 sq. ft.
Weight of Engine .... 252,500 lbs.
Tractive Force .... 45,327 lbs.

Pennsylvania Railroad

History Center—Schenectady

H 10s, Alco, Pittsburgh 1913

Cylinders .... 26"x 28"
Drivers .... 62"
Steam Pressure .... 205 lbs.
Grate Area .... 55.2 sq. ft.
Weight of Engine .... 247,500 lbs.
Tractive Force .... 53,197 lbs.

Pennsylvania Railroad

H 10s Baldwin 1915, built for Lines West

Cylinders .... 26"x 28"
Drivers .... 62"
Steam Pressure .... 205 lbs.
Grate Area .... 55.2 sq. ft.
Weight of Engine .... 247,500 lbs.
Tractive Force .... 53,197 lbs.

For example, P-RSL locomotive 6073 H 9s (ex-PRR 5265, 6269, 270) became PRR 9384 H 9s, while PRR 9384 H 10s was gold-lettered P-RSL 6073 H 10s, and so forth, for the twelve 2-8-0's involved. All this illustrates very clearly the amount of re-numbering and re-assigning that occurred through the years.

Consolidations sometimes locked coupler knuckles with passenger trains and rumbled briskly along the Schuylkill Branch with Reading locals. The H 9s actually made faster time than the regular passenger engine (usually a E 6s or G 5s), because of its ability to dig in and get away from stops quickly. H 10s Number 8259 hauled a late 1940's railfan special out of Philadelphia, covering the Octoraro Branch, lowgrade freight lines, and main line to Harrisburg. High point of the day however, was a fast-flying eastbound run along the main line from Parkesburg to Philly. Top speed for H class engines was fifty miles per hour; the

8259's exhausts were a continuous roar and her driving rods a blur as she sped along at better than 50-per with cinders flying—a ride of rides, to say the least.

Consols have carried For Sale tags on numerous occasions when smaller railroads were in the market for engines. Among the many buyers were Bellefonte Central, Norfolk & Portsmouth Belt Line (which painted American flags on the cylinders during World War II), Central Indiana, Western Allegheny, and others. As previously mentioned, they also ran on controlled lines such as Long Island and P-RSL.

In closing, the 2-8-0 has fared best of all among engines saved for historical purposes at Northumberland enginehouse. In addition to Number 1187 H 3, already mentioned, locomotives Number 2846 H 6sb and Number 7688 H 10s have been retained.

1187 with a string of period coaches as they are today at Northumberland, Pa.

ERECTION SHOP

Pennsylvania Railroad

Long Island Railroad H10s 105 (former PRR 7558) backhead.

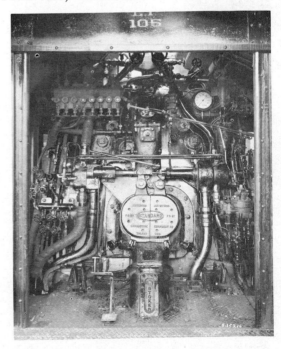

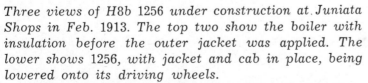

Three views of H8b 1256 under construction at Juniata Shops in Feb. 1913. The top two show the boiler with insulation before the outer jacket was applied. The lower shows 1256, with jacket and cab in place, being lowered onto its driving wheels.

This was indeed a familiar sight as the little "Consols" were turned out by the thousands.

DECEMBER 1942

Sometimes when a fan goes out to take pictures everything breaks just right. Such was the case for Paul Stringham as he captured H10 8421 rumbling across the Mackinaw River Bridge on a December morning in 1942. In addition to the usual winters smoke and steam we have the fresh snow being shaken loose from the bridge and track.

It is difficult to believe that this moment was repeated a thousand fold daily in the steam era.—It was a beautiful sight indeed!

H6sa, Baldwin 1905, shown in Logansport, Ind. 11, 1931.

Martin Flattley Jr.

H6sb 9102, Baldwin 1905, takes water at Chicago's 59th St. Enginehouse.

Martin Flattley Jr.

H8a 7535, Baldwin 1910, in Chicago—1938.

Martin Flattley Jr.

H8sa, Baldwin 1910, was built as class H8a.

Martin Flattley Jr.

H8c, was built by the Brooks Works of the American Locomotive Co. in 1910.

C. W. Burns

H8sc 9938, *Alco-Brooks 1910 at Ebenezer, N.Y., 1939.*

Martin Flattley Jr.

H8sb, *Juniata 1912, at Enola Enginehouse, April 1939.*
She was later rebuilt to H9s.

Martin Flattley Jr.

H9sc, *Juniata 1912, poses in Sept. 1936.*

Martin Flattley Jr.

H10s, *Juniata 1912, at Delray Enginehouse, Detroit, 1928.*

Staufer Collection

H10s, *Lima 1916, at the Peoria & Pekin Union Roundhouse.*
9624 was equipped with stoker.

Ken Schumacher

Above, Altoona bound 46 car mixed freight "braking" down the curve with a one H6a on the head end. below, Its a different story "up the curve". Two H6's are assisted by two more (out of picture) in this bit of 1910 DRAMA!

HORSESHOE CURVE

The beautiful semaphores tell the story as a pair of H6's (2578 H6s and H6b) battle towards the Curve. Needless to say, there are two sister Consolidations pushing on the other end. We can thank C. Chaney for being at trackside on this 31st day of May 1913.

above, As H9s 1196 waits between chores at South-port Yard, she looks like a Cyclops in the Night

right and below, H10s 7103 has just been put through the Altoona Shops, 1935. She still has the screw type reverse and small tender. Engine crews liked them as they were easy to fire, rode well and fast.

H9s 1145 is running eastward out of Thorndale, Pa. with West Chester WaWa local freight. She is on the mainline passenger track. The raised tracks to the right are the Trenton Cut-off lowgrade freight line which starts here separating the "main".

H9s gets a bath after a run in 1929.

below, H8a 7529 heads a Chicago Terminal Division W/B local out of Englewood.

Pennsylvania Railroad

Three Consolidations battle a blizzard with 33 cars in tow. It was a common practice to shorten trains and increase power during storms.

Test train of 100 loaded cars was handled from Altoona to Enola yards (127 miles) by a single H8b, 1221. Length of train was 4,888 feet, it carried 6,450 tons, and average speed was 12 M.P.H. It's a safe bet that little 1221 couldn't take the same train back.

Pennsylvania Railroad

above, It's the 4th of July 1917 and H9s 5217 is taking its 47 cars at the amazing speed of 40 M.P.H. This class was the "heavy" freight power on the Maryland and Baltimore Division until late 1923.

below, H6a 1995 heads a special train loaded with books for the J. C. Winston Co. —note the tenders back-up light.

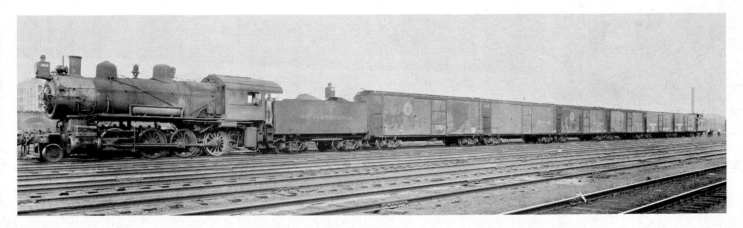

2318 H6sb and partner H6a drift back down to Altoona. They have just helped a freight over the Gallitzin summit, Oct. 1921.

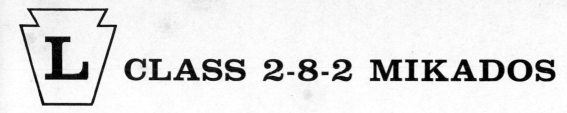

Identical boilers made them freight counterparts to the famous K-4s.

Descriptive phases come easy when thinking about the many-faceted fleet of 579 Mikados. This medium-sized freight-hauler and twin to the famed K-4s class Pacifics, was home-front heroes of two World Wars. Built originally to replace 2-8-0's in main line freight work, the L1s class was subsequently replaced, in turn, by far bigger engines.

The indominatable Mikados continued their useful service for many years on secondary assignments along main and branch lines. Their blueprinting was a twofold approach to the well-known alikeness of Pennsy motive power. First of all, the 574 strong armada embraced just one class, L1s, meaning they were identical. Secondly, their boilers were exact duplicates of boilers used on 425 class K-4s locomotives, both classes being drafted at the same time. This two-in-one maneuver gave the railroad a grand total of 999 engines with similar boilers, plus other common parts. All this occurred in years far removed from LaGrange (G. M. diesels) sponsored concepts of production line standardization.

The year was 1913. J. T. Wallis, Superintendent of Motive Power for Lines East, in collaboration with his mechanical engineers, especially Alfred Gibbs and Axel Vogt, planned out ideas for the double-duty boiler to be used on both Mikado and Pacific Type engines. The Belpaire fireboxed power plant was essentially an enlargement of the very successful E6s Atlantic type application. Many boiler details were derived from a giant experimental Pacific built by Alco (Schenectady) in 1911 (class K29s). The first Mikado was out-shopped by Juniata in April, 1914. It carried road number 1752 under its cab windows and shop construction number 2816 on its badge plate. Many non-boiler parts were also interchangeable with the K4s. Running gear components were hollow bored for weight reduction, and heat treated. This practice followed on succeeding engine designs.

L1s cylinder dimensions were 27" x 30," boiler pressure was 205 pounds, and the standard freight driving wheel, sixty-two inches, was used. Total weight was 314,-600 pounds, rated tractive effort was 61,465 pounds and potential horsepower was 2,712. Years later, stoker-firing upped the horsepower figure by at least one thousand. On a comparison basis with class H9s Consolidations, which it was designed to replace, the big new Mike produced an impressive twenty five percent increase in power with a thirty percent increase in weight.

Between the years 1914 and 1919, erecting shops at Baldwin, Juniata, and Lima joined forces to assemble a total of 574 identical sisters of No. 1752. Their road numbers were widely scattered throughout vacant spots in Lines East series below No. 7000, and a few got Lines West digits above No. 7000. Absent were feedwater heaters, stokers and power reverse. A screw reversing mechanism was used to operate Walscheart valve gear. Simplicity keynoted both K4s and L1s specifications; the only modern appliance being Schmidt superheaters. It was years before additional appliances were installed on 2-8-2's. Heavy wooden pilot beams supported passenger engine style cowcatchers. These had slanting, vertical bars which were pointed at bottom center. KW style trail-

ing trucks rolled underneath the ashpans. Mikados started out with low-sided (9000 gallon and 17½ tons) tenders, however, most of these were replaced by others with larger capacities. The most common of latter day tenders was class 90-F-75, carrying 9700 gallons and twenty-one tons, equipped for stoker application. Some were equipped with class 70-F-66A tenders carrying 7200 gallons and 17 tons.

The K4s half of this twin breed has won such high praise that its lesser-known, freight-hauling first cousin, is often overlooked. Identical boilers however gave them the same high steaming capacity and speedy running abilities in their class of service. A prime contributing factor to these qualities was the large heating surface provided by seventy square feet of grate area, a dimension that was retained on far larger boilered Decapods and Mountains.

Modernization through appliance installations didn't get under way until the late 1920's. One of these, the power reverse gear at boiler-side, shoved air tanks up front. This project was completed in the early 1930's under ICC orders to all railroads. Far more lethargic were stoker applications. These were done very slowly and some Mikes never got them. For example, in July of 1947, there were 513 stoker fired, thirty-nine hand fired, and ten oil fired L1's on the roster. The oil fired engines operated out of 46th Street enginehouse in Philadelphia and were an experiment prompted in large part by post-World War II coal miner's strikes which seriously affected Pennsy operations. Mechanical stokers, needless to say, increased performance greatly, since hand firing of seventy square feet of grate area was inadequate. Some of the older, early models of Duplex stokers were real clunkers. Their throbbing motors vibrated so strongly the whole engine cab would be shaking.

Steel pilot beams and footboards were another change made through the years. Feedwater heaters were never applied en masse, although locomotive No. 1543, and possibly several others, had the Worthington models. Several L1s engines were equipped, experimentally, with booster engines, once during the 1920's and again in the early 1940's. Locomotive No. 2861 participated in one of the most unusual experiments of all; it was sent to Baltimore & Ohio's Mount Clare Shops for installation of an Emerson water tube boiler.

The Mikado story concerns itself chiefly and most importantly with the top-heavy mass of standard builds. Five USRA light 2-8-2's classified L2s were the only exception. This minute contingent was built by Alco (Schenectady) in 1919 and assigned to Grand Rapids & Indiana District, carrying Lines West road numbers 9627-9631. They had radial stay fireboxes which were never replaced with Belpaire type. L2s stayed pretty much at home, for years working out of Pendleton, Ohio (near Cincinnati), on the southern end of the GR&I. An additional batch of thirty-two USRA light Mikes was assigned, briefly, to Lines West, but was soon sold to Missouri Pacific and Frisco Lines.

Urgent World War I freight demands hastened L1s construction, while its first cousin the K4s was pigeon-

air of L1s's team up on the Williamsport Division.

Milton A. Davis

The first L1s, 1752, Juniata 1914, with 7000 gallon tender.

L1s 1372, Baldwin 1918, note the oil burning headlight.

L1s 9722, Baldwin 1917. The word LINES on the tender tells us she was built for Lines West (of Pittsburgh).

L1s 7345, Lima 1917. Her dimensions were as follows: driving wheels 62", cylinders 27 x 30", steam pressure 205 lbs., grate area 70 sq. ft., tractive force 61,500 lbs., engine weight 327,500 lbs.

holed and didn't appear in quantity for several years. These powerful new Mikados were a welcomed lot throughout mountainous central portions of the railroad, where 2-8-0's were vainly struggling to pull and push wartime volume over the hills. Engine crews dubbed L1s engines "lollipops." We are not exactly sure why but it was probably their added length as compared to contemporary power.

Most 2-8-2's stayed in the Central Region until the 598 fleet of Decapods was completed in 1924. This released a number of L1s engines to points all over the Eastern Region, again replacing Consolidations. As late as 1923, for example, the H9s class 2-8-0 was the main line freight hauler between Jersey City and Washington. L1s engines hadn't yet made their appearance even though the Mikes had been running for nine years. All this shifting of motive power came down the line to low men on the tail end, notably hundreds and hundreds of little H-6 classes of Consols which were gradually cut up between the years 1925 through 1935.

The mid-1920's saw 2-8-2's pretty well spread around throughout Central and Eastern Regions, with heavy concentrations of them all over the eastern flatlands. Few ever got into the Western Region. 1930 depression years, and to some extent, eastern electrification, gradually made hundreds of L1s engines surplus and they were pushed onto storage tracks along with many other locomotives. Two large storage yards were at Hollidaysburg and Marysville, both in Pennsylvania. World War II's traffic crisis descended upon Pennsy, as it did on all railroads, and the L1s engines were at hand to play a monumental role in saving the railroad from disaster. Hundreds were still hand fired and stokers were added as quickly as possible. Even so, this took time, and when hand fired 2-8-2's were dispatched to haul main line freights, two firemen were usually in the cab. L1s engines were everywhere, filling the gaps in motive power.

They not only helped electric engines move tonnage east of Harrisburg, but after completion of electrification, were used constantly on many runs operating partially over non-wired trackage. Of course they were standard power on lines like Belvidere, Delmarva, Schuylkill, Cumberland Valley, etc. Quite a few ran out of Philadelphia on various assignments, some pushing freights westward on the main line to Paoli. Pushers were called "snappers" by operating men. On level or undulating routes, an L1s could do very well with seventy to eighty car trains.

An interesting incident once had an L1s hauling two passenger trains coupled together, through a ten mile dead wire section of the Philadelphia Division. After a freight wreck had pulled the wires down the L1s was coupled to the GG-1 electric of the "Gotham Limited". Eighteen cars back, "The Juniata's" GG-1 and train were coupled to the Gotham's last car and the 2-8-2 hauled the whole business from Parkesburg to Thorndale along westbound track No. 4. It was an unusual sight indeed. Another occasion saw L1s triple-headers hauling a twelve car section of a Philadelphia-Wilkes-Barre "Off the Beaten Track" excursion around the year 1940. This occurred over the Frackville grade to Pennsylvania's Anthracite coal fields. The return run out of Wilkes-Barre boasted one L1s and two K4s engines. The lead engine on these trains was 2-8-2 No. 4030, was derailed and rolled over in a Schuylkill Branch freight wreck just a week later. Several years hence, the No. 4030 was among three L1s engines sold to far-off Santa Fe.

Other L1s' left the PRR bailiwick to operate under the heralds of Lehigh & New England, Cambria & Indiana, and Interstate. As late as 1956, the L1s was running on Enola-Harrisburg-Rutherford (Reading Co.) transfer freights. Many a "Mike" was hastily dispatched to rescue a stalled M1 from the center of Rockville Bridge. Long waits for track at Rockville Tower, on the Susquehanna's east bank, would stiffen up car journals in cold weather; this, plus a sharp curve, combined to create possible stalling conditions.

On October 20th of 1957, very near the end of steam operations, L1s 520 pulled one of the last steam-powered passenger train. A railfan special out of Baltimore was given the L1s power between Enola and Northumberland. She raced along at high speed, leaving highway traveling photographers far behind, and arrived at Northumberland with a hot front truck journal. The historical collection of PRR steam power was on display for that rare occasion. 520 ran back to Enola, completing her active service, and eventually was returned to Northumberland in the role of 2-8-2 historical representative.

L1s 2861, Baldwin 1918, shown here in 1932 after having her Belpaire firebox replaced with Emerson watertube firebox.

H. L. Broadbelt Collection

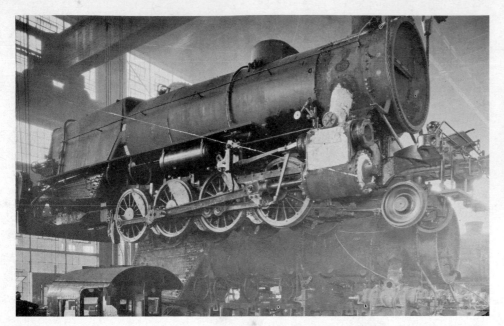

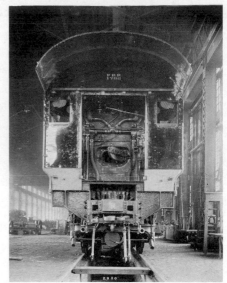

"Mike" getting heavy repairs at Altoona.

right, back view of the first L1s 1752.

The first L1s stand completed in the Juniata Erecting Shop. She has extended piston rods (later removed) and has not yet been painted black.

1752 passed road tests at Altoona testing plant with flying colors.

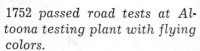

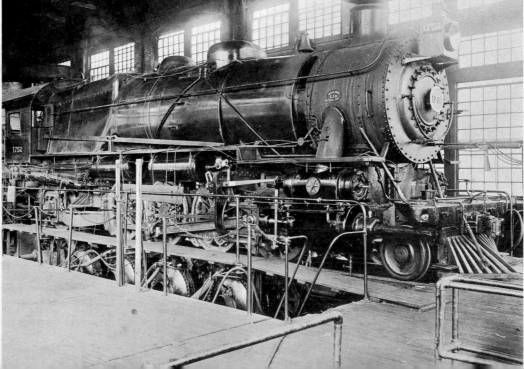

BOOSTERS

right, Pennsy didn't fool much with gadgets but they did give boosters a try. All L1s boosters were formerly applied to sister K4s class.

right below, Hostler opening snifter. The snifter was simply a steam bypass valve that prevented the locomotive from drifting in case of steam build up in the valve chamber.

lower right, Engineer's view as approaching signal bridge.

below, 1369 with an early application of train phone aerial.

Dr. Phillip R. Hastings

Pennsylvania Railroad

JULY 4, 1922

William H. Foster, of New York Central calendar fame, painted this powerful "oil" showing a wintertime freight meet.

Westbound tonnage passes the Altoona Cities watershed on its climb towards the Horseshoe Curve.

It has been our observation that on double power it is usually the second locomotive that is smoking. Our guess as to a plausible explanation would be that because the lead engine would be the helper, it would tend to have a better fire then the regular locomotive.

The steamer was surely a living thing. Diesels and Electric Locomotives have a sameness about them but each steam engine had enough variables to create quite distinct personalities.

Anyone who spent much time near steam locomotives will agree that their night time presence was unforgetable.

Jim Shaughnessy

H. L. Broadbelt Collection

Business was dull across the U.S.A. in 1923, so someone hit on the idea of some snappy publicity when Southern Pacific's order of 50 2-10-2 types were shipped westward. The train was decked out with banners proclaiming her the "Prosperity Special" and throngs gathered to watch her pass.—Above, Preparing to leave Baldwin's Plant, and below, half of the order gets a lift up the curve with six Pennsy Locomotives.

Pennsylvania Railroad

Although a number of USRA (United States Railroad Administration) locomotives were assigned to the Pennsy during World War I, the road never cared for them and most were disposed of. A few of these Mikado's were kept and classed L2s. 9630 was built by Schenectady in 1919.—No Belpaire Here!

Built by Baldwin Locomotives Works in 1916, L1s 1343 is still going strong here in Nov. 1956.

She heaves mightily on a westbound drag from Enola to Harrisburg.

Gallitzin—the high point of the Pennsy. The pushers on the rear will be cut off and the "Mikes" will handle the trains alone on the downward path to Pittsburgh, July 3, 1922.

LOLLIPOP AT ZOO. Mikados were nicknamed "lollipops" by Pennsy men, probably because of their length when first built in 1914. Here, 1695 has just passed Zoo Tower in West Philadelphia. Whenever possible, Pennsy named their towers after nearby towns or landmarks. Zoo Tower, obviously, is right next to Philadelphia's Zoological Gardens.

Don Wood

above, L1s 1627 blasts off Rockville Bridge going into Enola Yards. The track branching the other way is the mainline to Altoona.

left, Scooping water at Long Branch, N. J., on the New York and Long Branch R.R.

John M. Prophet III

below, Mikado action in twilight after lineside poles had been erected, but not yet in service, 1933.

Rail Photo Service

Pennsylvania Railroad

Bud Rothaar

An L1s gets a good cleaning at Philadelphia's 46th St. Enginehouse.

right, Post war look had air tanks on the pilot, generators on the face, and headlights on the boiler. This increased efficiency, but certainly not appearance.

The small tenders were the crews only complaint on an otherwise popular locomotive.

Don Wood

Silhouette at dusk, is created by 1882 pushing freight.

Dr. Phillip R. Hastings

4190 explodes through the tunnel that cuts under the B & O mainline at Halethorp, Md.

The L1s was one of the most displaced type on the system, being moved or put into storage every time a new steam type appeared or electrification was extended.

H. W. Pontin

below, Triple Header fan trip has L1s and two K4s going up the 4% grade to Hazelton Pa. Oct. 15, 1939.

Martin Flattley Jr.

I CLASS 2-10-0 DECAPODS

Not a favorite type nationwide, but PRR had 598 huge ones.

When a railroad's roster contains a 598-unit fleet having one given wheel arrangement, you would expect divisions segregating them into half a dozen or more differing classes. Pennsylvania-bred concepts of standardization, however, dictated that its six hundred - minus - two Decapods be identical and classified I1s. The 2-10-0 wheel arrangement was definitely not a favorite with most roads but in its Decapods, PRR found what it wanted. It was rugged with brute strength.

Western Pennsylvania's rough Allegheny Mountain topography had always presented operating problems. Grades were usually too steep, engines too small, and traffic volume heavy. Hundreds of Consolidations and Mikados were struggling with tonnage till the year 1916. A replacement engine packing a minimum twenty-five percent increase in power over the L1s class 2-8-2's was needed.

The first Altoona-built 2-10-0 rolled through Juniata's erecting shop in December of 1916. Following the usual test plant and road trials, the stamp of approval was affixed to design blueprints and a subsequent 122-unit order was placed with Juniata.

Elsewhere in the mountain-climbing experimental category, several types of Articulated engines were tried out between the years 1911 and 1919. None of these proved satisfactory and the Keystone Road was destined to hurdle the Alleghenies with two-cylindered power. The fleet of big, sure-footed Juniata I1s engines generated faith in its achievements to the extent of a 1922 order for 475 duplicates. It was placed with the Baldwin Locomotive Works and was the largest order ever, for a single class of power. It was only natural that the buyer was Pennsy.

By 1924, I1s's were considered the standard heavy freight hauler of the railroad. In spite of its huge size and drag freight appearance, I-class power was allowed a top speed of fifty miles per hour. This was quite typical of Pennsy requirements. The initial group of 123 engines built at Juniata carried widely scattered numbers throughout Lines East series below 7000. The 475 Baldwin-builts got a consecutive block of numbers running from 4225 to 4699.

In the mountainous Central Region, they replaced three smaller types of motive power: Consolidations were either transferred to lighter service or retired, Mikados were sent East, and USRA Santa Fe's were sent West.

Alfred W. Gibbs and Axel S. Vogt, two of the railroad's ablest standard design mechanical engineers, tailored I1s specifications and dimensions to meet requirements of operation. These basic "specs" developed back in 1916 proved entirely adequate to meet traffic demands for forty-one years. Their boilers were the largest applied to any PRR class up to 1916. The 69.6 square feet of grate area was fed by mechanical stokers and the 250 pounds steam pressure flowed into two massive 30½" x 32" cylinders. The sixty-two inch size drivers were powered by a ponderous main rod 11 feet 1½ inches in length and more than 8½ inches thick at the crankpin. Total engine weight was 386,100 pounds and tractive effort was 90,000 pounds. Only one other railroad had slightly larger Decapods. These were Western Maryland's twenty class I 2, but no one ever owned more Deks than Pennsy!

Locomotive No. 790 was the first I1s; its curving smokebox flanks carried Juniata Shop badge plate No. 3165. Before it got road trials, Altoona test plant recording instruments wrote a success story of the design. The L1s class 2-8-2 was out-performed by a whopping forty-one percent more horsepower while consuming twelve percent less steam (at full throttle and the amazing speed of seven miles per hour.) At that speed, I1s horsepower was 1,740, while the maximum indicated drawbar horsepower hit 3,486 at a speed of 25.3 miles per hour. Decapods were designed to operate at fifty percent cut-off, which, in the year 1916, was considered very efficient and economical in producing tractive effort while conserving steam. A 1930 revision of cylinder steam vents on 2-10-0's was changed to admit steam for seventy-eight percent of the stroke. This boosted tractive effort from 90,000 pounds to 96,000 pounds and made a new class I1sa. Through the years, many I1s engines were changed over to I1sa. By July of 1947, the 598-unit fleet was divided as follows: Class I1s, 109 locomotives; class I1sa, 489 locomotives.

Jim Shaughnessy

Reflections!

Although they were big and powerful, dimensions were kept within clearance limits of most freight routes. To get them over some of the more crooked branches, as well as around Horseshoe or Muleshoe Curves, only the two end pairs of driving wheels were flanged, the three center pairs being blind.

Decapods were husky-looking engines to say the least. Fat boilers and centipede-like row of drivers told the story of power. Their most distinguishing feature was probably the twin bulky air reservoir tanks riding up front on the pilot deck. Originally, these tanks weren't there as the 123 Juniata-built engines carried them in the normal boiler-side location. At that time, a screw reversing mechanism was used to operate Walscheart valve gear. Beginning in the year 1919, air power reversers were applied and this left insufficient space for air tanks. They were then moved up front.

Juniata-built 2-10-0's had no feedwater heaters, while the 475 Baldwin products were equipped with Worthington's. One air pump was standard equipment throughout, but some engines got complete new airbrake systems in later years and these featured two pumps. Two types of medium-sized tenders were used. During the early 1940's new long-distance tenders were built for a number of I1sa's for use on long runs such as East Altoona to Elmira, New York, via Bald Eagle line and Lock Haven. The three tender types were as follows:

Class 90-F-82 (11,940 gallons, 18 tons)
Class 130-F-82A (13475 gallons, 21 tons)
Class 210-F-82B (20,500 gallons, 30 tons)

The Decapod breed was built especially for, and used most extensively throughout mountainous territory north and west of Williamsport, Penna., west of Altoona, and stretching as far west as Central Ohio. Most of this general area was the Central Region between the years 1920 and 1955. The 2-10-0 also found itself at home in lesser numbers at innumerable locations all over the railroad system. It was power in demand for a variety of jobs, from pushing long strings of hoppers uphill onto South Amboy's coal dumper to Enola hump engine to coal hauler out of Columbus.

They were rather rough riding engines and the few that got to Western Regions were hated by engine crews who much preferred their smoother riding N2sa class Santa Fe's. Amidst the rough-and-tough Allegheny Mountain landscape, it was THE engine of all work. It looked the part and delivered the goods. The most spectacular assignments were of course those along the Pittsburgh Division main line, up the eastern slope from Altoona to Gallitzin, or the western slope from Johnstown (Conemaugh) to the same summit. The standard formula for mountain climbing tonnage out of Altoona consisted of two I1s engines on each end of every freight.

Wherever there were hills, there were usually Decapods not far away, pulling pushing; their shrill banshee whistles and deep-throated exhausts echoing across the mountains. In later years, some got passenger whistles. One of their last (1956-1957) and best-remembered assignments was the iron ore train runs out of Northumberland, Penna. They pulled and pushed nine thousand ton trains over 1.31 percent grades of the Shamokin Branch to an interchange with Lehigh Valley. Locomotive No. 4483 remains in storage at Northumberland as a part of the railroad's historical collection.

"Comin' right Atch-ya". This is an unusually rare one, probably because of the dangerous attitude that must be taken by the photographer. The brave one who was proving the old cliche' about "anything for a good picture", was Don Wood.

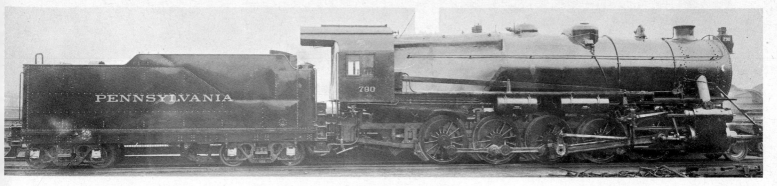

11s, DECAPOD, JUNIATA 1916

Cylinders	30½ x 32"	Grate Area	69.9 sq. ft.
Driers	62"	Engine Weight	386,100 lbs.
Steam Pressure	250 lbs.	Tractive Force	90,000 lbs.

This was the pilot model 2-10-0 type. She was duplicated by the hundreds with but minor machinery improvements.

Experimental aluminum side and main rods applied to I1s 4375.

As it turned out, this was one place where there was no substitute for steel. Aluminum was too brittle and had little or no give under stress and pounding. It would have been ideal, though, to have rods and mains of such light material. Lighter weight rods did appear much later in the form of super-strong Alloy Steel.

I1sa 4409, Baldwin 1923, shown here after being put through the Altoona Shops in 1938. She had been converted from class I1s. This merely involved piston-valve changes that admit steam for 78% of the stoke instead of 50%.

The "Deks" were definitely not favored by crews because their long frame, heavy parts and huge counter weights made them extremely rough riding. Their great steam consumption made them rather hard to fire and many times a "heel" had to be put into the corners by hand.

Compensating these disadvantages was their BRUTE STRENGTH—They could pull anything in sight!

Pennsylvania Railroad

above, The first I1s does her stuff on the Altoona test plant. Note the huge bar-reverse lever and air tank mounted on the side instead of front.

lower left, Back view of cab with old type fire door.

below, The 475 I1s' built by Baldwin had feedwater heaters. We see one here with its huge Worthington pump mounted boiler-side. The feedwater heater works as the name implies. It pre-heats the boiler feedwater—thus increasing the locomotive efficiency.

The place is Roaring Branch, north of Williamsport on the Elmira Branch in mid-state New York. We see here how the Pennsy moves 96 hoppers loaded with coal up a grade. This tonnage is moving to the lake steamers waiting at Sodus Pt., N. Y. on Lake Ontario.

Jim Shaughnessy took up a key position and recorded this beautiful sequence of the same train. All three I1sa's are working their "guts" out!

ELMIRA BRANCH

A tired 34 year old Baldwin built I1sa gets repairs at the Elmira, N. Y. roundhouse. Instructions are written on the cylinder jacket.

above, Fresh out of a boiler-wash at Northumberland Enginehouse. 4587, with Q2 tender, was used on the Sunbury to Mt. Carmel "tortuous ore run". below, 4273, waiting at the Columbus, St. Clair Ave. Enginehouse.

ERECTION SHOP

One of the most beautiful and dramatic sights in all railroading is that of the huge steam locomotive under construction or back in the shop for class repairs.
  Overhead cranes roam the immense interior, lifting and moving these giants with apparent ease.

right, I1s 4408 under construction at Baldwin's Eddystone, Pa. plant in March 1923.

below, Mammoth Decapod being lowered onto its drivers at Altoona's Juniata Shops, 1918.

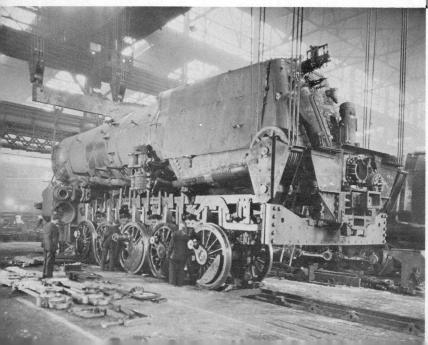

190 tons being gently lowered onto the pit at Juniata. We note with interest that only the main pair of drivers are blind. They were built with the center three pairs flangeless.

above, "Big Hippo" puts out a little smoke.

right, The brute size of the I1s can be felt in this Engineer's-View. The Belpaire says "Pennsy" and the running boards show she's been busy.

The Pennsylvania Hills are reverberating to the deep throated exhausts and shrill-wailing banshee screams, created by these moving giants. You can almost hear them thundering out of the past!

The house and buildings are shaking, in fact, the earth is trembling, as 4612 heads an end-less line of hoppers towards Williamsport, Pennsylvania.

Jim Shaughnessy

Pennsylvania's coal loading facilities at Sodus Pt., N. Y. Coal is shipped to Montreal, Toronto and all parts along the seaway from this point.

With despair the fireman from the I1s, observes the Cylinder Head that his "Hippo" has just blown off. This was the helper engine & the train stalled immediately. This takes power!

Dr. Phillip R. Hastings

The engine crew has just finished replacing a bent eccentric rod on its I1s 4352. (bent rod on ground) The train was S/B on the Elmira Branch.

I1sa 4587 *pierces the black night of Elmira, N. Y.*

left, 4528 *and* 4619 *start a Mt. Carmel bound ore train. 10 below zero temperature has engine wheezing steam at every port while stiff journals resist their efforts.*

below, Above the curve and bound for Pittsburgh, train of 88 cars has 3 engines, all I1s class, 1922.

Rough riding Hippo—They were built for lugging but they could be pressed to 50 M.P.H.

above, Scooping water at Latrobe, Pa.

right, May 27, 1934, Eastbound freight approaches Summit Tunnel at Gallitzin, Pa.

I

right, The powerful Decapods probably spent as much time on the rear of trains as the front. Here, one is so doing to 105 cars below Troy, Pa.

below, It takes a lot of power to get them up the hill and it takes a lot of "brakin" to get them down. 74 car E/B from the Curve to Altoona are shrouded in their own brakeshoe smoke.

I1sa 4230 has a 210 F 82A tender.

79

Mainline, U. S. A., Pennsy's 4 track main is all "high iron" boasting the greatest traffic density in the world.

below, Circus train being shifted on the Eastern Division. Note the circus people on the flat cars and the brakeman is in his "doghouse". All road-freight engines were so equipped.

Comin' round the Curve, a beautiful sight that occured over a hundred times a day during the steam era.

Eastbound Schuylkill Branch symbol freight S-12 gets a hefty boost just east of Norristown, Pa. Notice modernized cabin car of the late 1940's with port hole windows.

Bert Pennypacker

4221W/B into Altoona. From here she'll get plenty of help "over the hill", maybe from the Baldwin centipede diesels, left.

Milton A. Davis

New I1s poses for a company publicity shot.

Pennsylvania Railroad

CLASS 2-10-2 SANTA FE

The only major type not built at Altoona.

Quantity acquisition of a locomotive design usually carried with it a standard credo of principles. The locomotive was first of all, planned by the railroad, and, at least some of the units were built at Altoona. It was built for a period of years and used over wide areas of the System. An exception to all this were the 190 Santa Fe's (2-10-2 Type), comprising two different classes, which represented a marked deviation from the beaten path of conformity. Two thirds of this fleet was not of standard design. None were built at Altoona, and the entire group was assembled in less than one year's working time.

Although it featured the usual line-up of standard appearance trademarks, Lines West-designed class N1s exploded the timeworn remark about Pennsy engines, that "after you've seen one, you've seen them all." Its proportions were dis-similar to most other breeds of Keystone-conceived power. There was no mistaking an N1s at a distance with that massive blown-up air reservoir tank riding the pilot deck, or that highly-perched cab, or the Lines West tender with a square and high coal bunker.

Class N2sa (originally N2s) was of foreign design, being USRA (United States Railroad Administration) planned and equipped with radial stay fireboxes. It subsequently got cross-bred into a very Pennsy-looking, Belpaire-fireboxed hybrid that disclaimed much resemblance to its non-Altoona design ancestry. For the Standard Railroad of the World, 109 Santa Fe's was a modest-sized fleet. For most of its useful days, the 2-10-2 plied rail routes of well defined limits. They were all built for Lines West, and assigned to Central and Western Regions with a mere handful getting as far east as the Elmira Branch.

Class N1s was born when mechanical engineers at Fort Wayne Shops were given a green light to develop a heavy drag freight engine for coal and iron ore train service operating to and from lakeport terminals. Following the blueprint stage, Alco and Baldwin locomotive salesmen left Fort Wayne with orders for thirty-five and twenty-five engines, respectively. Delivery began from Alco (Brooks) in December of 1918 with the first engine being 7008, carrying a PFW&C-assigned number. Its construction number was 58556. All sixty N1s's were received from the two builders during the year 1919 and their road numbers were widely scattered throughout Lines West series. Extremely large dimensions accented N1s features, making it entirely capable for its weighty lugging chores.

Belpaire fireboxes possessed 79.9 square feet of grate area, there was a five foot long combustion chamber, boiler tubes were almost twenty-one feet in length, and maximum outside boiler diameter was ninety-nine inches. There was no feedwater heater, but stokers and power reverse were definite necessities on engines of this size. N1s was able to edge around 23-degree curves, first and fifth driver axles being equipped with lateral motion boxes, with the third (main) set blind.

Lines West—sponsored front end appearance deviated slightly from the familiar PRR pattern, which seldom bracketed headlights at smokebox center. An overhanging bell completed the Fort Wayne motif. A later face-lifting raised headlights and shoved bells back, atop boilers and behind stacks. Still later, headlights rode completely on top of smokeboxes. The usual heavy duty KW style trailing trucks rolled along in a location that appeared to be far below highly-placed cabs. Class 100-F-85 tenders carried 9600 gallons and twenty tons. Their high, eighty-five inches-above-rail decks were very typical of Lines West planning, as were their high coal bunkers with catwalks and overall larger tender capacity. Tenders got brakeman's doghouses in later years.

N1s boiler pressure was set at 215 pounds, although its boiler was supposedly designed to operate with up to 250 pounds. This higher pressure, however, was never achieved. An increase in pressure with its corresponding increase in tractive effort will actually decrease factor of adhesion if weight on drivers is not also increased. Since these engines were used exclusively in slow, drag freight work, perhaps the railroad considered a 4.13 factor of adhesion to be most desirable.

The N1s was similar to I1s class Decapods in many respects with the principal differences being slightly smaller boiler and 250 pounds pressure on the 2-10-0. This produced a higher tractive effort (84,890 lbs. vs. 90,000 lbs.) and lower FofA of 3.91 (later reduced to 3.67 on class I1sa.) Both "Deks" and "Santa Fe's" had similar drivers (62-inch) and nearly identical cylinders and weights on drivers. All these comparison figures illustrate reasons for building I-class engines by the hundreds for fifty miles per hour service, while sixty N1s units remained in low-gear status quo with a top speed rating of only thirty-five.

The Santa Fe's probably remained in one restricted area more than any other class. Nearly all of them could usually be found operating out of Ashtabula, Cleveland, Erie, Buffalo, Mahoningtown, and Conway, hauling iron ore from the lakeports and coal toward them. Pennsy has always been the largest Eastern ore carrier and N1s engines were kept busy trundling ore extras away from ship-

Smithsonian Institute

7646 with a caboose, hop crossing the N.Y.C.
in at Erie, Pa.

Paul W. Prescott

N 1s 2-10-2 FREIGHT LOCOMOTIVE, AMERICAN LOCOMOTIVE CO., 1918

History Center—Schenectady

Cylinders .... 30"x 32"	Grate Area .... 79.9 sq. ft.
Drivers .... 62"	Engine Weight (empty) ... 389,000 lbs.
Steam Pressure .... 215 lbs.	Tractive Force .... 84,890 lbs.

N 1s FREIGHT LOCOMOTIVE, BALDWIN 1919

Pennsylvania Railroad

side docks at rates usually exceeding twenty million tons per year. In wintertime, when the Great Lakes froze over and ore moved only from ground storage piles in lesser volume, surplus N1s locomotives might be found running along Eastern and Pittsburgh Divisions. Once springtime came, back to the Lake Region they'd go in full force. They were the first class of large power to be retired in numbers when diesels started to come on the scene; they were getting pretty scarce by 1949 but just one year previous, they had been very much in evidence.

Class N2s consisted of 130 locomotives having USRA specifications and were built by Alco and Baldwin during the year 1919. Locomotive No. 7909 rolled in from Alco (Brooks) in March of 1919, resplendent in its coat of shiny, new paint; the first N2s to arrive. Her road number was a Little Miami assignment, and construction number was 60948. The rugged and rakish-looking N1s had far better aesthetic lines than its USRA counter-part. Many dimensions equalled, or surpassed, those of sister class N1s, but modest steam pressure of only 190 pounds and lighter total weight made N2s less powerful. Appli-

ance equipment was similar to N1s class engines with stokers and power reverse. Some had Southern valve gear, while others used Walschaert gear. Class 120-F78 tenders carried 12,000 gallons and seventeen tons.

N2s arrived on Pennsy rails with the look of a foreign intruder. Radial stay fireboxes, non-standard tenders and cabs, and light-duty trailing trucks were strictly taboo. Smokebox centered headlights and overhanging bells were permissable applications, since these were for Lines West. The Pennsy look was due to make its inevitable appearance, and it did just that beginning in 1923. A major operation transformed boilers to standard styles and produced re-classification to N2sa. PRR shop surgeons carefully cut away radial stay fireboxes and sutured into place the ever-present Belpaire. This added 252 square feet of heating area, while grate area remained unchanged at 88.3 square feet. Standard smokebox fronts went on, together with raised headlights and relocated bells to boiler tops. Tenders were later equipped with brakemen's shacks. On some long runs in the Western Region, water tank cars were pulled to provide extra capacity. Like the N1s, N2s(a) was considered to be a slow-speed drag freight hauler with top allowable speed of thirty-five miles per hour.

In the year 1923 there were eighty N2s engines assigned to Central Region operations and fifty to the Western Region. As new Decapods began rolling in from Baldwin in quantity, most N2s engines were gradually moved into the Western Regions. (One exception was on the Elmira Branch, where eight N2sa's remained until the early 1930's. In later years they were especially numerous around Indianapolis. After bigger power came, they were the general utility engine of the West, just as the L1s class 2-8-2 was so-used in the East.

Pennsylvania Railroad

N2sa on the Panhandle Division 1926

Front view of U.S.R.A. 7139 N2s.

World War II pipe line. When the chips are down, this is it. Surprising as it may seem, the railroads are the most flexible form of transportation. In addition to mountainous capacity, they are easiest to get going after battle damage.

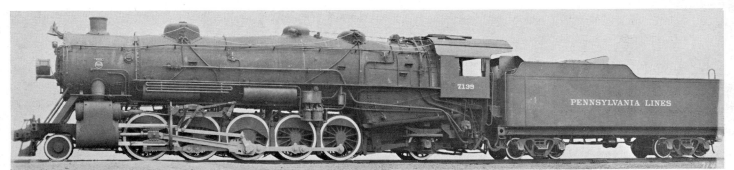

N 2s 2-10-2, BALDWIN 1919—U.S.R.A. DESIGN

Cylinders	30"x 32"	Grate Area	88.27 sq. ft.
Drivers	63"	Engine Weight (empty)	336,900 lbs.
Steam Pressure	190 lbs.	Tractive Force	73,829 lbs.

N 2s SANTA FE TYPE, AMERICAN LOCOMOTIVE CO. 1919

The N1s, above, was a far more handsome engine than its rebuilt cousin, N2sa. Almost every time a Railroad alters a class of power it has an adverse affect on its appearance. The Railroad though, is more concerned about operation than aesthetics.

below, A pair of N2sa's, with trains, wait to cross the Wabash R.R. at Logansport, Ind.

William Swartz

Logansport, Indiana, Nov. 1934. The USRA designed cab looks out-of-place behind a Belpaire firebox. The N2sa gained 252 sq. ft. of heating area when the Belpaire's displaced the radial stay type.

Martin Flattley Jr.

above, N2sa 7917, still in steam as she hangs in the Columbus, Ohio shops for class repairs.

right, a pair of USRA rebuilds, lug their tonnage through Canton, Ohio, 1935.

below, Two N1s with their high-sides tenders apply plenty of HEAVE-HO to their mixed tonnage.

With tourists, watching the "show", 6439 battles her way up the Horseshoe Curve.

J CLASS 2-10-4 TEXAS

Borrowed C&O plans gave Pennsy an outstanding modern class.

Bert Pennypacker

America's largest fleet of 2-10-4 (Texas Type) locomotives boasted an unusual genealogy. Its direct and distant ancestral designs transcended from two other railroads, two decades back. The superb J1 and J1a classes were PRR's World War II freight hauling babies, conceived not by the yardstick of railroad standards, but from urgent necessities of wartime restrictions. Since they were based wholly upon previously proven principles, their outstanding performance was to be expected even before blutprint copies reached the hands of Altoona Shop gang foremen. They took the railroad's longtime proving ground (Pittsburgh Division) by storm, replacing Mountain Types entirely and dominating the heretofore redoubtable Decapods. Truly the best motive power built in modern steam years, the 2-10-4's were equally at home anywhere west of Altoona, on heavy grades and level stretches alike.

Midway between World Wars I and II, Lima-built super power for Erie and Chesapeake & Ohio was destined to inject a blueprint-inked blood relationship into PRR 2-10-4's. To start at the beginning; C&O wanted a high-horsepower machine to move its 160-car long, Toledo-bound coal trains northward across Ohio. A new Erie Berkshire was borrowed in 1929 for test runs, but it proved incapable of doing a good job with 12,000 ton consists. Lima draftsmen however slide-ruled the Erie 2-8-4 into an enlarged version of the Texas Type (2-10-4) for C&O. The Pocahontas Coal Hauler was well satisfied, so it acquired forty engines in the year 1930 (numbered 3000-3039, class T-1). C&O operated them on moderately-graded lines east and west of its mountainous center districts. They did fine work on Russell, Kentucky-Toledo, Ohio coal trains for which they were built.

World War II traffic volume descended upon all railroads with vehemence but because of Pennsy's size and strategic location, it had far greater impact. The Pennsylvania Railroad chalked up an admirable war record, but new engines were badly needed to do it. Since government restrictions made new designs taboo, and there was no time for locomotive development anyway, the railroad went shopping to locate an existing breed that could be duplicated for its purposes. The selection had to possess two differing inherent capabilities. It had to be a Pittsburgh Division mountain climber and a fast-running hotshot elsewhere. 4-8-4's were ruled out because their highest capacity wasn't equal to Altoona-Gallitzin hill. A C&O 2-10-4 was borrowed and demonstrated its prowess in all fields. The selection was made and in 1942 Altoona Shops went to work on a 125-unit fleet.

C&O and PRR specifications were, of course, very similar:

	C & O	P R R
Cylinders	29" x 34"	29" x 34"
Drivers	69"	70"
Pressure	265 lb.	270 lb.
Wt. on Drivers	373,000 lb.	377,800 lb.
Total Weight	566,000 lb.	575,880 lb.
Tractive Effort	93,350 lb.	93,750 lb.
Booster, TE	15,275 lb.	15,000 lb.
Tender	23,500 Gal.	21,000 Gal.
	30 Tons	30 Tons

December, 1942 saw the first J1 class locomotive, No. 6450, roll into bright Altoona sunlight for the first time. Her construction number was 4399. Similar data on the first J1a was: locomotive No. 6475, March of 1943 (construction No. 4429). The 125 Texas Types, all built at Altoona Shops from 1942 to 1944, were numbered and classified as follows:

Class J1 No. 6150-6174, No. 6435-6474
Class J1a No. 6401-6434, No. 6475-6500

Acceptance of someone else's locomotive plans brought with them a number of new or little used features that were heretofore, noticeably absent from standard designs. Commonwealth outside journal front trucks, Baker valve gear, Commonwealth Delta four-wheel trailing trucks, radial stay fireboxes, and boosters were especially evident departures from the normal. The "Pennsy look" was by no means lost; there were rounded, solid pilots with drop couplers, smokebox front mounted keystone number plates, and standard type 210-F-84 tenders. This all helped very well to mask C&O heritage. New cab styling with partially rounded windows, and a front end, pilotdeck mounting of signal equipment boxes and after-cooler units gave a further new design look to the J1's. Total length was 117 feet 8 inches.

Some J1's had fabricated bar frames, while others had cast steel underframes and all J1a's had cast steel underframes. Both J1 and J1a had stoker engines located on the tender.

Texas Types operated over main freight routes anywhere west of Altoona. They replaced Mountain types on the heavy-graded Pittsburgh Division and did a wonderful job over this toughest of main line divisions, frequently double-heading out of Altoona with 5,400 tons (plus pusher). Outside the mountain climbing areas, seventy-inch drivers provided speedy running to match the best eight-drivered dual service machine. Texas Types were the ultimate in latter-year two-cylinder super-power locomotives. One of PRR's last J1 class assignments was at Columbus, Ohio, where they spent a memorable 1956 summertime working in company with leased Santa Fe 2-10-4's.

Bert Pennypacker

Chesapeake & Ohio's T-1 was the prototype for Pennsy's fleet of superb J's. Two un-Pennsy traits were the radial-stay firebox and booster engine.

Bert Pennypacker

Three views of Pennsy's wonderful War Babies.

above, J1's 6432 and 6155 lugging upgrade around the curve. To illustrate how PRR powers trains, this one stopped on the curve for reasons unknown, then started again on the 1.86% grade with no great difficulty. There were pushers of course.

below, Dramatic view of two mighty J pushers, clawing their way around the bend.

above, The brakeshoe smoke is drifting up as the mammoth engine resists the grade.

below, Even the huge locomotive and train are dwarfed by immense scenery surrounding the most famous railroad landmark in the world, Horseshoe Curve.

left, Underway out of Marion, O.

above, Little Attica Junction is a summertime hot spot where Pennsy's ore-coal traffic crosses the B&O mainline.

below, Gray smoke from grinding brakeshoes as train of hopper cars pushes 6165 down the Curve.

Bud Rothaar

A really great class of freight power was the universal praise extended to this type, by all the crews. They had everything: brute strength, speed and easy steaming.The only minor problem was stay-bolts and crown bolts leaking.

One old timer said you could burn anything in them and keep them hot, even mud.

above, At Carrothers, Ohio and below on the Altoona ready track waiting to drag a freight "up the hill".

Don Wood

Poppin' Off! With a full head of steam, 6464, eagerly awaits her run out of Chicago. She'll be heading for Columbus.

above, 6495 getting serviced at Sandusky, Ohio.

below, J1, moving a freight on the Pittsburgh Division.

above, In the summer of 1956, Pennsy leased a dozen 2-10-4's from the Santa Fe. Two are setting here with an I1s and a J class at Columbus, Ohio.

right, 6418 is getting eased under the coal chutes.

below, Cab interior of new J1 at Altoona.

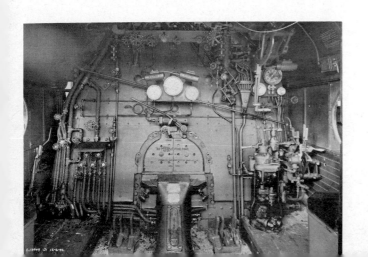

Milton A. Davis

J

left, White capped engineer waves a greeting when he spotted the photographer overhead, Portage, Pa.

below, "Working the throttle" through the Ohio flatlands with a coal drag from Columbus to Sandusky. 6482 is doing about 40 m.p.h.

Dr. Philip R. Hastings

above, Drifting downgrade in a scenic section of the Pittsburgh Division. The gently rising brakeshoe smoke is shrouding the train.

right, 6488 is getting under way after a coaling stop about 3 miles north of Marion, Ohio.

99

above, Two of the largest 2-10-4 type in America team up on their Columbus, Ohio ore drag. Pennsy crews liked the mammoth western oil burners, particularly the roomy cabs.

below, 70" drivers are whirling to the tune of 50 m.p.h. As the track pan is reached the scoop is lowered. Is there a man who doesn't miss the steam locomotive!

In everyday railroading, it's a rare occasion when a photographer captures a train meet. Not quite so rare though, in the middle of Pennsy's Horseshoe Curve. Two mighty J's are about to pass.

To satisfy the J's insatiable thirst, the Pennsy used auxiliary tenders on their Ohio run. This one did former service behind an M1 type locomotive.

D CLASS 4-4-0 AMERICANS

Several remained in use as late as World War II.

Throughout the Ninteenth Century years of development and far-flung growth of America's railroad industry, predominate motive power designs featured utilitarian simplicity embodying a four-wheel leading truck and four driving wheels. Although other types of locomotives were also used, most railroads found the 4-4-0 best suited to haul a wide variety of trains including passenger and fast freights. The type's wide-spread popularity earned it the well deserved name of "American." The Pennsylvania Railroad had its share in, fact, it probably out-numbered all other contenders.

Among the various wheel arrangements used by Pennsy, Americans hold the record for total years of service. They were the principal main line passenger hauler for over fifty years, and their total span of service was more than eighty-five years. As late as July, 1924, there were still 309 "D-class" 4-4-0's on the roster, most of them, by that time, being assigned to purely local and branch line runs. An exception was the four-car passenger express run between Philadelphia and Stroudsburg over the Belvidere Branch, connecting with through cars for Lackawanna Railroad points. This run rated D16sb power until 1925.

One of the earliest 4-4-0 class was the sixteen unit "Juniata" group of woodburners out-shopped by Baldwin in 1849. These little 22½ tonners had 15" x 20" cylinders, 54 inch drivers, and were equipped with hook motion valve gear and half stroke steam cut-off. The railroad and its subsidiary lines acquired a wide variety of 4-4-0's from many builders and there were many differences between groups. The 1857 locomotive inventory listed 148 Americans out of a 217 roster total. It was also the year numbers replaced names on locomotives.

Standard designs were introduced in the year 1867 to overcome costly maintenance of the wide variety present in the roster. Each standard design carried a capital alphabetical class letter and until 1895, fourteen of the twenty-five standard designs were American Types. The 1895 re-classification system abolished different class letters for the same type and assigned one given letter to each wheel arrangement. 4-4-0's got the letter "D," and their classes ran from D1 through D16. Small suffix letters were also used to denote variations where necessary.

With standard classes introduced, Altoona Shops assumed its role as a locomotive builder. All power built there and elsewhere, with few exceptions, was to standard specifications. The Altoona mechanical engineers knew their stuff, as their class C (later D3) 4-4-0 proved. It was of 1869 vintage, a very successful main line passenger and fast freight hauler, built in quantity for nearly ten years. It had 17" x 24" cylinders, 62-inch drivers, 125 pound boiler pressure, weighed nearly forty tons, and exerted 11,890 pounds tractive effort. C class engines were especially notable because they initiated long distance, non-stop runs by scooping water from track pans "on the fly." This was a Pennsy invention, first tried in 1870 and adopted on a system-wide basis several years later. The heavy water scoop underneath all road locomotive tenders became standard equipment, a practice lasting to the largest tenders used on modern day steam power.

Back in 1876, the first day of June saw C class locomotive 573 coupled to the head end of a Jarrett and Palmer theatrical special enroute from Jersey City to Pittsburgh, (a distance of 438.5 miles). The gallant, little American established a distance record by making the run non-stop in ten hours and five minutes, average speed being 43.5 miles per hour. Such a run was made possible by scooping water into the 2400 gallon capacity tender, but accounts of the run fail to mention what provisions were made to carry extra coal. The standard C class tenders held only four tons, so at an average consumption of thirty-five pounds per engine mile, twice the normal tender capacity was required.

Pooling of motive power was also started in 1876, with only a few trains running across more than one division without engine change. Long distance runs covering more than three or four divisions were never achieved on a permanent basis.

Pennsy Americans were among the very first locomotives to be equipped with Westinghouse air brakes, the first tests being made in September of 1869. Class A (later D-1) engines pulled some of the original test trains. The first air brake was a straight air version; automatic types came along by 1875, and they were adopted as standard three years later,

Pennsy's long-time and outstanding locomotive design trademark, the bulky-looking Belpaire firebox, made its initial appearance on passenger engines in the year 1889. Altoona Shops applied new Belpaire boilers to some 4-4-0 engines in classes O and P, which subsequently became D8a and D11a.

Although many standard design 4-4-0's were in service during early years of the Twentieth Century, the longest-

D16sb moves a local out of N. Elizabeth, N. J. 1917.

Smithsonian Institute

The 80" drivers are a blur and the dust is swirled up from the track. Original 30" x 22" oil painting by *Alvin F. Staufer.*

Pennsylvania Limited.

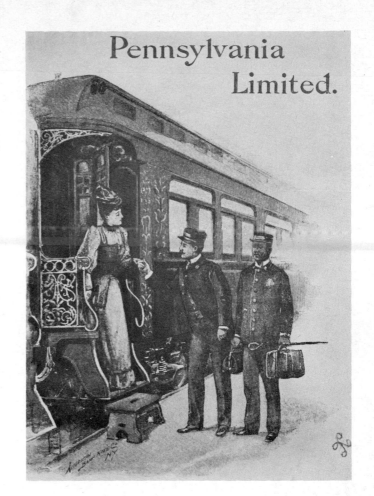

Pennsylvania Railroad

Pennsylvania Limited.

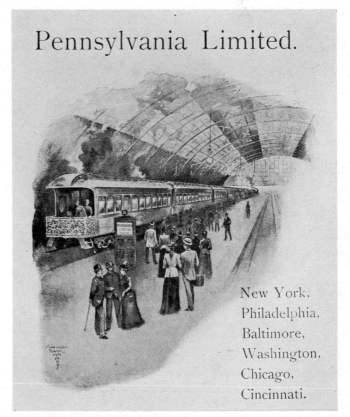

New York,
Philadelphia,
Baltimore,
Washington,
Chicago,
Cincinnati.

Pennsylvania Railroad

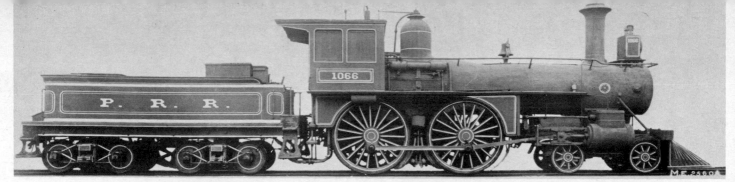

The first class K, No. 10 Altoona 1883. Changed to D6, 1066. 78" drivers, cylinders 18" x 24", engine wt. 97,600 lbs.—retired Nov. 1905.

Odd D, Baldwin 1892 disposed of by early 1911.

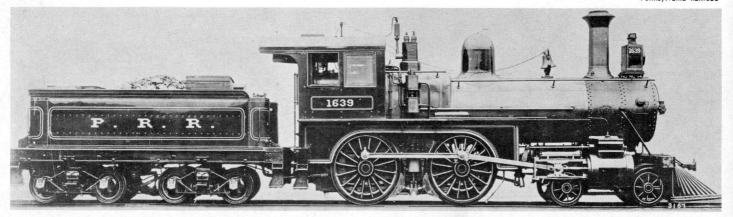

D13, Altoona 18½" x 24" cylinders, 68" drivers, engine wt. 114,500 lbs. and tractive force 17,968 lbs.

lasting, most-remembered, speediest development of all PRR Americans, were the magnificent D16 classes. Designed and built originally by the railroad at Altoona in 1895 as second class L, they were an enlargement of preceding class P (later D14), and were considered an extremely large passenger hauler of the late '90's. The railroad's do-it-yourself craftsmen at Altoona turned out one of their best that time. The dimensions speak for the engine: 18½" x 26" cylinders, 80-inch drivers, 185 pounds boiler pressure, weight of 134,-500 pounds, and tractive effort of 17,500 pounds. This was truly a neatly-packaged speed merchant in steam and steel.

A mountain-climbing modified version, rolling on smaller 68-inch drivers, was also produced with a resultant tractive effort boost to 20,500 pounds. Previous Americans had carried relatively low-slung boilers with fireboxes riding

between engine frames, however, class L was a departure from that practice, carrying its boiler and firebox completely atop the frames. Fears regarding this high center of gravity soon proved groundless as the engines rode well and steady at high speeds, fully proving the skill of her designers. Class L was planned jointly by three well-known Pennsylvania motive power experts, including T. N. Ely, Chief of Motive Power; Axel S. Vogt, Mechanical Engineer; and F. D. Casanave, General Superintendent of Motive Power, Lines East (of Pittsburgh).

Under the re-classification system adopted in 1895, L class engines having 68-inch drivers became class D16, while those with 80-inch drivers were assigned D16a. A grand total of 429 D16's, covering five sub-classes, all built at Altoona, were turned out between the years of 1895 and

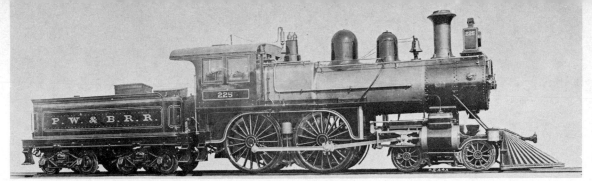

D14, *Juniata* 1893, 78" *drivers, 175 lbs. steam pressure, engine weight 122,600 lbs. and tractive force 15,665 lbs.*

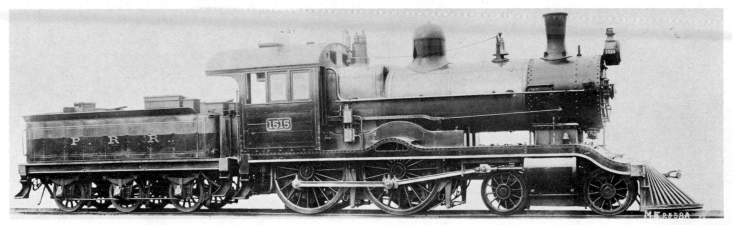

D15 *compound, cylinders* 19½ *and* 31" *x* 28", 84" *drivers, 205 lbs. steam pressure, 145,500 lbs. engine wt. and 20,800 lbs. tractive force.*

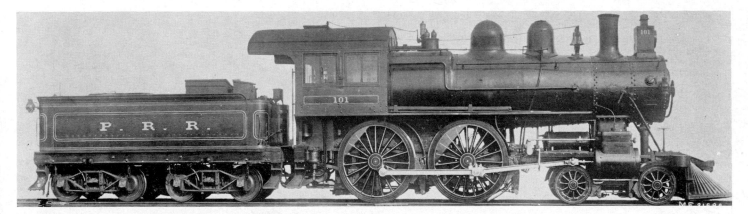

D16a, *Juniata,* 18½" *x* 26" *cylinders,* 80" *drivers, 185 lbs. steam pressure, 134,500 lbs. engine wt. and tractive force 17,491 lbs.*

1910. Aside from the two classes mentioned above, there were also D16b (80-inch drivers), D16c (68-inch drivers), and D16d (80-inch drivers). All classes were similar in most dimensions with the exception of driver sizes. The very fact of their building in great numbers is a self-explanatory success story.

Old timers who might be familiar with the superb mechanical perfection of the D16 in conjunction with its operation over the Middle Division, might recall the record of D16a 816. This locomotive piled up more than three hundred thousand miles of service along that division in a period of three years and four months, without shopping or heavy repairs of any kind. It was quite an unusual feat in those days.

D16's were the chosen steeds to match high-wheeling prowess with Atlantic City Railroad (Reading) speed de-

mons along the famous 58½-mile-long parallel "racetracks", between Camden and Atlantic City. On the New York Division between Jersey City and West Philadelphia, the gloved hand of engineman Martin Lee on a D16 throttle lever, became a legend of high-speed running. One of his most spectacular sprints was an eight-mile fling between Metuchen and Rahway at a recorded speed of 102 miles per hour. On another occasion, he pulled President A. J. Cassatt's special train on a hurry-up journey from Broad Street Station, Philadelphia, to Jersey City, a distance of ninety miles, cramming the time into seventy-seven dizzy minutes. Mr. Cassatt was probably impressed, for it was Martin Lee's running abilities which the President requested to pilot D16 1395 on the initial run of the "Pennsylvania Special" for its twenty-hour Jersey City to Chicago trip in 1902. Needless to say, Lee recorded an on-time performance

D16B, Juniata 1906, 68" drivers and weight 138,000 lbs. Note huge combination sand and steam dome, later replaced.

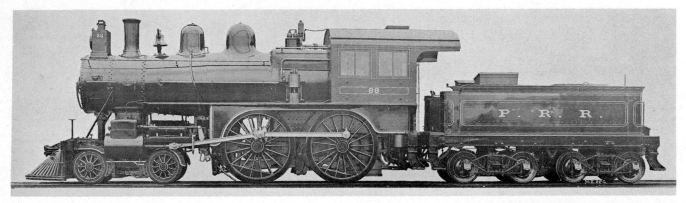

D16d, Juniata 1900, 80" drivers and 138,000 lbs. wt.

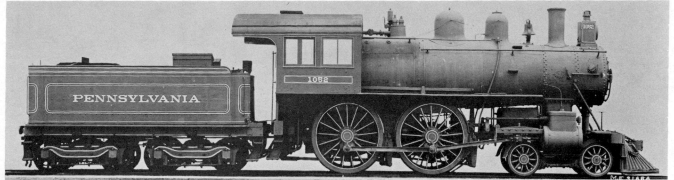

Former P class, Juniata Shops.

Former P class.

over his division.

Progressive events of the early 1900's gradually bumped 4-4-0's and wooden cars from their top dog position on main line limiteds. The crack "Pennsylvania Special" of 1905 rated larger power in the form of Atlantics (4-4-2) with steel cars in the offing. Americans were employed for lesser services, hauling main line commuter locals and branch line trains for many years. Class D16d was actually built at Altoona until 1910.

The D16 saga got a shot in the arm by way of a 1914 Altoona metamorphosis featuring a combination face-lifting and upgrading which increased both efficiency and years of service. The prototype rebuild subject, D16b 178, built in 1900, was wheeled into the shops and torn down. Her old square-top slide valve cylinders were replaced with new, and slightly larger (20½" x 26"), piston valve cylinders. A new invention, the Schmidt superheater, went into her boiler, and steam pressure was reduced ten pounds to 175. The driver size was set at sixty-eight inches for all D16 rebuilds. Tractive effort was increased to 23,900 pounds creating a new class, D16sb. During several following years, more than two hundred D16sb's became converts from classes D16b, D16c, and D16d. There were also a very few rebuilds to class D16sd, retaining eighty-inch drivers.

The doughty D16sb's puffed along through the years and by December, 1929 there were still 143 of them on the roster. Most were hauling Central and Eastern Region locals. Several were sold to the quaint Kishacoquillas Valley Railroad, running out of Lewistown, Penna. The D16sb class ended its serviceable days tucked away on several obscure Eastern Shore branches like Easton and Maryland, on the Delmarva Division.

There were three 4-4-0 sisters left down there during the first years of World War II—engines 1035, 1223, and 5079. Two were equipped with pilot footboards, but the 1223 continued to sport a slatted passenger pilot. 4-4-0's seldom got the keystone number plates that were introduced about 1927. By that time, Americans were in such minority that keystones were considered an unnecessary extravagance.

The 1223 was selected for historical preservation and sent to storage at Northumberland, Penna., after laying at Wilmington, Delaware, until about 1951. It was built by Juniata Shops in 1905. Then, in the year 1960, arrangements were made, and 1223 was carefully pulled to the well known tourist attraction, Strasburg Railroad, where it remains today as an exhibit in the Amish country hamlet of Strasburg, Penna.

Pennsylvania Railroad

This engine found fame in the 1939 movie "Broadway Limited".

Pennsylvania Railroad

Slick and shiny after 1937 re-shopping.

D16sb 1223, at Northumberland, Pa.

Bud Rothaar

109

Water and smoke fill the air as D16a 96 rips over the track pan with the first section of No. 21.—1902.

Train 326 with D146 5068 on the head end, pulls into Loudon Park, 1911.

"Winters aren't what they used to be" —and these two pictures prove it.

above, D16a and E2a meet in an unknown station on the New York Division in 1914.

below, D16sb 2222 and three coaches are really buried on a N. Y. Division branch line. Note the brave passenger who ventured out to survey the situation.

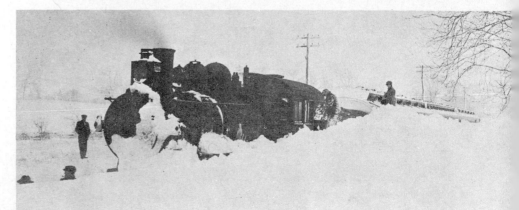

above, The beautiful semaphores guard the train below, It's the turn of the Century and the place is Orangeville (Baltimore).

left, Dec. 29, 1910, few people bothered to take train pictures then, but C. Chaney tried a twilight shot. Powering train No. 282 is D16a 5049.

below, The Americans hauled everything. White coated engineer handles a string of reefers out of Washington, D. C., July 6, 1912.

111

above, D16sb 676 rips through East Elizabeth, N. J. on an extra train, May 31, 1920.

below, 80" drivers, D14 wheels a two-car train on the Maryland Division.

D

Born at Altoona 1900, and still working hard 38 years later in Easton, Maryland, 5079 D16sb.

The shiny new Pennsylvania Limited pauses, the crew gets out, and the picture is taken. The place is Rockville Bridge near Harrisburg, Pa. In 1902 this structure was replaced by the stone arch one.

D16a 4131 waits with sister engines near Baltimore's Passenger Station—about 1910.

Big number for a little engine, D8a Juniata 1887. Pennsy's practice was to add a fifth diget to excess equipment before being scrapped. Taken at Ft. Wayne, Indiana.

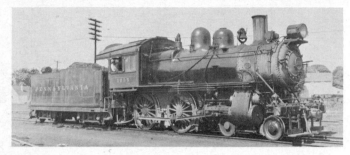

above, left, 1046. This was the last P.R.R. 4-4-0 type used on a regular passenger train. It operated from Corry to Oil City and Oil City to Warren, Pa. She ran till the end of 1936.

left, one of the last surviving 4-4-0's, 1035 D16sb.

A D16sb heads a Trenton to Camden local, just south of Trenton, N. J. August 1927. This was photographed from a boat in the old P.R.R. owned Delaware & Raritan Canal.

above, Train No. 1 "Fast Mail" speeding near Merion, Pa. The beautiful high-drivered American is 1634, as D16a.

below, A beautiful mass of Smoke! Steam! and Steel! the old 32nd St. Enginehouse, Philadelphia.

A gathering of Americans in Baltimore, Md. 1903. Note that the front left engine, D16B, has its air tank behind the stack.

115

GCLASS 4-6-0 TEN WHEELERS

They saw limited usage in mainline and secondary service.

Although it was built for both fast and slow service, freight or passenger trains, the Ten Wheeler (4-6-0 Type) was used only in small to moderate numbers. It was never built by the hundreds, as were most Pennsy wheel arrangements. Most early models were freight haulers, capable of out-pulling the standard 4-4-0 type. Later designs matured into fast passenger pullers, such as class X (later G3). They used to whisk trains like the six car "Pennsylvania Limited" of 1898 over the Pittsburgh, Fort Wayne & Chicago (Lines West). Turn of the Century heavyweights in the form of classes G4 and G4a, for passenger and freight hauling respectively, spoke well for continued development of the species.

The Ten Wheeler was doomed to near oblivion when Atlantic Types got the nod for further main line passenger power and Consolidations began head-ending tonnage trains. The 4-6-0 became practically a dead item for more than a generation; none were built from the year 1901 through to 1923. This refers to Standard Designs built for Pennsy main lines. There were a few odds and ends scattered about; two examples being Long Island Rail Road and Grand Rapids & Indiana.

One of Pennsy's earliest 4-6-0's were a group of little, balloon-stacked teakettles of the "Berks" class, out-shopped in cast iron by Baldwin, circa 1852. These pint-sized freight haulers had 18" x 22" cylinders, 44-inch driving wheels, and topped the scales at just 32¼ tons. Still in the freight lugging category, 4-6-0's evolved into two of the original Standard Locomotive Classes of the year 1868. These included classes D (later G1) and E (later G2), for regular service and mountain work, respectively.

Total weight was up to about forty-two tons with a tractive effort averaging fourteen thousand pounds. Progress in the year 1893 saw fast stepping passenger models of class X (later G3) built at Fort Wayne Shops for use along the PFW&C route. They were a standard class, having Belpaire boilers and sixty-eight inch drivers. The Fort Wayne road figured it needed something bigger than 4-4-0's to make fast scheduled time along its 189 miles of slight grades stretching from the Steel City to Crestline, Ohio (later PRR Eastern Division). There was also a class G3a with sixty-two inch drivers, for freight service.

G4 classes of Ten Wheelers, built between the years 1899 and 1901, possessed features indicating the steam locomotive was beginning to flex its muscles and develop into modern day concepts. Steam pressure, total weight, and pulling power were all unusually high for their day. Engine crews kept anxious eyes focused in the direction of steam pressure gauge needles, quivering at 225 pounds; previous average boiler pressures had been around 180 pounds. G4 weight was up to ninety-two tons, while its tractive effort was 29,750 pounds, which represented a forty-four percent increase in power over D16 and D16b Americans. Incidentally, it was also a 150 percent jump from class D3 4-4-0's of the year 1868. The G4 group included the following:

G4 —25 built by Juniata, 1899 through 1901
    5 built by Baldwin, 1900
G4a—46 built by Juniata, 1899 and 1900
    10 built by Baldwin, 1900
G4b—G 4a with Belpaire firebox (1 engine)
G4s—G 4 with superheater and piston valves

These were Lines West designs, built first for PFW&C, although some were used to conquer Pittsburgh Division grades. As usual, their road numbers were scattered about. Big boilers with radial stay fireboxes, riding atop relatively small drivers, gave them a heavy, powerful look. This show of strength was a very necessary element for any locomotive assigned to do battle with the Altoona to Gallitzin grade of 1.86 percent. Gold-striped class G4 was the passenger version with seventy-two inch driving wheels and 29,750 pounds tractive effort. Class G4a was built for freight work and had smaller drivers measuring sixty-two inches in diameter, with a corresponding boost in tractive effort to a hefty 34,550 pounds. An innovation about that time was placement of air reservoir tanks underneath cabs, and that's just where they were located on G4 classes. This practice extended to a number of classes through the years, along with pilot mounted air tanks on some later classes.

Subsequent rebuilding affected a small number of these engines. Locomotive No. 7306 had her radial stay firebox replaced with a Belpaire (the only such guinea pig among G4's), reclassifying her G4b. Slide valve cylinders of the square top style, and Stephenson valve gear, were standard equipment as built. However, ten G4 engines were later rebuilt with new piston valve cylinders, superheaters, and larger (23" x 28") cylinders, changing their class to G4s. This modernization occurred sometime after the year 1911 and greatly expanded the usefulness of the rebuilds. Following the 1920 Regional operating re-organization, class G4s was used in the Central Region on Buffalo, Allegheny and Pittsburgh Divisions, in local service.

Classes G4 and G4a were built specifically for the job of pulling trains over heavily-graded main lines, which they did well. They were replaced, eventually, by Pacifics and Consolidations. The 4-6-0 might well have been developed into larger, highspeed machines for use along level sections, but the railroad preferred to build 4-4-2's instead.

In the year 1924, the locomotive inventory listed 164 Ten Wheelers for passenger service and four assigned to freight work. This was a period of change for the 4-6-0, as the new G5s class was being built at Juniata.

By the year 1929, class G5s reigned supreme as the one and only 4-6-0 representative. This excludes the Long Island, which still had a few odd non-standard engines like class G53sd, built as late as 1917. Other non-standard 4-6-0's which the G5s replaced were a couple dozen old cabbage cutters operating over the GR&I, classed as G34, G35, G36 and G37. A new suburban power was born in 1923, when W. F. Kiesel pulled out a thirteen year old E6s class boiler blueprint, dusted it off, and fitted its specifications to ride atop the underframe of a big, new 4-6-0, creating the G5s.

No ordinary engines were these. Their design was powerful and gutty, affording rapid starts on local runs with short trains. G5s turned out to be the heaviest and most powerful 4-6-0 class ever built. The men of Juniata constructed ninety of them between 1923 and 1925, for use on PRR lines. An additional thirty-one were put together for Long Island between 1924 and 1929. PRR road numbers were scattered, with one solid block of fifty numbers running No. 5700-5749, while L1's carried digets No. 20-50. The first G5s rolled out of Juniata Shops in June of 1923, its number being 987, and the shop number on its builder's

Pennsylvania Railroad

G4, JUNIATA, 1900

Cylinders	20"x 28"
Drivers	72"
Steam Pressure	225 lbs.
Grate Area	30.8 sq. ft.
Weight of Engine	184,300 lbs.
Tractive Force	29,750 lbs.

Pennsylvania Railroad

Pennsylvania Railroad

G5s, JUNIATA, 1923

Cylinders	24"x 28"
Drivers	68"
Steam Pressure	205 lbs.
Grate Area	55 sq. ft.
Weight of Engine	237,000 lbs.
Tractive Force	41,330 lbs.

plate was No. 3769.

The drivers weren't exceptionally large (only 68 inches), designed purposely to provide the desired power, and adding an almost freight engine look. What's more, the last pair of drivers was separated by a wide space from the second pair to allow for proper rear-end weight balance. Machinery details were similar to those used on previous heavy duty power. The 4-6-0's had 24" x 28" cylinders, 205 pounds boiler pressure, weighed 237,000 pounds, and exerted 41,330 pounds tractive effort. They were built with superheaters and power reverse gear, but never got stokers or feedwater heaters. The small steel cabs were very evident, as were newly-devised heavy iron-legged electric marker lights on pilot and tender.

An unusual trait of the species was pilot-mounted air reservoir tanks. This was a "now you see it, now you don't" affair, with some engines equipped this way, and some not. Tenders were class 70-P-82A, carrying 8300 gallons and sixteen tons. These were rebuilds from the original version which held only 7700 gallons and twelve tons. Notice the high firing deck (82") which equalled or bettered, much larger engines; this was necessary to accommodate the firebox entirely on top of underframes.

Generally, G5s' were scattered all over the system, although there were a few particularly heavy concentrations. Western Region usage included Chicago-Valparaiso locals and all passenger service along the Grand Rapids Division. Since they were built to handle exceptionally heavy Pittsburgh area commuter train volume, and so many were used there, the term "Pittsburgh commuter engines" was a familiar nickname. Twenty-eighth Street Enginehouse dispatched them in a continuous flow to pull locals running out of the Golden Triangle in all directions. They went to

Greensburg, Derry, Brownsville, Washington (Pa.), North Trafford, New Castle, Sharon, Beaver Falls and other points.

Early morning westbound locals along the Pittsburgh Division main line from Derry to Greensburg, played tag with several long-distance limiteds. It was quite a contrast to see a bulky G5s snort impatiently out of Pitcairn station with a three-car local, followed closely by a long distance limited, with its big T- engine heeling to the banked curve with double roller-bearinged rods flip-flopping.

Enginemen found the G5s to be extremely rough riding. Few of them had stomachs that were strong enough to remain unaffected by the bump and bounce of seatboxes, once the engine attained moderate speed.

The G5s at times assumed the role of backwoods branchline meanderer. A very typical case in point was the daily local that trekked from Sunbury to Bellefonte and return, a trip of 145 miles. In the year 1944, it consisted of a G5s pulling several Sheffield Farms (of New York City) milk tank cars, with a 54-foot, coal stove heated, combine car on the rear. Passengers were scarce; principal reason for the train's existence was the milk business. Westward from the broad Susquehanna River Valley the local plodded, snaking through mountianous and sparsely settled wilderness.

The only town of any size was Mifflinburg, population 2000. This was an area where a trackside wave of the hand was a passenger stop signal to the man with gloved hand on his G5s's throttle lever. A special stop was made at an indicated spot by a clearing amidst towering trees, to discharge a hunter and unload several hundred pounds of his camping equipment.

"Off the Beaten Track" excursions covering branch lines frequently drew G5s power, since larger engines were prohibited. One of particular interest was run out of Philadelphia in the year 1936. It covered parts of the main line, low-grade freight lines, and the weed-grown right-of-way of New Holland Branch, running between Downingtown and Lancaster, also called the D & L, or "Dark & Lonely" (which it was). G5s locomotive No. 5726 took the excursion trainload of daisy-pickers out of Broad Street Station. From Downingtown, it poked slowly along the branch's crooked rails, leaving a swath of bent and broken foliage in its wake. At Suplee station, an operating stop was necessary to telephone for permission before proceeding across the Reading Company's Wilmington & Northern Branch. A local Suplee resident, living in a farmhouse near the single track, observed with interest the panting G5s and its string of well-filled coaches. Being politically inclined, and not wishing to miss any opportunities to advertise his 1936 campaign choice for United States President, he hurried to trackside with a supply of Alf Landon posters and quickly tacked them to nearby trees and telephone poles, facing the train. This brought a continuous round of loud boo's from each coach as the train got under way and chuffed slowly across the W&N and on its way. It is doubtful if the excursionists were predominately Democratic; it just seemed like the thing to do at the time.

In later years, some G5s got onto the Delmarva Division and also the P-RSL over in New Jersey. Out of Philly, one could usually be found on a Reading local or Bordentown commuter train, and sometimes even a work train. The fine big Ten Wheeler breed is not extinct, for locomotive No. 5741 has been stored at Northumberland for historical purposes.

G5s, Juniata 1924, shown in 1940 with new style lettering. Their "bulldog" appearance was no deception but they were real back breakers, being hand fired. The spacing of the rear drivers caused heavy eccentric pounding at high speeds.

G5s, Juniata 1928, built for the Long Island Railroad.

Smoke haze outlines the speeding 5716 (G5s) and train as it whips through a curve near Birdsboro, Pa. on the Schuylkill Branch in Nov. 1948.

Derry to Pittsburgh Local, scooping water at La-trobe, Pa.

John M. Prophet III

Long Island G5s on a fan trip.

Husky G5s waiting to leave Broad St. Station.

Many G5s' had tender pilots, as they were not turned at the end of a run.

Beaver Falls bound local at Leetsdale, Pa. August 1949. The G5s class was originally designed for use in this area.

G3, at Wellsville, Ohio, 1920. She was built at Ft. Wayne in 1892.

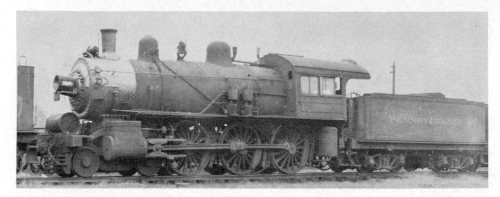

Centered headlight and radial stay firebox has 7080 looking more like New York Central power.

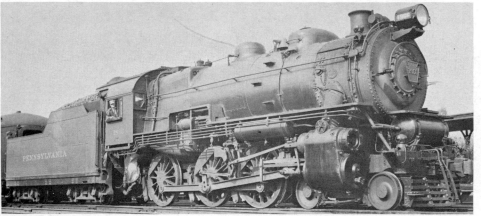

G5s ready to head a Valpariso Local out of Chicago. They were hard to fire, rough riding, but extremely good at accelerating their stop-start trains.

Squat and tough little G5s had 178,000 of its 237,000 lb. weight on its drivers, Chicago 1948.

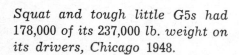

The small but powerful ten wheeler was ideally suited for "Off the beaten track" chores.

Above are two "daisy picker specials" that ran out of Philadelphia on the Susquehanna River low grade line in 1937. Knickers, straw hats and white trousers were the uniform of the day.

G

above, Long Islands G5s' were identical to parent Pennsys. Here is No. 20 making time with eight coaches on the Port Jefferson Branch.

right, G5s waiting in the Camden, N. J. roundhouse. The most "alive" hunk of machinery ever created by man was the steam locomotive. Each, though a duplicate of its class, had a distinct personality.

E CLASS 4-4-2 ATLANTICS

Easy-steaming pacesetters for high-speed passenger service.

Increased boiler pressures and better machinery design during twilight years of the Nineteenth Century fostered highspeed passenger train schedules. This, in turn, resulted in fast-wheeling, speed war competition with parallel railroads like the New York Central. Faithful 4-4-0's had just about reached their size and capacity limits.

New frontiers in passenger power were required to meet, and, if possible, surpass the competitor's speed challenges. Toward this end, Axel Vogt came up with an 1899-dated trio of wide fireboxed camelback Atlantics (4-4-2 Type). Class E1 proved highly successful on the Camden - Atlantic City run, where it would fly across 58.3 miles of flat Jersey lowlands in 55 minutes. This while towing train weights of 300 tons at 75 miles per hour. PRR however, wasn't about to embark upon a middle cab fleet with its inherent, unsafe separation of engineer and fireman. The road's first and last camelbacks went to Long Island after four years. Meanwhile, Mr. Vogt had pared down E1's wide Belpaire sufficiently to accommodate a rear cab, while retaining most of the other dimensions. The result was one E1a locomotive which became the prototype for most of Pennsy's 601 Atlantics.

In 1901, standard-styled Atlantics commenced rolling through Juniata's erecting shop doors with the regularity of a duplicating machine. Although a wide variety of successive classes resulted, mechanical specifications changed but slightly, with that same "look" remaining constant throughout E2 and E3 class groups. Distinguishing highlights included long, smooth boilers and fifty-inch, spoked trailing wheels placed far to the rear. The trailing truck, a Pennsy original, was equalized with the drivers on each side by means of two short beams with a half-elliptic spring placed between them. Light machinery details, roomy twin-windowed cabs and long air reservoir tanks, were additional Altoona trademarks. Interestingly enough, E2 and 3 groups weren't successive; they were simultaneous. 1½-inch differences in cylinder diameters, plus a few minor changes were the only difference. Boilers were identical in size and capacity, as were steam pressure (205 pounds) and driver size (80 inches). Two cylinder sizes were employed for light and heavy work.

Pennsylvania Railroad

This overall similarity among eight E2 and 3 classes represented standard design as practiced by masters of the art. E2d and E3d classes were the first passenger power to have Walschaert valve gear. PRR entrusted the creation of very few passenger engines to outside builders, and Atlantics were no exception. Alco built a few, Baldwin barely made a showing with four, while Juniata craftsmen lavished their unusual skills upon hundreds. Class E7s (rebuilt from various E2 classes) pulled 70-P-58 tenders which held 7100 gallons and nearly nineteen tons. E3sd ten-

Pennsylvania Railroad

ders were 55-P-58A, holding 5800 gallons and 15½ tons.

Atlantics occupied the middle spot among three major passenger locomotive wheel types used in great quantities during PRR's century-plus steam history. Most of them carried more than sixty thousand pounds per driving axle, a heavyweight feature initiated by Juniata in 1901 with class E2, and continued throughout its 4-4-2 building era. E-class engines were capable of hauling train weights that required small Pacifics on many other railroads.

The only small Atlantic was the 1904 deGlehn import. That French experimental compound was said to have had development values; however, judging by the length of time it stood idle near the master mechanic's office building in Altoona, it had little train pulling values.

Atlantics quickly became standard, heavyduty main line power, replacing Americans and successfully meeting

t, E3a heads the "Atlantic City Excursion", 1920.

E6s and driver.   Pennsylvania Railroad

fast schedule requirements with trains of increasing tonnage. The fastest of long distance schedules was probably "Pennsylvania Special's" eighteen hour stint in both directions between Jersey City and Chicago, established on June 11, 1905. This required an overall average speed of 50.2 miles per hour. The 189 miles from Jersey City to Harrisburg, however, was timecarded for 196 minutes, at an average clip of 57.8 MPH. Only one intermediate stop was listed (North Philadelphia), but there was probably an additional operating stop at Thorndale to load coal. E2 7002 has been highly publicized for its 127.1 MPH run with the "Pennsylvania Special" on its maiden westbound trip. The record was made over a three mile section west of Crestline, between AY Tower and Elida, Ohio. More recently, Pennsy produced the "famous 7002" as an exhibit at Chicago's lakefront Railroad Fair of 1949. It was clearly an imposter— engine 8063, one of the last remaining E7 s's easily recognized by railroad historians. At any rate, an E7s was saved, and remains preserved at Northumberland enginehouse.

Class E3a was big passenger power along the Pittsburgh Division until K2 Pacifics came in 1910. In fact , quite a few E3a engines remained on the division until K4s power was available at the end of World War I. Although 4-4-2's made their best highspeed showing on level divisions, they were standard, heavy duty power along the entire main line for a number of years.

Except for the New York Division main line, Atlantics remained in possession of most New Jersey routes and particularly the seashore runs. Most Atlantics built prior to 1910 were slowly done away with during the '30's, as branch line and other locals they pulled were lopped off the schedules. By 1947, there were only five E3sd's left, and these were in work train service. The author was particularly intrigued by an E3sd that worked the Thorndale wire maintenance train for several years during World War II. That big, fifty-inch, outside trailing wheel would revolve in an unusually fascinating manner, unlike anything else anywhere, simply because there were no other classes like that in existence.

The Hercules of Atlantics, and second only to K4s in fame, was created by the prolific Alfred W. Gibbs. E6 made its appearance with one experimental model in 1910. After four years, including exhaustive tests, three changes of cylinder diameters, application of superheaters, and building of two additional samples, eighty E6s locomotives were built by Juniata in 1914. Considering the fact Pacifics were an accepted engine in quantity by 1910 and K4s was initially produced in 1914, the E6s story points up one of Pennsy's many unusual traits. Why would a railroad spend money to develop and acquire an 83-unit fleet of Atlantics under such conditions? It was no hasty decision, as the four-year lapse

between the first experimental and the subsequent order for eighty, bears out. Road tests on the Fort Wayne Division showed Mr. Gibbs that his protege, the E6, could actually equal a K2's performance at speed, on level terrain! After that fact was established, and with several improvements, it was an economic boom for the operating department to have E6s Atlantics pulling trains that would otherwise require six-drivered Pacifics. All E6's's were employed on nearly level eastern seaboard divisions (east of Altoona).

E6s's rapid steaming power plant was extraordinary in its multi-fold, near duplication among three wheel types and five major classes. In addition to Atlantics, its recipients included more than twelve hundred Consolidations and 121 Ten Wheelers. Grate area tube numbers and dimensions within the boiler, heating and superheating surfaces all tallied exactly, or were close enough to make differences unmentionable. It could only happen on PRR. And, there's more—that gem of a boiler not only proved capable of powering three increasing sizes of 2-8-0 cylinders, but did likewise on E6s engines. While the 4-4-2's cylinder stroke remained constant at 26 inches, Mr. Gibbs tried diameters of 22 inches, then 23 inches, and finally settled for 23½ inches. The boiler took it all in stride.

Another remarkable E6s feature was its KW style trailing truck, used initially in 1910, on classes E5 and E6. KW's heavy frame served as the rear equalizer, with the locomotive underframe supported directly upon it, by means of sliding bearings. Riveted fabrication was used to assemble the first KW's, but steel castings soon became standard. This trailing truck was used on all railroad-designed classes until 1930. E6s pulled two principal classes of tenders. 70-P-66 held 7150 gallons and 15 tons, while 90-P-66 carried 9700 gallons, 17½ tons.

The first and only E6 engine, 5075, chalked up an impressive performance record during stationary and moving test runs. Her designers' know-how was underscored by the maximum indicated drawbar horsepower of 2488, achieved on Altoona's test plant. In September of 1911, road tests were run along the "flat as a table top" Fort Wayne Division, between Fort Wayne and Valparaiso, 105 miles. Performance with various train weights was as follows:
(1) Nine car train averaged 75.31 MPH, start to stop
(2) Thirteen car train averaged 66.6 MPH, start to stop
(3) Fifteen car train averaged 58.05 MPH, start to stop

At forty miles per hour and above, on level track, 5075 equaled a K2 Pacific. That was using saturated steam in the smaller sized (22" x 26") cylinders. It doesn't take much figuring to see why an F6s fleet was built.

E6s engines quickly became prime movers of main line limiteds, working chiefly on Jersey City or Manhattan Transfer to Washington trains. They also ran westward to Harrisburg, once in a while farther west to Altoona. They worked shoulder to shoulder with E3sd and K2 classes, handling heavy World War I traffic. Since New York's Penn Terminal was opened in 1910, steel cars were employed on all trains tunneling underneath the Hudson. E6s locomotives made two round trips daily on hourly clockers between Philadelphia and New York. In Railway & Locomotive Historical Society Bulletin No. 91, Mr. Charles E. Fisher relates a 1917 memory wherein E6s 1321 was seen passing Torresdale, Philadelphia, at 55 miles per hour with a 21 car mail/express train in tow.

As K4s Pacifics became numerous in the early 1920's, E6s' were gradually shifted to lesser assignments, although the fat-boilered Atlantics remained big power on Jersey seashore routes. E6s locomotive 13 ran for many years on the Williamsport Division, where engine crews shared the opposite opinion by considering her as good luck. In fact, the engine ran so well that it held the division mileage record. The day finally came when a K4s replacement was due on the scene. Well sir, 13's regular enginemen wanted nothing to do with a K4s; after all, what other engine could possibly replace their beloved and faithful 13-spot? The matter was finally resolved by a compromise, wherein No. 13 was exchanged for K4s No. 12, which was as close as the railroad could come without re-numbering. The E6s later found its way to Baltimore, and was changed into an oil fired job soon after World War II.

In later years, E6s handled quite a variety of local and semi-local runs. Ever skim alongside the broad Susquehanna behind No. 51 on its Wilkes-Barre-Sunbury run, or up the scenic and historic Belvidere Branch to Stroudsburg (located on Lackawanna rails), and how about the "Skooky" (nickname for Schuylkill River) from Philly to Reading on a Sunday afternoon? New Jersey saw the first Atlantics in 1899 and they were usually most numerous in that state (appropriately enough, were last used there.) They were everywhere, on PRR and P-RSL lines alike—Ocean City Branch, Hammonton locals, Haddonfield connections for Bridge Trains, Trenton-Red Bank local, Broad Street expresses, just name it and an E6s probably hauled it at one time or another.

1947's roster total of 74 E6s engines includes only those on Pennsy. Nine missing Atlantics were owned by P-RSL, where they carried road numbers 6009, 6028, 6056, 6064, 6084 to 6087, and 6092. Other PRR-owned E6s were leased as needed. Frequent doubleheaders of E6s occurred during World War II years. For anyone who might wonder, E6s in tandem was just as spectacular a scene as were the famous K4s teams. After all, what was an E6s, but a junior edition of the K4; both were justly famous and proud standard bearers of the Keystone herald.

In mechanical retrospect of all Atlantics, none ever had a stoker, a feedwater heater, or power reverse. Theirs was the PRR tradition of pure and simple design, with abilities to run fast with heavy trains. Two basic boilers were used principally, as were 26-inch cylinder stroke, 80-inch drivers and 205 pounds steam pressure. A super Atlantic, to be classed E8s, died on the drawing boards as K4s proved its necessity under increasing traffic loads. Aside from 7002, already mentioned, E6s 460 has been preserved at Northumberland.

"PUREST OF THE PURE, PRIDE OF THE FLEET". The E6s Atlantics were everybody's favorite, even though none ever had stokers, feedwater heaters or power reverses.

Bud Rothaar got this quote from an E6s engineer, "nicest hand fired engines ever built. Speed Queens rode beautifully, but at 75 m.p.h. started a 'tipsy' side motion that many times scared crews, as they felt top heavy. Once up to 80 m.p.h., they settled back down and could keep right on climbing with no effort or effect on riding quality. They were very easy on coal and water, and were the pace-setters for timetable operations".

Pennsylvania Railroad

E1, JUNIATA, 1899   Pennsylvania Railroad

E1, JUNIATA, 1899   Pennsylvania Railroad

E1a, JUNIATA, 1900   Pennsylvania Railroad

E2, JUNIATA, 1901   Pennsylvania Railroad

E28. BALDWIN, 1905, COMPOUND   Pennsylvania Railroad

E29, AMERICAN, 1905, COMPOUND   History Center—Schenectady

ATLANTIC DEVELOPMENT CHART

Class	Total Number Built	Builders	Years Built	Boiler Type	Valve Gear	Cylinder Type	First Engine Number	notes
E1	3	J	1899	B	SV	S	698	1
E1a	1	J	1900	B	SV	S	269	2
E2	88	J	1901-1903	RS	SV	S	WJ&S 65	3,14
E2a	88	J	1902-1905	B	SV	S	PFWC 166	4,9,13
E2b	45	A J	1903-1909	B	PV	S	8478	5,13
E2c	44	A	1903	B	SV PV	S	7376	6,13
E2d	88	J	1906-1910	B	PV	W	3005	7,9,
E2sd				B	PV	W	E2d superheated	
E3	8	J	1901-1902	RS	SV	S	621	
E3a	115	J	1902-1905	B	SV	S	2024	8,9,
E3sa				B	PV	W	E3a superheated	
E3d	88	J	1906-1910	B	PV	W	2997	9,4,7,8
E3sd				B	PV	W	E3d superheated	
E5	12	J	1910-1913	B	PV	W	1750	11
E6	1	J	1910	B	PV	W	5075 (1067)	10
E6s	1	J	1912	B	PV	W	89	10
E6sa	1	J	1912	B	RV	YA	1092	10
E6s	80	J	1914	B	PV	W		10
E7s				B	PV	S		13,4,5,6
E7sa				RS	PV	S		14,3
E21	4	A	1902	RS	SV	S		15
E22	5	A	1903	RS	SV	S		16
E23	10	A	1906-1910	RS	PV	S		17
E28	2	B	1905	B	PV	S	2579 7451	18
E29	2	A	1905	B	PV	S	2760 7452	19
de Glehn	1		1904	B	PV	W	2512	20
ODD	2	B	1907	RS	PV	S		21

By 1947 5 E3sd, 7 E5s, 74 E6s

Total 601

128

Class Development Chart - notes

J - Juniata
B - Belpaire Boiler
RS - Radial Stay Boiler
SV - Slide Valve Cylinders
PV - Piston Valve Cylinders
S - Stephenson Link Motion
W - Walschaert Valve Gear
YA - Young-Averill Valve Gear
RV - Rotary Valves
A - American Locomotive Co.

Notes:
1 - Camelbacks, sold to Long Island 12-1903.
2 - Gone by 12-1917.
3 - Lines East and West. Twelve L.W. E2 converted to class E7sa. Class E2 gone by 1918.
4 - Lines East and West. Nine E2a converted to class E3sd. Other E2a were among 92 converted to class E7s.
5 - Lines West. First Juniata engine built 1906. Many E2b were among 92 engines converted to class E7s.
6. Lines West. Many E2c were among 92 engines converted to class E7s.
7 - Lines East. Class E2d and E3d built simultaneously, some E2d changed to E3d, exact figures not available. Total number of both classes was 88 engines, shown twice on chart.
8 - Lines East. Six E3a were converted to class E3d.
9 - Lines East. Nine E2a and six E3a engines were converted to class E3sd. Classes E2d and E3d were built simultaneously, some E2d were changed to E3d, exact figures are not available. Total number of both classes was 88 engines, shown twice on the chart.
10 - Lines East. E6 5075 was re-numbered 1067 when rebuilt with superheater and larger cylinders in 1912 to become class E6s. However, locomotive 89 was the first E6s built. E6sa engine 1092 had rotary valves as built, later changed to piston valve cylinders, Walschaert valve gear, class E6s. E6s class evolved as follows: 1910, one engine; 1912, two built new and one converted; 1914, eighty built.
11 - Several were class E4 at first, with 20½x26" cylinders, soon changed into E5.
13 - 92 engines from classes E2a, E2b, and E2c converted to E7s.
14 - Twelve Lines West E2 engines were converted to class E7sa.
15 - Ex-Vandalia 20-23, became PRR 8720-8723.
16 - Ex-Vandalia 24-28, became PRR 8724-8728.
17 - Ex-Vandalia 29-38, became PRR 8729-8738.
18 - Two experimental compounds, one for Lines East, one for Lines West.
19 - Two experimental compounds, one for Lines East, one for Lines West.
20 - Built by Societe Alsacienne de Constructions Mecaniques, Belfort, France. Balanced compound. Tested on PRR's Vogt-designed loco test plant at Louisiana Purchase Exposition in St. Louis. Far too light for Pennsy use, out of service by 1912.
21 - For New York Philadelphia and Norfolk.

E3sd, JUNIATA, 1908   Pennsylvania Railroad

E3sd, JUNIATA, 1907   Pennsylvania Railroad

E5, JUNIATA, 1910   Pennsylvania Railroad

E6, JUNIATA, 1910   Pennsylvania Railroad

E6s, JUNIATA, 1914   Pennsylvania Railroad

E6sa, JUNIATA, 1912, rotary valves   Pennsylvania Railroad

129

"Monkey motion" to satisfy the gadget lovers, This is a rare one tried by Pennsy in 1912. It is a regular Walschaert valve gear actuating Young rotary valves. Designed by O. W. Young, about 1900, it really worked quite well. Its initial cost was rather high and like so many complex gears, it was discarded in favor of the tough, reliable piston valves.

E6

E6 No. 1 stands new at Altoona, Dec. 1910. She was not yet superheated so there is no letter "s" on the builders plate. She sports a wooden pilot beam and a heavy sand dome —both were later replaced.

History Center—Schenectady

E2a 7375 stands waiting for an eastbound limited at Crestline, Ohio. Built by American in 1903, she was later superheated and classed E7s, 9714.

below left, the deGlehn (French built) compound. They just didn't build them tough enough in Europe for American's heavy railroad requirements.

below right, Beautiful E2c, American 1903, ready to depart from Chicago. All engine wheels were spoked making them a pleasure to behold.

Paul W. Prescott

Paul W. Prescott

E7s 7907 (former E2a 8907) looked like the 7375 (top-this page) when first built in 1902.

Pennsylvania Railroad

131

Engineer Jerry McCarthy poses with the Locomotive (E7sa 7002) that won him world-wide fame. It was June 11, 1905 and the "Pennsylvania Special" on its maiden trip rolled late into Crestline, Ohio. 7002 was coupled onto the "Special" and the orders were to make up as much time as possible. Make up time they did, for as they were speeding toward Ft. Wayne they averaged 127.1 miles per hour between AY tower and Elida, Ohio.

Pennsylvania Railroad

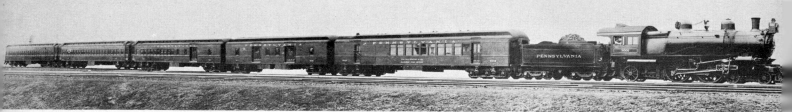

All steel train in 1908 with E3d 3006 on the head end.

Pennsylvania Railroad

Manhattan Transfer—where steam power was exchanged for electric power on trains bound for Penn Station. The reverse is happening here as E3d 3156 prepares to speed to Philadelphia.

Pennsylvania Railroad

E3

E3sd is wired with recording instruments on the Altoona Test Plant.

One month old E6s 1645 at the Meadows, N. J. enginehouse. Later the huge sand dome was replaced as were the extended piston rods, oil headlights and marker lights.

left, The "Metropolitan Express" hits 60 m. p.h. through Bellewood, Pa., May 30, 1914.

below, Nine car—No. 723 moves through East Elizabeth, N. J., Sept. 16, 1916. The E6s was a thing of beauty from any angle.

Train No. 822 with E6s 779, scooping water at Long Branch, N. J.

George Ritz, the photographer, is about to be bathed in smoke as his subject, E6s 6513, roars by.

The E6s was designed for a purpose; it was to haul trains at speed on level terrain. Here No. 759 is so doing with 13 steel coaches at Hammonton, New Jersey in 1942.

The brand-new catenary gets a little smoke from a W/B local at Rahway, N. J. in 1932.

135

E2 1979, and smoking helper head their string of varnish west on the Philadelphia Division.

Smithsonian Institute

below, Indiana suburban train leaves Union Station, Chicago, August 4, 1929. Powering the local is E7s 8588.

"Nellie Bly" April 10, 1914, New York to Atlantic City, southbound through Haddonfield, N. J. E3sd 3158 C. Z. Vaughan
is the gem on the head end.

Smithsonian Institute

. W. Johnson

Leaving a beautiful arc of smoke in her wake, this light E3sd is hauling 9 steel cars at 55 m.p.h.

137

Charles B. Chaney—Born in Baltimore, 1875, died in 1948.

Is there a lover of trains who at sometime or another didn't wish he could turn back the calendar and stand trackside with camera in hand? We of this era owe this man a deep debt of gratitude, for he spent his every spare moment photographing the railroad he loved—the Pennsylvania. With antique equipment, he did a remarkably good job. People who saw him must have questioned his sanity, for who in his right mind would bother taking pictures of steam locomotives.

He was wise enough to will his collection to the Smithsonian Institution, where we can all share it. So many private collections of old have been discarded by unknowing heirs.

The pictures on these two pages, and all others credited to the Smithsonian Institution, are the work of this man, Charles B. Chaney.

above, With two P54 steel and one wooden coach, E3sd 5165 rips along at 60 m.p.h.

right, July 2, 1916, E3sd 5120 at Williams, Md.

WASHINGTON

above, Juniata built (1902) E2a 1413 passes beneath the beautiful array of semaphores, that are guarding the throat of Washington's Terminal, Dec. 1, 1911.

right, The semaphore is just beginning to drop as the Washington-Philadelphia express passes below. Dec. 26, 1916, Loudon Park, Maryland.

Troop Train extra hurries through N. Elizabeth, N. J. Aug. 8, 1919.

Hittin' the beautiful curved water pans.

above, Whoa! Driver of the shiny, new model T-Ford leans forward to watch E3sd 700 at Asbury Park, N. J. about 1924.

right, E6s chugs into Haddonfield, N. J. on a mist shrouded summer morning, 1946.

C. Z. Vaughan

April 3, 1915 (*the day before Easter*) *the East Coast was hit with a late, crippling snow storm. The southbound Atlantic Express fights her way into the Haddonfield Station. Power is an E6s.*

Engines 7408 (E7s) and 7515 (K2s) battle their way out of Chicago with Pennsylvania Railroads crack "Manhattan Limited". Because of the severe snow, this train will have double power all the way to the Manhattan Transfer. Jan. 24, 1920.

A. W. Johnson

CLASS 4-6-2 EARLY PACIFICS

Alco experimentals led the way.

Seven years and 259 K-class engines prior to the renowned K4s' 1914 birthdate, Pennsy took delivery of its very first Pacific locomotive. That single Alco-built, class K28 experimental of 1907 was truly an infinitesimal beginning for a 4-6-2 fleet that was to eventually reach a grand total of 686 units. In that year, 1907, the handwriting was on the wall. Lines West operating men were already yelling loudly for bigger engines. The pressures of long trains, fast schedules, and drawbar drag of new steel cars, too frequently forced doubleheading of Atlantics. PFW&C-assigned K28 was an expanded version of two big experimental J28 class Alco passenger 2-6-2's, which had come to PRR rails two years previously. The new Pacific was also a monster when compared in size to contemporary Atlantics of the time. This explains why the engine crews dubbed her "Fat Annie."

Standardized fleet construction got underway at Juniata Shops in 1910, following exhaustive K28 tests, including differing proposals for two classes, K1 and K2, worked out by Lines East and West, respectively. The Fort Wayne K2 was selected. This was a "Pennsyfied" version (complete with Belpaire firebox) of the K28, using most of its dimensions. The K2 class group, built principally by Juniata Shops, reached a total of 227 locomotives by 1913, after which thirty K3s were contracted to Baldwin. K3s had slightly larger cylinders, but was otherwise similar to its predecessor classes. Although these early Pacifics were lightweights by modern day standards, they possessed really fantastic factors of adhesion, which made a whale of a difference when getting heavy trains under way or hauling them over mountain grades. Class K2s had 5.76, K2sa was 5.86, and K3s boasted 5.13.

Meanwhile, back at Alco's Schenectady locomotive laboratory, in the year 1911, energetic fashioners of steam and steel super power were readying another mighty experimental Pacific for Keystone delivery. That one was 3395 class K29s, which has been generally (and accurately) credited with being the K4s prototype. Compared with the K2, its total heating surface was 5650 square feet against 4629; total weight and tractive effort were up by 12 percent and 24 percent, respectively. Interestingly enough, even though its engineering brilliance helped materially to develop heavy PRR passenger power, Alco shared little in the expected fruits of its work. Most 4-6-2's were built by Juniata Shops, a few by Baldwin, and only twelve by Alco (including the two experimentals). Another unorthodoxical locomotive planning maneuver at Altoona featured side-by-side efforts at producing the K2 Pacific and E6 Atlantic—a

normal course of events on most railroads would have the former supersede the latter. PRR Lines East however believed in the 4-4-2 so wholeheartedly, that the heavy E6 4-4-2 was actually built to equal a K2's performance at speeds above forty miles per hour over level terrain!

Following is a brief run-down of Pacific classes planned and/or built during the period 1907-1913:

K28—Pennsy's first Pacific. Experimental locomotive 7067 built by Alco (Pittsburgh) in May of 1907. Assigned to Lines West (PFW&C). Radial stay type firebox, piston valves, Walschaert valve gear, saturated as built. Superheated later, became class K28s. Class 70-P-66 tender carried 7350 gallons, twelve tons.

K1—Ghost engine, Lines East design proposed by Alfred Gibbs for quantity production as a standard Pacific class. Would have had 175 pounds boiler pressure, smaller boiler than class K28; plans showed an elongated version of the E3d Atlantic. Blueprints rejected in favor of class K2.

K2—153 built by Juniata Shops in 1910 and 1911 for Lines East and West. First engine 7510 (PFW&C), built January, 1910. Fort Wayne design, accepted in lieu of Lines East's proposed K1 class. Except for substitution of Belpaire firebox, similar to K28. Some built saturated, others superheated, all later superheated as class K2s. Many had class 70-P-66 tenders, which held 7100 gallons, sixteen tons.

K2a—62 built by Juniata Shops between 1911 and 1913, 10 built by Alco (Schenectady) in 1912, for Lines East and West. First engine 86 (Lines East, PRR), built December, 1911. Identical to class K2 except for higher firing decks to accommodate stokers, which were applied only to some Lines West engines and subsequently removed (Street underfeed type). Some built saturated (K2a), others built superheated (K2sa), all later became superheated (K2sa). 70-P-77 tenders held 6800 gallons, sixteen tons.

K2b—Two built by Juniata Shops in 1911 for Lines East, road numbers 3371 and 3375. Similar to K2 except for 72-inch drivers instead of 80-inch. Also had KW style trailing truck (later replaced by Commonwealth Delta) in place of the usual K2/K3 fabricated type. Superheated later, making class K2sb.

K3s—30 built by Baldwin in 1913 for Lines West. First engine 7546 (PFW&C), built March, 1913. Incidentally, K3s 8661 was the 40,000 locomotive built by Baldwin. Similar to K2 except for cylinders being two inches larger in diameter, Crawford underfeed stoker (later removed), and superheaters as built. They also sported distinctively square-and-high Lines West style tenders, class 80-P-79, loading

K28, Pennsy's first Pacific Type Locomotive.

History Center—Schenectady

8100 gallons, seventeen tons.

K21s—12 built by Alco (Schenectady) from 1911 to 1913 for old Vandalia Line. Non-standard design, inherited when Vandalia was absorbed into PCC&STL in 1916. Vandalia road numbers were 1-12, became Pennsy 8701-8712. Somewhat similar to K28 in many respects, but smaller in size.

K29s—Experimental locomotive 3395 built by Alco (Schenectady) late in 1911 for Lines East. It led the way toward K4s and L1s standard classes. Aside from its monster of a boiler (for the year 1911), it embodied a radial stay type firebox with brick arch, larger cylinders, outside steam delivery pipes, stoker, screw reverser, superheater, and other modern innovations of the day. The class 80-P-83 tender held 8280 gallons, fourteen tons.

K5s—A ghost proposal of the year 1914, never carried out. Lines West planned to upgrade classes K2s and K2sa by increasing cylinder diameters one inch. This would have made classes K5s and K5sa. Do not confuse with class K5 of 1929.

Mechanical and structural changes through the years gave Pacifics varying personality traits. Coming of the Schmidt superheater while K2 engines were being assembled led to a fast-moving program that saw superheaters applied to those already built, plus those under construction. K2 locomotive 8637 got the first superheater, making it the first K2s, however, 3393 K2s was the first new engine built with a superheater; both occurred in the year 1911. Square-cased headlights and pointed cowcatchers eventually gave way to rounded illuminators and slatted, steel pilots. On Lines West, headlight locations changed several times on some engines, from high level to smokebox center, and in later years, back to high level.

K2 classes had inside cylinder steam delivery pipes, which was standard practice until Alco's experimental K29s introduced outside steam delivery pipes. These were incorporated into K3s specifications, and later applied to K2 classes. Years passed, came 1930—lo and behold!—the inside delivery pipes were back on M1a engines. Lines West Pacifics were equipped with that old reliable back-breaker for reversing, the Johnson bar, while Lines East enginemen enjoyed the refinements of twirling the screw reverse. This status quo remained unchanged until the mid 1930's, when all Pacifics got power reverse, as per ICC orders. K3s class, without stokers since removal of their short-lived Crawford underfeeds, also got new Standard stokers. K2 classes remained hand bombers.

K2 classes were probably the most graceful-looking and well-proportioned examples of Pennsy Pacifics, with their smooth, trim boilers. Juniata rushed work on many of the first ones for Lines West, where the need was greatest. They were soon out-shopped in quantities sufficient to be seen steaming along main lines with through expresses anywhere between Manhattan Transfer and Chicago. Tripleheaded K2 power was a common sight on the Pittsburgh Division. East of Harrisburg, E6s Atlantics and K2 classes shared passenger hauling honors, but west of Pennsylvania's capitol city, the scenic Middle Division's curvaceous Juniata valley reverberated to choppy K2 exhausts until the mid-1920's. They were big power there until about 1927, when K4s engines displaced them. They (K2s) then made their initial appearance on the Atlantic Division.

Smaller-drivered (72-inch) set of K2b's was assigned to heavily-graded upstate Renovo and Buffalo Divisions and turned up years later in Baltimore and West Philadelphia. Although never labeled experimental, no more were built, even though it would seem that smaller drivered power would surely give a far better account of itself in mountain work. Could the standard 80-inch passenger engine driver size be irrevocable to the extent of denying its use where needed? Such was not the case in pre-1900 years, when passenger power was planned with two driving wheel

Pennsylvania Railroad

K2s with Manhattan Limited, scooping water, 1922. Note—keystone is retouched in photo.

sizes. The answer came in 1914 when K4s, with 80-inch drivers, was so powerful at that time to obviate any necessity for reducing wheel sizes.

K3s stayed pretty well within its Lines West bailiwick for many years, hauling varnish between Pittsburgh, Columbus, and Crestline (Central Region). Later, some got farther west, and, during World War II, several actually got east of Jamaica on the Long Island, which is just about as far east as an engine can get on Pennsy. Their boxy-cowled tenders gave them a heavy look. In 1930, five were sold to Norfolk & Western, where they plodded over West Virginia bituminous feeder branches as N&W numbers 500-504, class E-3.

The big K29s probably stayed in one spot to a higher degree than any other 4-6-2. Its entire working lifetime was spent on the Pittsburgh Division main line, tugging uphill against the straining drawbar drag of limiteds, or coasting downgrade with redhot brakeshoes and wheel tires smoking. 3395 was reportedly capable of dragging thirteen cars, unassisted, uphill from Altoona to Gallitzin. Train speed must have been quite low. It also did helper service out of Altoona.

All the early Pacific designs, including experimentals, were highly successful, which was very unusual. Most of them lasted for many years; 1929's roster showing only two ex-Vandalia K21s gone, plus K29s. By July of 1947, the many passing years had taken their toll, leaving only seven engines a piece in classes K2s and K2sa, plus twelve K3s on the roster. In June of 1949, K2sa 1387 was still in steam, running out of Enola on a work train. At that time, she looked almost proud and racy enough to once again be marked up on the board for the "Iron City Express" or "Manhattan Limited." The year 1949 was just about "trails end" for K2/K3s engines.

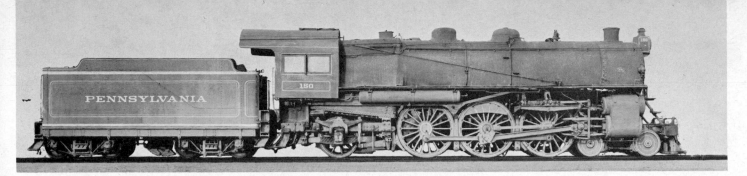

K2 PACIFIC, JUNIATA, 1910

Cylinders	24"x 26"	Weight on Drivers	185,900 lbs.
Drivers	80"	Engine Weight	278,800 lbs.
Steam Pressure	205 lbs.	Tractive Force	32,620 lbs.

K2sb PACIFIC, JUNIATA, 1911

Cylinders	24"x 26"	Weight on Drivers	192,500 lbs.
Drivers	72"	Engine Weight	286,600 lbs.
Steam Pressure	205 lbs.	Tractive Force	36,244 lbs.

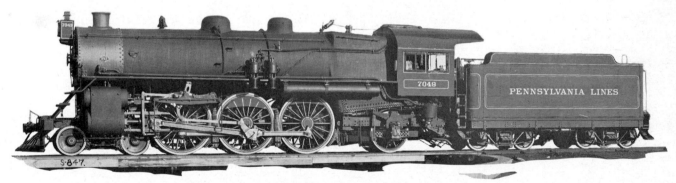

K2a PACIFIC, AMERICAN LOCO CO., 1912

Cylinders	24"x 26"	Weight on Drivers	178,500 lbs.
Drivers	80"	Engine Weight	272,000 lbs.
Steam Pressure	205 lbs.	Tractive Force	32,620 lbs.

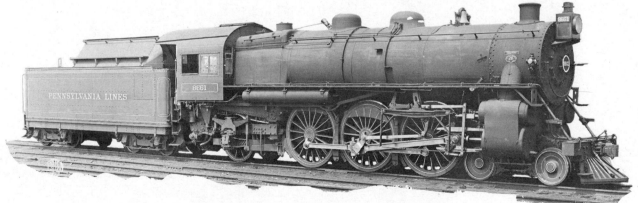

K3s PACIFIC, BALDWIN LOCO. WORKS, 1913

Cylinders	26"x 26"	Grate Area	55.38 sq. ft.
Drivers	80"	Engine Weight	293,600 lbs.
Steam Pressure	205 lbs.	Tractive Force	32,283 lbs.

K29

History Center—Schenectady

A shaft of brilliant sunlight pierces the skylight and hits the beautiful, almost completed, K29, Oct. 1911.

We can't help but wonder what the men of the American Locomotive Co. must have thought of the Pennsylvania Railroad. Everything they created for Pennsy was a supreme achievement in design and performance, but when the actual orders were passed out, Alco was almost completely overlooked.

We can only offer a layman's guess that Alco (American Loco's present name) knew full well it had no chance for large Pennsy orders, because the Railroad would naturally favor their Juniata Shops. Furthermore, Baldwin was a good customer right on the mainline.

The K29 was one of the most successful demonstrators ever built. This engine, not the K2s's and K3s's, was the prototype for Pennsy's famous fleet of K4s class.

History Center—Schenectady

K29 PACIFIC, AMERICAN LOCOMOTIVE CO., 1911

Cylinders	27"x 28"	Weight on Drivers	197,800 lbs.
Drivers	80"	Engine Weight	317,000 lbs.
Steam Pressure	200 lbs.	Tractive Force	43,375 lbs.

J28

Pennsylvania preferred to handle most of its locomotive planning and development, but the ingenuity of the major commercial builders was by no means overlooked. Various experimental engines were purchased, and had definite bearing upon succeeding Altoona-planned standard designs. In the year 1905, an experimental sextet of mighty Alco-built, guinea pigs were delivered. There were two Atlantics (E29), two Prairies (J28), and two Consolidations (H28). They were the first engines on the railroad to have really big boilers, a step leading to subsequent applications on a wide variety of power.

Each set of engines was divided (one unit going to Lines East and the other to Lines West) for testing purposes. The two Prairies (2-6-2 Type) were especially interesting since they represented the only power of this wheel arrangement that PRR ever owned. Schenectady turned them out in September 1905, and it was said they were very similar to some power built for the Lake Shore & Michigan Southern. Lines East got J28 2761, while 7453 went to Lines West.

Although the radial stay firebox on J28 had a grate area of fifty-five square feet (which was, by no means, an enlargement over existing engines), total heating surface of 3,881 square feet was a huge jump. Piston valves were used, with the Lines East engine having vertically-canted cylinders and Walschaert valve gear, while the Lines West version sported cylinders that slanted at a 45-degree angle, with Stephenson valve motion. 200 lb. boiler pressure, 21½" x 28" cylinders, and eighty-inch driving wheels completed the picture.

The big J28's were assigned to the Fort Wayne and Pittsburgh Divisions, hauling trains over terrain that didn't exactly duplicate their name (Prairie). These afforded widely divergent test situations. 2761 also worked east to Jersey City and over the undulating terrain east of Altoona, handled various "named" trains. One was still carried on the roster of 1924; probably a local suburban engine by that time. Although the wheel arrangement wasn't worth duplicating, future standard boilers possessed features employed in these classes.

Cylinders	21½"x 28"
Drivers	80"
Steam Pressure	200 lbs.
Grate Area	55 sq. ft.
Weight of Engine	233,500 lbs.
Tractive Force	27,504 lbs.

History Center—Schenectady

J28 PRAIRIE

AMERICAN LOCOMOTIVE CO., 1905

Lines West J28 had slanted cylinders with Stephenson valve motion. Ft. Wayne, Ind. 1912. The Prairies ran well, but the four-wheel pony truck did a better job on leading the locomotive into a curve at speed.

Paul W. Prescott

147

80" drivered K2sa speeds along with its New York Division Express train in 1916. One of the most important, and often overlooked, aspects of motive power development is the track work. Pennsy's excellent road bed and heavy rail allowed them higher axel loadings then would have been otherwise permissable.

No. 25 pulls into Chicago's old Union Station beneath the rumbling Interurban that is crossing on the "L" bridge overhead. P.R.R. train No. 40 with double power is waiting to depart. All engines here are K2s's and the date is August 31, 1919.

A. W. Johnson

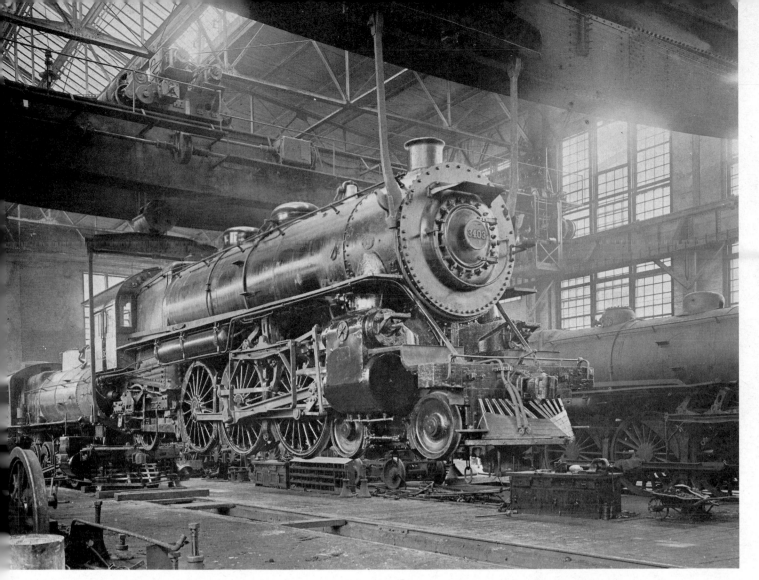

The early part of the 20th Century was the twilight of the fancy Victorian Period. It is paradoxial that the motive power of that period was beautifully clean and uncluttered. Here we have a superb example, K2sa 3403, that has returned home for class repairs. She will soon be back on the busy Middle Division at the more familiar spot of heading the Limiteds. Juniata, 1917.

K2 3349 has not yet been superheated as she heads No. 7 westbound on the New York Division in 1911. In 1914 she was superheated and classed K2s.

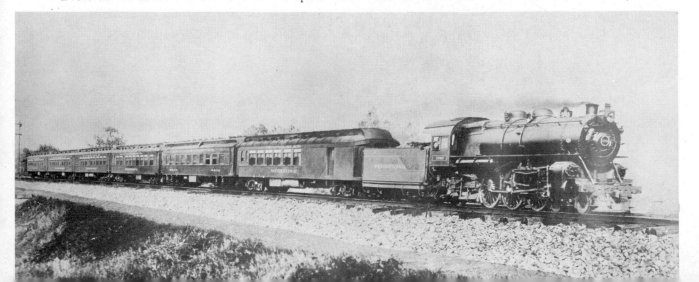

K2s 3359 assists K4s up-grade from Altoona to Gallitzin with train 13, July 5, 1922.

3325 appears to be leaning into its task as it wheels the Philadelphia Express near Rahway, N. J. 1933.

K2

Eastbound down the Curve is Train No. 2 with K2 3380 offering the resistance. May 31, 1914.

Four modes of transportation in one picture—far left has a trolley line and horse carriage, while on the right, the Pennsylvania Special races behind a beautiful old touring car. We can identify the locomotive as a K2 Pacific, but we are at a loss on the automobile.

PHILADELPHIA

Pennsylvania Railroad

Engineer's view of Broad St. Station's outbound track from a cab of a K2 Pacific.

Sometimes a photographer has the ability to impart a "special" mood that somehow takes the viewer back in time—back to a world he never knew. This bit of work by A. W. Johnson seems to have that unusual bit of magic. It's July 22, 1921 and Pennsylvania's No. 5 is heading east through South Chicago with a K2a Pacific.

CHICAGO

K2a 9999, the highest regular engine number used on the Pennsy. She was built by Juniata in 1911.

May 23, 1936, 7301 (K3s) leaves Akron, bound for Cleveland after coming from Columbus.

Waiting to take a train from St. Louis to Indianapolis is K21s. She rolled out of Schenectady in May 1910. Why is the steam locomotive such a thing of beauty? Probably because it follows the old architectural cliche "form follows function".

K3s, Baldwin 1913, sets at 28th St. in Pittsburgh.

A shorter Belpaire firebox and straight boiler were the major exterior differences between the K2 and K3 and their more famous K4s cousins. K2s 3799 is the product of Juniata, 1911.

The trailing truck is another mark of the early Pacifics. We are not sure of its exact style and type, but it appears to be a Pennsy design somewhat similar to the then popular Hodges type.

155

K2s in full stride.

Everybody works during a snowstorm. The man in the foreground is pouring oil on the fires that are keeping the switches free. Background is a K2 locomotive.

156

The centered headlight gave the Lines West engines a New York Central look. No. 22 the "Manhattan Limited" leaves Chicago with a bell-ringing K2s on the headend. April 24, 1921.

K2s 7519 backs No. 22 into Chicago's old Union Station. The green flags tell us that this must be the first section. These were the glorious days before freeways and Government subsidized airlines.

K4s CLASS 4-6-2 PACIFICS

America's most famous Pacific type.

Through the years, frequently-elusive ingredients of chance have blessed a select group of the chosen few locomotives with widespread fame. Although a number of Pennsy engine classes were quite successful and well known, none was so outstandingly successful and widely recognized as the 425-unit fleet of K4s Pacifics. This principal hauler of the railroad's vast passenger train armada was no super-horsepowered machine; rather, its basic dimensions and equipment were modest, plain and simple throughout. Perhaps the K4s's secret popularity weapon was its uncanny

The late Ralph Maxson and his engine. Bud Rothaar

ability to keep pace with more modern power on competing railroads—a controversially-flavored subject, as we shall see shortly.

At any rate, the K4s was definitely an engine among engines, every standardized pound of it, and anyone who has seen on in full flight (at 75 per) has never doubted its abilities. The time-honored image of PRR's named Blue Ribbon trains carried the traditional K4s power up front, complete with train name sign affixed to its red and gold keystone number plate. Later year changes altered the familiar K4s look on many engines, but most of them remained basically unchanged from the lasting 1914 design. Much has been said and written about this wondrous Keystone idol; its further presentation upon these pages can only serve to emphasize, once again, glory days associated with the K4s story.

The famed K4s family's first member was locomotive 1737, out-shopped at Juniata in May of 1914, carrying construction No. 2825. Her development was one half of a two-pronged, simultaneous effort to produce new, heavy freight and passenger classes utilizing a common boiler design (L1s Mikado and K4s Pacific). Motive power chief, J. T. Wallis, together with his able assistants, Alfred Gibbs and Axel Vogt, drew upon firm foundations of previous classes to evolve the K4s. Alco's huge experimental K29s of 1911 provided most of the basic "specs," while lightweight, heat treated machinery of E6s Atlantics was another inclusive asset. Fifty-five square foot grate area, used on many classes since 1907, went out the window in favor of a new

standard size, seventy square feet, which was subsequently carried on most heavy road power.

The K4s was superheated, equipped with screw reverse, and hand fired. It had square-cased headlight, wooden cow-catcher, KW style trailing truck, and low-sided tender, class 70-P-75, holding only 7000 gallons and 12½ tons. Early versions of K4s had the breather located in the cylinder side; this was later changed to a top-of-cylinder location, together with Pennsy's familiar, bulky steam delivery pipes.

A three year time lag existed between pilot engine 1737 and her sisters. Exhaustive road and test plant tryouts were run during that time, but the real stopper was the top priority construction of L1s Mikados. Finally, in 1917, Juniata found erecting shop's clear to assemble K4s' en masse. The first 168, carried the usual, widely scattered road numbering, while later groups (built since 1920) were kept within consecutive series. The first engines went to three "problem divisions" having heaviest line grades: the Pittsburgh, Eastern and Panhandle.

Below is a listing, by years, of K4s construction:
1914—one engine—1737
1917—41 engines—assorted numbers
1918—111 engines—3667 to 3684, 5334 to 5349, plus assorted numbers
1919—15 engines—all Lines West, assorted numbers
1920—50 engines—3726 to 3775
1923—57 engines—3800, 3801, 3805 to 3807, 3838 to 3889
1924—50 engines—5350 to 5399
1927—92 engines—5400 to 5491
1928—8 engines—5492 to 5499
Note: 5400 to 5474 built by Baldwin, all others by Juniata Shops.

Bud Rothaar

Andy Fountain and K4s at 78 m.p.h.

The original 1914 ingredients were a design engineering masterpiece, so well-planned, that the fourteen year span saw only minor alterations made to the basic formula. All locomotives, no matter how good, undergo certain modernization and superficial changes as time passes. The final 207 K4s' got power reverses as built, but the rest had to wait until the mid 1930's. One exception to this was a small group of Lines West K4s, built in 1919 with both power reverse and

hauling a P-RSL express near Zoo Tower.
Bert Pennypacker

Fireman's view from 2nd K4s.   Bud Rothaar

Street underfeed stokers. The stokers didn't last long and were removed as unsatisfactory. It wasn't until the mid 1930's that dependable Standard stokers were fitted to all K4s.

Although stokers were the biggest single improvement from an operating standpoint, several other changes were also made during the '30's. They got table grates, mechanical lubricators, star exhaust nozzles, and the small steel cabs which characterized standard designs of the mid 1920's. Eight different tender styles were used at various times, starting with the low-sided midgets and going upward in size to mammoth "coast-to-coast" ones. The 1930's modernization included larger tenders designed by W. F. Kiesel, Jr., Mechanical Engineer. These were called Kiesel tenders, and sometimes referred to as Baldwin tenders. Three major classes were:

    90-P-75 (9700 gallons, 21 tons)
    110-P-75 (11,980 gallons, 18½ tons)
    130-P-75 (13,475 gallons, 22 tons)

At first, most K4s engine runs were limited to one division, but runs were gradually increased to cover two or three divisions when hauling long-distance, named trains. The longest regular through runs never got above 450 to 500 miles in length. Prior to Eastern lines electrification, a N. Y.-Chicago Limited, usually got the following K4s assignments:

    Manhattan Transfer-Harrisburg, three divisions, 187 miles
    Harrisburg-Pittsburgh, two divisions, 245 miles
    Pittsburgh-Crestline, one division, 189 miles
    Crestline-Chicago, one division, 279 miles
      (engines were occasionally changed at Fort Wayne, breaking this run into 131 and 148 mile sections, respectively)

Lubricating.   Pennsylvania Railroad

Water was scooped on the fly about twice per division. Before stokers were applied, and even with large capacity tenders, each through run required at least one on-line stop to load coal, and sometimes two. This wasn't because tenders were empty, the coal supply simply got too far away from firebox doors to be fired efficiently by hand at high speed, and PRR had no coal pushers on its tenders.

The high point of heavy-duty, main line operation was reached during the 1930's, when stoker installations boosted performance to unbelievable levels. By the year 1933, electrification had crept westward to Paoli and a long distance pool of K4s engines was running through from Philadelphia or Paoli to Pittsburgh, approximately 350 miles. This run lasted until catenary reached Harrisburg in 1938. Top-notch mechanical shape was the prime requisite for long distance pool assignments. These engines also carried a white star stenciled on their pilots, in addition to the usual regional and enginehouse symbol letters. That Pittsburgh run was the toughest on the railroad; it was a fight all the way, totally unlike the racing speeds attainable across western Ohio and Indiana.

Let's follow the operation of a westbound "star" K4s out of Paoli. It would be serviced at West Philadelphia enginehouse and run light to Paoli, twenty miles west, to pick up its train coming from New York with electric motive power. Westward from Paoli, over the Philadelphia Division, the K4s would scoop water at Atglen and load it from a standpipe, if needed, at Lancaster. Out of Harrisburg, the Middle Division engine crew scooped water at Bailey, Hawstone, Mapleton, and Bellwood. One or two of these locations might be run by without scooping if sufficient water was in the tender. After running approximately 140 miles, about twelve tons of the twenty-two tons aboard a 130-P-75 tender were gone, and an on-line stop was made at Denholm coal wharf, several miles east of Lewistown. Water could also be loaded there at the same time, eliminating two scoopings, which put far less water into a tank than standpipe refills. The one coal stop was usually sufficient to take her through to Pittsburgh, 184 miles and around sixteen tons. Coal might also be loaded at Conemaugh (Johnstown) if needed.

After loading water at Altoona station and attaching helpers, the train was battling its way across the saw-toothed Pittsburgh Division, scooping water at Wilmore and Saxmans, plus a stop at Conemaugh if required. In most cases, doubleheaders ran the length of Pittsburgh Division.

The K4s did its best work pulling trainweights of one thousand tons or less over relatively level routes, not exceeding 0.3 percent ascending grades. Average speed range was usually 60-75 miles per hour. Accounts of their fast runs over Fort Wayne Division, eastern seaboard divisions, and other relatively flat routes would fill many pages. In Oc-

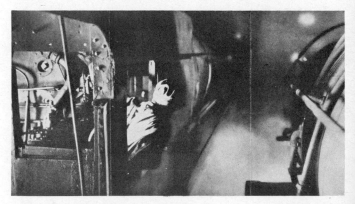

Pennsylvania Railroad

K4s passing a freight. This is before indicator lights were inside the cabs.

tober of 1938, a special test train, consisting of sixteen cars, weighing 1005.2 tons, attained a top speed of 92 MPH along the Fort Wayne Division racetrack, using engines 5354, 5362, or 3876, on various runs. (This test was conducted for the Association of American Railroads to determine horsepower requirements for pulling trains at various speeds. Similar tests were also run on Chicago & Northwestern and Union Pacific, using their engines.

This was the maximum attainable performance for a conventional stoker-fired K4s.

As good as it was, the K4s represented only a moderately-powerful machine, possessing limitations that could be overcome only by doubleheading heavy trains. This was especially true of long distance East-West limiteds, carrying Pullmans. With the introduction of air conditioned cars, the standard K4s assignment formula settled into a routine of two engines per train. All this leads to frequently expressed opinions doubting the wisdom of building hand fired K4s in the first place, and using them for so many years in main line doubleheaded work. This viewpoint goes even farther, stating the final one hundred K4s might better have been eight-drivered machines, possibly passenger M1's. After all, most other large railroads had adopted this type of power for passenger work during the mid 1920's. A PRR official, looking back a few years, made no bones about lamenting the huge expense of continually doubleheading K4s engines west of Harrisburg. "That hand fired engine was designed to haul eleven, 1914-style cars over the river graded Middle Division," he stated. "Cars not only increased greatly in weight, but it was also very seldom we had trains as short as eleven cars."

No one ever doubted the snappy, mile-eating performance of two K4s with sixteen or more cars tied to their combined tails. Perhaps the motive power men were dubious about getting that sort of work from anything short of a mammoth articulated. Two K4s' per train was always amply justified on the Pittsburgh Division. For example, what other engine(s) could possibly haul eighteen cars eastbound through Cresson on 1.5 percent ascending grade at better than fifty miles per hour?

The early 1930's saw thirty M-class 4-8-2's doing a fine job hauling passenger trains over the hilly, central divisions. Electrification however, sent dozens of K4s west of Harrisburg during the 30's, and most M class Mountains went into freight work. A further reason for not acquiring super passenger power was one of economics. Let's look at the facts: 425 K4s on hand, the big depression, one hundred new M1a engines, Eastern electrification program (cost $175 million). Is it any wonder then, that the railroad didn't embark on a project of a hundred or so super-locomotives. The K4s was not big enough, but under the circumstances (in our opinion) the Pennsy had no other alternative. Thus endeth the controversy.

South and east of Trenton, New York-Atlantic City Flyer No. 1077, the "Nellie Bly," was hauled by a K4s. Her engineman proudly told the author about being clocked at 98 MPH for several miles near Egg Harbor with 1546. A personal look-see revealed the train's passage that day at an unbelievable speed which seemed to confirm her throttle artist's claims. It was reminiscent of the Chicago-bound "Trail Blazer's" fast-flying dash (a few years earlier) across the 148 mile racetrack separating Fort Wayne and the Windy City, when speed was a steady 80-85 MPH.

The end was near early in 1956. Only 72 K4s remained in existence; twenty of these were in service, in New Jersey. New York & Long Branch, running between South Amboy and Bay Head Jct., was the final stronghold. This extended usage occurred because diesel units were too scarce to assign two per train, while one old K4s could handle a train. Figured on a horsepower basis, a K4s topped one 2000 HP diesel by a wide margin. Of course it was only a temporary thing, but their last stand was great while it lasted!

Pennsylvania Railroad

Thundering out of the darkness with scoop lowered! The engineer leans far out of his K4s as she picks up water on the Pittsburgh Division, in 1930. Note the reflections.

K4s VALEDICTORY

LOCOMOTIVE 8309—First K4s to be scrapped. On December 27, 1937, it was derailed in Pittsburgh, fell over a cliff and landed in the street below. Damage was so heavy that it had to be scrapped.

LOCOMOTIVE 612—Class K4sa, last passenger engine to haul a railfan special. On October 20, 1957, the trip ran in North Jersey coast area, along NY&LB.

LOCOMOTIVE 5351—Last K4s to haul a regular passenger train. In November 1957, it chuffed leisurely from Pemberton, N. J., into Camden on a short, morning commuter local and wrapped up the active K4s story for all time.

LOCOMOTIVES 1737 and 3750—The first K4s (1737) was sent to Northumberland for historical preservation, and its original tender was even dug up, probably off an H9s. 1737 however had laid idle so long and deteriorated to such a point that she wasn't even fit for saving. 3750 was selected as her stand-in, and received important 1737's masquerading parts, such as number and builder's plates. Apparently it wasn't enough just to save a K4s, it had to be the first one, regardless.

LOCOMOTIVE 1361—K4s presented to the City of Altoona and placed upon permanent exhibition at Horseshoe Curve trackside. On Saturday, June 8, 1957, the exhibit was dedicated and a special train carried 1600 passengers up from Altoona to witness the event. 1361 had only recently run her last miles out in New Jersey, and was completely refurbished by Altoona Shops before being placed at the Curve.

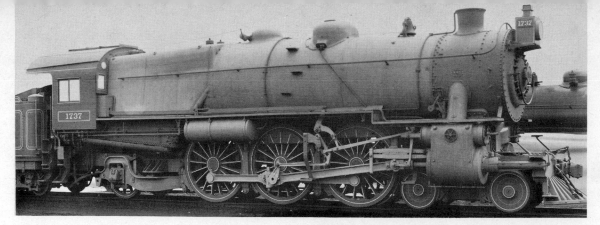

K4s 1737

May 1914, Juniata Shops turned out the first K4s locomotive, 1737. They knew they had a good one, but little did they realize how good! She was so perfect that she was copied 424 times over the next eighteen years.

The top photo shows the right side, still painted the flat gray official portrait color. Next, 1737 is in steam and painted shiny black. Below finds her at the Meadows, N. J. Enginehouse getting a high pressure bath of oil and water, 1923.

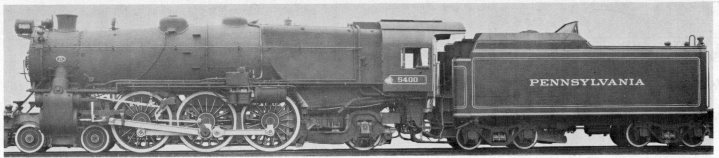

K4s, BALDWIN LOCOMOTIVE WORKS, 1927

Cylinders	27"x 28"	Grate Area	69.89 sq. ft.
Drivers	80"	Engine Weight	308,800 lbs.
Steam Pressure	205 lbs.	Tractive Force	44,460 lbs.

5471 *was a Baldwin sister to 5400 (above). Here at Altoona in 1956 she was one of the last 20 left in service. Except for stokers and front end alterations, they remained unchanged through the years.*

Westbound with No. 205-19 out of Altoona. Within the hour 3872 with its six cars in tour, will battle the Horseshoe Curve unassisted.

163

A night "meet"—probably depicting the East and West bound Broadway Limited.—oil.

K4s as seen by Artists

William Harndon Foster painted the first three New York Central calendar pictures, the last being the world famous "As the Centuries Pass In the Night". He and Central must have had some sort of disagreement, because he did advertising paintings for Pennsy after 1924. A superb fine artist, who had a deep love of trains, he was at his best with "dramatic action" containing masterful plays of lights and darks. We know very little else about this man.

"Night on the servicing pits".

—oil

A Chaney photograph was the inspiration for this 28" x 22" oil. It has three K4s Locomotives ascending the Allegheny Grade with No. 25, the Metropolitan Express.

Looming up out of the mist, a K4s hits the track pans.—oil.

1917

1120 as built, except the headlight has been converted to electricity.

1928

The one we remember best, with large raised headlight and slatted pilot.

1936

The face of Pennsy's first streamlined locomotive 3768.

TENDERS

Pennsy tender classification is not as complex as it may appear. The tender shown below is a 110-P-75. It carried 11,980 gallons and 18½ tons. The first digit represents water capacity in hundreds—so 110 represents 11,000 or more gallons. The letter P or F simply stands for passenger or freight service. The last number is the deck height above the rail in inches, thus 75 equals 75". So, 110-P-75 means, 11,000 or more gallons of water, P for passenger service and a deck that is 75" above rail level.

Beautifully striped 110-P-75 class tender for use on K4s class. William F Kiesel, Jr., mechanical engineer, designed both the tender and trucks.

OF THE K4s

1940

120, 2665, 3678 and 5338 were treated to very beautiful shrouds this year, 1120 is also on the far left.

1941

Early adaptions of the drop coupler pilots were quite handsome.

1947

The ugliest of them all— bulky pilot and cluttered face.

1954

Some were partially altered, 5497 retains her "Bar Pilot"

Don Wood

Ghost-like apparition as she sits bathed in her own steam.

"Black Knight" shrouded in darkness.

Ed Kospriske

167

CHICAGO

Engines 5358 and 3876 head No. 58, the combined *Liberty Limited* and *Golden Arrow* past 18th St. The "Windy City" skyline is the misty backdrop. April 28, 1934.

Pennsylvania Railroad

NEW YORK DIVISION

The heaviest traffic in the world rolls over Pennsy's New York Division. Working with a clean stack, in this pre-electrification picture, is K4s 5404.

The Railroad's capacity to move people and tonnage is beyond belief. For example: these four tracks have the capacity of a forty (yes we said forty) lane super highway—all this and no parking problem!

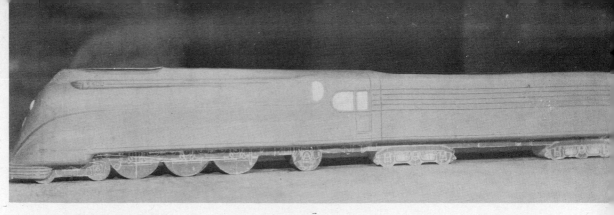

Clay wind tunnel test model for 3768.
below, 3768 as streamlined in 1936. Part of the side skirt is removed.

The mid-thirties saw American design ruled by the advocates of streamlining. Almost every major Railroad had a locomotive or two so treated. Pennsy's fling was quite small (five K4s and its lone S1), small that is, until the 52 T1 class appeared. 3768's shroud is rather bulky, but handsome none the less.

below, Special first run of the new Broadway Limited with members of the Traffic Club of Chicago passing 103rd St., June 7, 1938. The aerodynamic styling was supposed to reduce wind resistance, but they were a nuisance to maintain and were all later removed.

170

Dec. 14, 1940—23 year old K4s shows off her new styling. Four K4s's: 1120, 2665, 3678 and 5338 were so treated. These were beautiful, tastefully done shrouds. They were reminiscent of the streamlining applied to New York Central's Hudson type, two years previously.

2665 blasts out of Chicago with stainless steel cylinder covers glistening in the sun. The "South Wind" will reach Cincinnati via Ft. Wayne, Ind.

171

1361

The Pennsylvania Railroad, in the interest of history, has wisely preserved one or two locomotives of most major wheel arrangements. What more appropriate spot than the Horseshoe Curve could have been picked for the display site of a K4s? The exhibit was dedicated Saturday, June 8, 1957.

How many times she and others of her class powered Limiteds by this very spot!

below, 1361, when she was alive and running, roaring over the crossing south of Red Bank, N. J., May 1955.

SUPERHEATERS

The greatest single improvement, bar none, of the steam locomotive was the superheater. Prior to its development, steam would collect at the steam dome atop the boiler and be piped directly to the cylinders. This "raw steam" is referred to as saturated or wet steam.

The superheater is simply a collecting chamber (superheater header) with a series of tubes that run inside the large boiler tubes (designed for that purpose). As the steam is re-routed or detoured through these tubes, it is dried and greatly heated, causing no appreciable effect on the pressure. This ingenious but simple device upped locomotive efficiency by about 20%.

Pennsy began superheating locomotives about 1911. They were, of course, an instant success and were applied to all new locomotives and to most engines that came back for class repairs. All locomotives so treated were then sub classed "s". This little letter "s" was dropped as superflous after 1923, since superheaters were as common as wheels by then. An exception to this were the 100 Pacific's built in 1927 and 1928. They were classed K4s, making them similar to their earlier built sisters.

above, Partly completed K4s clearly showing the superheater tubes and the huge main steam delivery pipes.

below, Heavy—heavy!—Juniata Shops 1924, showing two K4s's under construction before being assigned to the western region.

above, A well dressed gentleman passenger has walked forward to view the charger that will speed him from Ft. Wayne to Pittsburgh. The locomotive blends very well with the Victorian-Gothic architecture.

below, One of the Baldwin built K4s Pacifics on the 46th St. Enginehouse turntable in Philadelphia, 1938. Many serious students of motive power disagree with Pennsy on this one. They believe the Railroad should have expanded its fleet of 4-8-2 Mountains, rather than order 100 K4s's in 1927-28.

Just ask any Pennsylvania fan and he will readily admit that this is the most beautiful steam locomotive in the land—We agree! 5487, built by Juniata in 1927, is impatiently waiting in East St. Louis.

below, In 1923 this beautiful train shed at Broad St. Station Philadelphia was destroyed by fire. This 1921 scene has the train crew visiting the busy engineer. Within two hours 3731 will have delivered all of them to the Electrics at Manhattan Transfer.

R. L. Long

While Western Railroads were forced to lug heavy water capacity tenders, Pennsy used small ones and relied on picking up their water from 22 strategically placed track pans. Their greatest concentration was on Lines East of Pittsburgh. The taking of water on the fly was just another bit of drama created by the steam locomotive.

left, STAND BACK! Sometimes the lowered scoop puts on a show more spectacular than the photographer bargained for. Ancora, N. J. 1953.

below, Scooping water at Long Branch, N. J. on the New York & Long Branch R.R. between Bay Head Junction and South Amboy. July 1949.

WATER ON THE FLY

John M. Prophet III

Pennsylvania Railroad

5455 leads its train through one of the many curves on its Baltimore to Harrisburg run in 1937. This 83 mile segment of the Pennsy is a series of high-degree curves and stiff grades running through rolling farm country, just east of the Allegheny Mountains.

An Atlantic City Express train (No. 1073) rips through Elizabeth, N. J. before electrification, May 23, 1931.

Ted Gay

In the early 1930's a few K4s's were painted Tuscan Red instead of Brunswick Green (Pennsy official passenger locomotive color). We don't know if 3761 was so treated, but we can use our imagination and "deck-her-out"—red with gold stripes and letters.

below, New York to Pittsburgh flyer on the mainline, midway between Philadelphia and Harrisburg. In 1938 this section was electrified.

178

Pennsy's pride, the "Broadway Limited" rolls along near Andalusia, Pa. in 1923. 1985's headlight has been electrified, but she still retains her small tender and oil marker lights.

below, 5415 wheels a long string of Varnish on the Pittsburgh Division. Pennsy didn't fool much with fancy gadgets like booster engines and feedwater heaters on their K4s fleet. To compensate these omissions, they were designed with huge 27" x 28" cylinders. It took a heck of a good boiler to supply steam to them and it took a h - - - of a good fireman to supply coal to the firebox! The K4s' were not built with stokers either.

179

The cold December day accents 5372's heavy exhaust plume as she races through Middletown, New Jersey at 65 m.p.h., with No. 787 on the N. Y. & L. B. Railroad. This Sunday-only train is bound for Bay Head Junction, N. J.

3858 pauses at Frankford Junction, Philadelphia, with special train bound for the Atlantic City racetrack. This affords an excellent view of class 130-P-75 (with trainphone aerial) tender, that was used on many K4s'.

"The Nellie Bly" races w e s t w a r d across the Jersey flatlands at 75 M.P.H. After reaching Trenton, a GG1 will relieve 8378 (the highest numbered K4s) and take the train to New York City.

Pennypacker

Warm, summer Sunday mornings saw hourly seashore trains running out of Philadelphia in two or more sections. Here, K4s 5412 blasted through Zoo Tower's interlocking plant and was on her way to Atlantic City with coaches filled with ocean-bound travelers.

Don Wood

If you cared to "brave it", severe winter conditions afforded the greatest rail-photography potentials. On this crystal clear January day, it was 5° above zero at Matawan, New Jersey, as 612 heads No. 709 bound for Bay Head. 612 incidently, was one of five K4s' fitted with larger piston valves and classified K4sa.

One K4s could handle a train up the Curve very easily; if it were short enough, that is.
3768 is so doing here, with the four-car Pittsburgh Express on Oct. 5, 1920.

below, The same locomotive shown above has a new attire here, in 1936. 3768 is speeding
along under the beautiful, semetrical curved trolley wire.

The decision facing J. Edgar Thomson, who staked out the Pennsy mainline over one hundred years ago, was: should the Railroad attack the Allegheny Mountains gradually or suddenly? The latter was chosen; so to gain altitude in a short distance, the now famous Horseshoe Curve was devised.

above, Six car train, 602 descends Thomson's Trail on June 25, 1920.

below, The first and second sections of the W/B Manhattan Limited pause at Paoli, Pa. Neither K4s has yet been fitted with stokers.

25

PITTSBURGH DIVISION

Three brand new K4s Pacifics head the 17 car "Metropolitan Express" (No. 25) towards the Horseshoe Curve. After the train reaches the Gallitizin summit, the lead engine (helper) 5448, will be cut off.

Pennsylvania Railroad

C. Z. Vaughan

Jan. 17, 1953, New York to Atlantic City Express rips by West Haddonfield's Vernon Tower.

In addition to giving the K4s a drop- coupler, the post war ... t added desired front end ... ght.

Don Wood

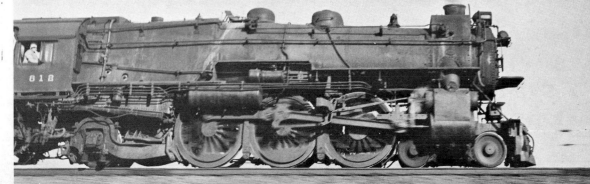

COULD THE K4s BE IMPROVED

As the years slipped by, a few K4s' assumed the role of guinea pigs, sporting all manner and kinds of gadgetry for test purposes. Various innovations included streamlined shrouds, poppet valve gears, cross-counter balanced disc drivers, front end throttles, roller bearings, huge tenders, tuscan red livery, smoke deflectors, and many others. Just name it and PRR probably had it on the K4s locomotive at one time or another. More K4s's carried more different kinds of test equipment than any other class.

Strange as it may seem, most changes did not alter the K4s classification. Only five engines got switched to K4sa; and these because of fifteen-inch piston valves instead of the normal twelve-inch size. Improvements such as front end throttles, disc drivers, and circulators (which added forty-two square feet to total heating surface) were used on K4sa's and K4s's. Steam distribution tests showed that front end throttles helped materially to deliver steam into cylinders with very little drop in temperature and/or pressure. Locomotive 5399, rebuilt by Lima in 1939, with Franklin valve gear and poppet valves, along with many other improvements, showed the greatest increase in hauling capacity. Its drawbar horsepower, between sixty and eighty miles per hour, topped conventional piston valved K4s power by 24 to 44 percent.

Selective experimentation began in the mid-1930's, soon after most K4s had been upgraded to include stokers, mechanical lubricators, larger tenders, etc. Inasmuch as the

PENNSYLVANIA LOCOMOTIVE, CLASS K-4-S, WITH TIMKEN BEARINGS ON THE CROSSHEAD AND ALL CRANK PINS; ALSO THE MAIN AND SIDE RODS, PISTON AND PISTON ROD, CRANK PINS AND CROSSHEAD ARE MADE OF TIMKEN HIGH DYNAMIC STEEL. THE RECIPROCATING PARTS WEIGH LESS THAN 1,000 LBS. THIS ENGINE IS ALSO EQUIPPED ON ALL AXLES WITH TIMKEN BEARINGS. THE DRIVING AXLE AND TRAILER TRUCK BOXES FIT INTO PLAIN BEARING PEDESTAL OPENING. BEARING AND ROD APPLICATIONS WERE MADE IN APRIL 1934, AND THE LOCOMOTIVE AVERAGES 12,000 MILES PER MONTH. THE LOCOMOTIVE HAULS THE "CINCINNATI LIMITED" AND THE "AMERICAN" BETWEEN COLUMBUS AND PITTSBURGH.   TIMKEN R-325.

G. Grabill Jr.

There is no denying the worth of roller bearings. The K4s fleet was built before their development. Two engines, 20 and 5371, were equipped with them.

425-unit fleet was built and retained in relatively plain and simple form, installation of ultra-modern test equipment was bound to boost efficiency. On the other hand, K4s's original, built-in design was so perfect that any appreciable increases in power were almost impossible. After all, any type of motive power had its capacity limits. Souping it up could (and did) produce satisfactory marginal success, but, was no cure-all to solve doubleheading problems. Something much larger was required for that, and it came, eventually, in the duplex-drive T1 (which K4s experimentation helped develop.)

Paul W. Prescott

Smoke deflectors were designed to lift the smoke up and over the engine cab.

Coast to Coast tenders were fitted to ten K4s' in the thirties, but proved a liability because the added weight meant dropping a car from the trains length. Loaded, they weighed 14 more tons than the locomotive. It is interesting to note that Pennsy engines usually operated on one, two, or three divisions, rather than over the entire Line, as did locomotives of most other roads.

Pennsylvania Railroad

Only three K4s' (5399, 5436 and 3676) were equipped with Booster Engines. Note the big booster pipe coming from the top of the boiler. right, Close up showing booster pipe and cylinders on trailing truck.

BOOSTERS

Other roads preferred using smaller main cylinders, relying on Booster Engines to help start trains. Pennsy chose to by pass this expensive gadget and bet on its free steaming Belpair Boiler delivering enough steam to the two huge 27" x 28" cylinders. For comparison, New York Central's J3a (built in 1938, with Booster) had 22½" x 29" cylinders.

History would probably bare Pennsy out on this one, for on some of the very last locomotives built, the Booster was left off as unnecessary.

Pennsy's K4s fleet was built with spoked drivers. A few were refitted with disc types, as shown here.

DRIVERS

One of the bad features of a steam locomotive was the damage to rails by wheel and rod pounding. The disc drivers were an attempt to reduce this.

POPPETS

Pennsy had three K4s' fitted with three different actuated poppet valves. Poppets are similar to the valves in a regular diesel or gasoline engine, having a stem and head construction.

Pennsylvania Railroad

The various named poppet valves are much the same, but the differentiation is their powering.

5399 had the Franklin O. C. (oscillating cams) arrangement applied in 1939 by the Lima Locomotive Works. This proved to be almost unbelievably successful producing 44% more draw-bar horsepower at 80 m.p.h.

In 1940, 5436 received steam accuated valves, designed by Lloyd B. Jones, Engineer of Tests, at Altoona.

In 1945, 3847 was treated to the unusual Franklin Type B system, that has the eccentric turning an exterior cam.

The poppets were applied to these three K4s's with a definite eye towards future class development, rather than any wholesale application to the 4-6-2 fleet.

Summing up: Poppets were good, in fact, excellent at higher speeds. They were, however, complex, rather expensive and definitely required "looking after". Piston valves were inefficient at higher speeds, but were simple, proven and durable. Had reciprocating steam power held reign, a better steam distribution system would have evolved—probably in some simple poppet form.

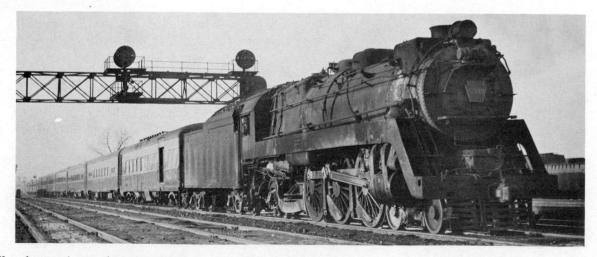

Harold Stirton

The fantastic performing 5399 heads the "Trail Blazer" through Englewood, Feb. 15, 1948. This was probably the most disasterous success on record, for had 5399 not been so great, the Pennsy might have built their T1 fleet with Walschaert piston valves instead of Franklin Poppets.

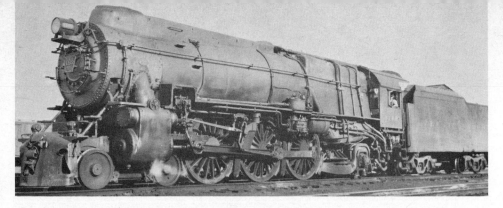

K4s 1188 got a boiler-top face lifting in the form of a long, smooth cowling which is reminiscent of the type applied to Southern Pacific engines. The men referred to her as "The Skyline".

Front end throttle and Franklin rotary-accuated poppet valves on 3847, made her the most unusual looking K4s of all. She was a wonder to watch, with everything in motion except the heavy outer valve frame. She is powering the Florida Arrow out of Chicago, March 1949.

Probably the largest smoke deflectors ever added to an American engine was applied to K4s 5038. The huge "ears" and shrouded stack were enough to make the aesthetically sensitive, look the other way. They did, however, do an excellent job of lifting the smoke up and over the cab.

189

K5 CLASS 4-6-2 PACIFICS

Could the K 4s be improved upon?

A year after the last K4s was built, (1929) two whopping big experimental Pacifics rolled into service. These were class K5, road numbers 5698 and 5699. The K5 seemed to be Pennsy's challenge to the Hudsons (4-6-4 Type) that were extremely popular on the New York Central.

The K5 topped the K4s with just about bigger everything except driver size (80 inches) and grate area. (69.89 sq. ft.). A comparison follows:

	K4s	K5
Cylinders	27" x 28"	27" x 30"
Boiler Pressure	205 lbs.	250 lbs.
Total Heating Surface	4041 sq. ft.	4285 sq. ft.
Superheating Surface	943 sq. ft.	1634 sq. ft.
Weight on Drivers	201,830 lbs.	208,250 lbs.
Total Engine Weight	308,890 lbs.	327,560 lbs.
Tractive Effort	44,460 lbs.	54,675 lbs.
Factor of Adhesion	4.54	3.80

Notice K5's lower factor of adhesion which produced less sure rail footing when starting and working at low speeds. Factor of adhesion is simply the ratio between tractive force and weight on drivers. The factor of adhesion was less on the K5 than K4s because its power increase was far greater than corresponding weight added to drivers. It would be something like putting a heavier, more powerful motor in an automobile. You would have a lot more power but you would also have a greater tendency to slip on wet pavement.

Since they preceded the M1a Mountain by one year, it's safe to assume that K5's huge, one piece cast steel cylinder saddle, with inside steam delivery pipes, was a successful trial balloon. The K5 and 4-8-2's were also identical in cylinder dimensions, boiler pressure, and superheater size. The K5's had power reverse, Worthington feedwater heaters, unflanged main driving wheels, nickel steel boiler shells and they were (believe it or not) hand fired.

Class 130-P-75 tenders carried 13,475 gallons and twenty-two tons. Tender trucks differed from those used on most Kiesel-designed tenders, being arched with equalizing springs underneath the arched center portion. Aside from their extremely large boilers the K5's were instantly recognized by the unique bell location, beneath the headlight on the smokebox front.

Although classified identically, the two K5's had striking differences, as shown below:

Engine 5698—Built at Altoona Works in 1929. Piston valves, Walschaert valve gear, one piece, cast steel underframe, tractive effort 54,675 pounds.

Engine 5699—Built by Baldwin in 1929. Poppet valves, Caprotti valve gear, fabricated underframe, tractive effort 58,092 pounds.

Caprotti valve gear and poppet valves were removed from 5699 in 1937. These were replaced by piston valves and Walschaert gear, making it identical to its sister engine.

5698 and 5699 were originally assigned to haul the Philadelphia-Pittsburgh through trains. After electrification reached Harrisburg, they were re-assigned to the twisting Northern Central line between Harrisburg and Baltimore. On this 83 mile segment, they were even doubleheaded with H9s Consolidations. The K5 ended its days on Pittsburgh Crestline runs.

As it was with so many experimentals, they were not always complete successes or "end answers" in themselves, but the results aided immeasurably in future decisions and class developments.

Thru Timonium, Maryland, by Milton A. Davis.

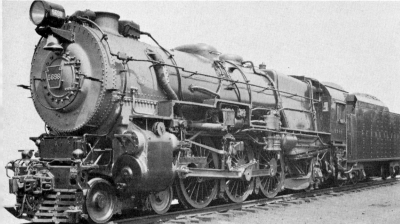

Three views of Kiesel designed, Altoona built K5 after stoker engine was added in 1940. 5698 and 5699 were the only Pennsy Pacifics with feedwater heaters. The huge cylinder saddle was used the following year on 100 new M1a mountain type locomotives.

Baldwin built K5 had Caprotti poppet valves, and was called (kiddingly) Mussolini. Senior Caprotti, (the Italian designer) was quite shocked the first time he saw an American freight train. "Your locomotives haul houses, not cars!", was his apt comment.

left, Altoona Shops, January 1929, find K5 5698 under construction. The one piece, cast steel frame and cylinders were built at Commonwealth's Granite City, Ill., plant.

below, The most striking feature about the K5 was its Decapod sized boiler. Note the feedwater heater behind the stack.

April, 1941 has a vastly improved K5 speeding towards Baltimore between Glen Rock and New Freedom, Pa. Walschaert valve gear has replaced the delicate Caprotti and stokers are now feeding the 70 sq. ft. grate area. It's hard to believe that they were built hand-fired.

Milton A. Davis

Baldwin built 5699 hefts a Harrisburg-Washington train near Timonium, Maryland. The engine crews didn't particularly care for the two K5's, probably because they had a lot more "git" than "dig".

In the mid thirties, about the time the streamlining fad was running hot, 5698 had shroud covering placed behind the domes and stack. The Worthington Feedwater heater is covered and the turret has a bit of sheetmetal art applied.

Pennsylvania Railroad

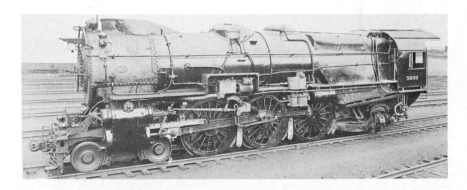

The K5's didn't escape the front end "beauty" treatment.

Milton A. Davis

CLASS 4-8-2 MOUNTAINS

Pennsy's gilt-edged investment in steam power.

Some frequently asked questions have been concerned with reasons for Pennsylvania's relatively late adoption of fast, high horsepower, dual service engines, as exemplified in its fleet of 301 4-8-2's. It has also been asked why more were not built. Facts of the matter are, soaring World War I tonnage volume, coupled with up-and-down topography made very necessary a 1916 to 1923 concentration upon acquisition of nearly eight hundred drag freighters of the ten drivered type.

New at Baldwin, 1930.   Pennsylvania Railroad

After the 1926 and 1930 additions of three hundred Mountain Types, depression years and long-range electrification plans obviated further needs for more. Since PRR did far more of its own locomotive research and development than the average railroad, an approach to fast dual service concepts was a cautious one. A single prototype model 4-8-2 was designed and out-shopped by Juniata in 1923. This was locomotive 4700, shop construction No. 3819, and classified as M1. She underwent more than two years of test plant and road trials before the design features were approved for fleet construction.

Following is a numerical list of the Mountains:
Class M1   1923   1 locomotive
    4700 (re-numbered 6699) Juniata Shops
Class M1   1926   200 locomotives
    6800-6974   Baldwin
    6975-6999   Lima
Class M1a   1930   100 locomotives
    6700-6749   Baldwin
    6750-6774   Juniata Shops
    6775-6799   Lima

Although a natural assumption might well place the M1 design into an enlarged K4s Pacific, such was not the case. The 4-8-2's standard features were actually transplanted from the I1s class Decapods. The M1 designers, J. T. Wallis, Chief of Motive Power, and W. F. Kiesel, Jr., Mechanical Engineer, took an I1s boiler blueprint and inked in a much larger combustion chamber leaving most other details unchanged. Other items of I1s derivation included

guides, crossheads, and various machinery parts. Characteristic highlights included: pilot deck-mounted air reservoir tank, 27" x 30" cylinders, 72-inch drivers, 250 pounds boiler pressure, KW type trailing truck, Belpaire firebox, small steel cab, total weight of 385,000 pounds, and tractive effort of 64,550 pounds. Incidentally, original plans called for 80-inch drivers, but experience has shown this would have been a fatal mistake.

M1 and M1a classes were basically the same in most respects; however, the M1a had several improvements, including two air compressers instead of one, and Worthington feedwater heaters. The M1 had one piece, welded cylinders, while M1a's cylinders were of one piece, cast steel with inside steam delivery pipes. The two hundred M1 engines were built with medium sized tenders having a capacity of 11,980 gallons and 18½ tons (class 110-P-75). The 1930-vintage M1a engines however, got PRR's first large capacity tenders, nick-named "coast-to-coast tenders" by employees. They rode on six-wheel trucks and carried 22,090 gallons and 31½ tons (class 210-F-75). On the Western Region, some M1's also pulled tank cars for extra water carrying capacity on long runs.

D. A. Fink II

Trails End, Altoona table in 1957.

b 6761 with 136 loads.

Bud Rothaar

"Buffalo Boxcar"—Millersburg, Pa.   Bud Rothaar

The original experimental engine, 4700, was built with a very small tender and no mechanical stoker. It didn't take long to see that under heavy service conditions, even a Jawn Henry would find himself in serious difficulties, hand firing the seventy square feet of grate area. Stoker and tender faults were soon corrected. In later years, many of the medium capacity M1 tenders were replaced with new class 210-F-75B long-distance ones, these being closely similar to the big M1a tenders, except that they rode on eight wheel, roller bearing trucks. Their weight, loaded, was 411,400 pounds, which was actually thirteen tons heavier than an M1. Some also got 250-P-75 tenders carrying 24,410 gallons and 25 tons. Railing-like trainphone aerials were added to most tender tops during the 1940's.

Mountains were the first classes of superheated power to drop the suffix letter "s" from class designation. Since all new engines were superheated by that time, the small letter was considered superfluous. All 4-8-2's were built with standard passenger type slatted pilots, but many were subsequently replaced by the less attractive, but more utilitarian, footboards. A further pilot revision featured rounded, solid pilots with drop couplers. Husky-throated passenger whistles were installed atop the boilers and keystone number plates replaced the original round ones. A prime lesson in how to mar the good looks of a locomotive was adequately demonstrated in the middle 1940's by exchanging headlight and turbo-generator locations, plus the addition of a smokebox-front mounted platform to stand on when servicing the generator. These features had their good points from an operating point of view only.

Beginning in the year 1946, a number of class M1a locomotives were upgraded and re-classified M1b. Important changes included a twenty pound increase in steam pressure to 270 pounds, and installation of circulators (somewhat similar to syphons) in fireboxes, which increased heating surface by thirty-five square feet. These improvements boosted tractive effort from 64,550 pounds to 69,700 pounds, however, since engine weight was not materially increased, factor of adhesion went down from 4.19

to 3.89. There were thirty-eight M1b engines. Interestingly enough, these changes occurred after the locomotives were sixteen or more years old, and their final years of service were spent pulling the heaviest tonnages of their careers.

Mountain types were so-named because they were considered big and powerful for such work when first designed during World War I days. However, by the years PRR acquired its M1's, the type had developed into a river-grade or level-route hauler. Although the M1 was built and used as a dual service machine, its greatest value proved to be in freight work. Electrification of most main routes east of Harrisburg during the 1930's displaced a large quantity of K4s class, which eventually took over most passenger assignments handled by 4-8-2's. Even so, the M1 could handle far heavier trains and it might have been better in the long run to have had more 4-8-2's and fewer K4s, to avoid expensive doubleheading.

Lowgrade freight line.   Pennsylvania Railroad

In freight work, the M-classes were practically worth their weight in diamonds, operating in fast service along most principal main routes. Although the railroad built a number of very successful engines through the years, PRR men have always maintained their M1/M1a classes were the best steam locomotives the railroad ever owned. They replaced Mikados, Decapods, and Santa Fe's. By hauling most fast symbol freights, they became the hallmark of Pennsy fast freight service. The 4-8-2's rapid exhausts echoed from the Trenton Cut-off or river-grades of Susquehanna and Juniata valleys or pancake flat Fort Wayne and St. Louis Divisions. Eighty miles per hour was top allowable speed along the New York Division, with seventy-five per being permitted on most other divisions.

Twenty M1 engines and ten M1a were assigned to passenger service, when built; the ten M1a's being 6700-6709 with beautifully gold-striped long-distance tenders. They sometimes ran through from Harrisburg to Columbus, a distance of 435.5 miles spanning three divisions, about the longest through runs ever achieved. Westbound out of Altoona, an M1 without helper could take a ten-car passenger train up the 1.86 percent average grade to Gallitzin. Eastbound on one percent grades climbing toward Gallitzin, an M1 was able to average thirty miles per hour with seventeen or eighteen cars in tow. Three 4-8-2's were assigned to the Cleveland Division and four to the Fort Wayne Division, leaving twenty-three for Harrisburg-Pittsburgh-Columbus passenger runs.

In the year 1932, for example, M1a 6707 hauled train No. 54 "The Gotham Limited" over the Middle Division from Altoona to Harrisburg. A Baldwin official was riding her cab and his records show the following: Sixteen cars weighing 1100 tons, running time 162 minutes non-stop for 130.8 miles at an overall average speed of 48.5 miles per hour. The run was completed five minutes faster, averaging fifty miles per hour, with top speeds of 65-70 MPH. During the 1940's, several M1 engines with class 110-P-75 tenders were used on passenger trains between Harrisburg, Williamsport, and Buffalo, though most 4-8-2's were, by that time, in freight service.

Most 4-8-2's were assigned to moderately-graded divisions, the largest blocks of them being operated east of Altoona over Middle and Philadelphia Divisions, which, in 1932, had sixty and seventy-three assigned, respectively. When the Philadelphia Division was electrified in 1938, many Mountains were re-assigned to handle practically all Middle Division traffic, including heavy coal trains. They were also sent up the Williamsport Division to Renovo or Wilkes-Barre. World War II traffic demands also made

and/or low-grade freight lines. The normal New York route was over the Trenton Cut-off from Thorndale to Morrisville, by-passing Philadelphia. This meant the Mountains also ran over New York Division main line east of Morrisville. On the eastern end, locomotives terminated at either Meadows Enginehouse (Kearny, N. J.) or South Amboy, N. J.

Enola and East Altoona enginehouses were always well supplied with Mountains. The continuous sweeping curves of the Middle Division were their special and long-time operating habitat, lasting here almost to the end of steam operations. When the new iron ore import pier was opened at South Philadelphia in 1954, westbound ore trains were hauled over the Middle Division with two 4-8-2's pulling and an I1s class Decapod pushing all the way. Previously, several fast symbol freights rated doubleheaders; one usually pulled out of Enola each mid-afternoon and whipped up speed like a passenger train as its 125 cars rocked along the Susquehanna's banks.

During their last years of service, they were given increasingly heavy tonnage to pull, while diesels were assigned to the faster runs. As usual, the M1 did a wonderful job; its rating of more than four thousand drawbar horsepower was sufficient to handle heavy trains. Nostalgic memories include the way a hard-working westbound 4-8-2 would vibrate house windows while passing through Coatesville and fighting the 0.6 percent grade, usually with an L1s class snapper blasting away on the rear end. A parting farewell note to these gallant Mountains is that locomotive 6755 has been stored at Northumberland for historical purposes.

Bob Lorenz

6971 lugs tonnage east out of Crestline, Ohio.

necessary continued use of some 4-8-2's east of Harrisburg, where they smoked up the catenary wires. Most other M1's pulled freight over the Eastern, Fort Wayne, and St. Louis Divisions, with very few negotiating the tough Pittsburgh Division grades.

The seventy-three 4-8-2's assigned to Philadelphia Division, running eastward out of Enola (Harrisburg), handled freights to Philadelphia and to the various New York terminal areas located on the west shores of the Hudson River. Routings were via any possible combination of main line

Bob Lorenz

M1 6925 and J1 6163 work up Tiro Hill near Carrothers, Ohio.

M1, *Juniata, October 1923, later numbered 6699.*

M1, *Lima, 1926. 27" x 30" cylinders, 72" drivers, 382,400 lbs. engine weight and tractive force 64,550 lbs.*

M1a, *Baldwin 1930, built and painted for passenger service.*

M1a, *Lima 1930 with 210-F-75 tender, 22,090 gallons and 31½ tons.*

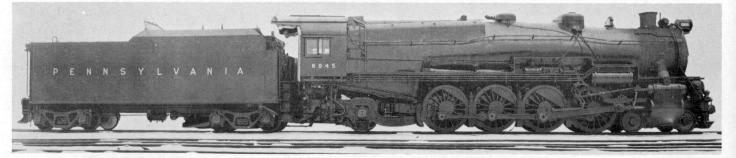

M1, *Baldwin 1926, shown here after re-shopping in 1941. Pennsy's President didn't care for this Futura lettering, so it didn't last long.*

M 1

Face of the "M" class before and after beauty treatment. left, Baldwin built M1a 6715. right, M1 with a string of hoppers waiting to cross Rockville Bridge. The new pilot served two purposes: It had a drop coupler and it increased front-end weight.

The first M1 waits on the Altoona test plant in Oct. 1923. The Pennsylvania Railroad, with its usual thoroughness, tested 4700 for two years before ordering more M's. She is one of, if not the, last locomotive built with extended piston rods. The extra bits of striping and trim certainly dressed her up.

M1a 6738 and M1 helper with 57 car freight, Chicago, September 1947. — This pictur[e] speaks for itself.

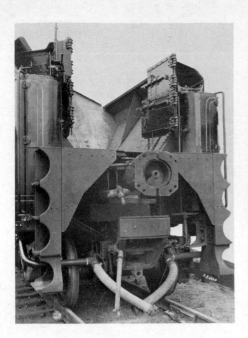  

Pennsylvania Railroad

left, front of 110-P-82 tender for the first M1 4700. She was built without stoker, but it didn't take long to see that no man could keep pace with its huge firebox.

middle, Rear of same tender. Note the letter P, indicating that the pilot model M1 was built with an eye towards passenger service.

right, huge 210-F-75A built in 1939. There was a definite trend in steam development towards larger and larger tenders.

M1a satisfying its thirst. This 210-F-75 tender holds 22,090 gallons and 31½ tons.

Bob Lorenz

Track pans weren't everywhere. Here at Leolyn, Pa. on the Elmira Branch, a pair of M1's get an "old fashioned drink".

right, Head brakeman leaves his doghouse as 6730 passes the water pan. Mapleton, Pa., Sept. 1949.

below, Mountains and Mountains, M1's are dwarfed by the immense Pennsylvania backdrop, Mapleton, Pa.

Everytime we see dramatic shots of scooping water, we think of the stories about unsuspecting tramps who would hitch a ride on the rear of a tender in cold weather. Everything was fine until the scoop was lowered and the poor chap was frozen stiff.

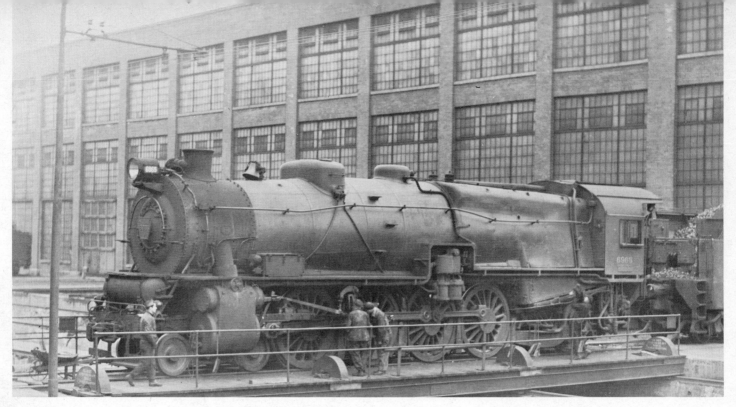

above, M1 6965 *has been separated from her tender. The transfer table will "spot" her, to be moved through one of the huge doors at the Altoona Works.*

right. Cab arrangement of an M1a. Note the set of cab indicator lights for both Engineer and Fireman. These duplicate the signals on the block ahead.*

below, M1a, 6766 *under construction at Altoona, 1930. in the foreground we have stacks of lagging (insulation), domes, air tanks, and other miscellaneous machinery that are yet to be applied.*

M

Pennsylvania Railroad

These two pictures capture much of the glory and drama that belong to steam. *above,* An M1, shrouded in its own steam, pounds out of Philadelphia's 52nd St. Yards.

below, M1b just north of Harrisburg bound for Williamsport passing electrified "slide fence". This safety device trips signal, should rock slide break the fence. Note the sand being applied to 1st and 3rd drivers.

Bud Rothaar

MIDDLE

DIVISION

Up the Middle Division with
an E/B coal drag, 1939. 6746's
huge stack is clean.

Pennsylvania Railroad

M1 6842 was pulling hard
past View Tower, Duncan-
non, Pa. with 125 car coal
t r a i n. The t o w e r was
named well, for it is located
on the west shore of the
broad Susquehanna River,
looking towards beautiful
mountain scenery.

Bert Pennypacker

6802 certainly has the look of power and speed about her as she heads her string of "reefers" near Valparaiso, Indiana. She's doing almost 60 m.p.h.

Marching up the beautiful Middle Division with a load of coal, is Baldwin built M1a 6703. It was hot, this June day in 1941, and the heat radiating from the backhead is making the cab interior a virtual oven.

A pair of M1a's stand ready at Enola Enginehouse. Pennsy hit the jackpot on this one. They were just about the greatest hunk of steam power they ever owned. They were designed with an eye towards passenger and dual service, but they possessed such power that they became the kings of the high speed freight. When the occasion demanded it, they could wheel 20 heavy Pullmans at speed.

Fat boilered M1 gets a good cleaning at Philadelphia's 46th St. Enginehouse.

POWER

East Altoona Enginehouse holds I1sa 2035 and M1a 6793. The relationship between these two classes was more than slight, for rather than being an "extended" K4s Pacific, the Mountain's "standards" were adapted from huge Decapods.

*The Enola Enginehouse contains 43 stalls for "grooming the iron horses".
Here, taking up four of these berths are M1's. After this minor shopping they will all be back heading Symbol Freights on the Middle Division.*

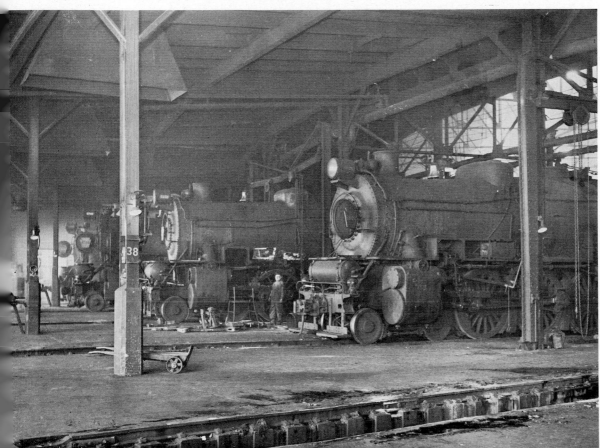

Rods flashing, drivers pounding, eccentric whirling and stack blasting—We can almost hear her as she roars towards Altoona from Enola, Pa. This was probably the most favored and loved class of power on the Pennsylvania Railroad. They were just about flawless and rode beautifully. At home on passenger runs or hot shot freights, they had everything: easy steaming, power and speed. Can anyone blame us for wondering why the Pennsy ordered its last 100 K4s Pacifics, when it could have had these instead?

A Bit of Nostalgia—M1 6825, on a cold November dawn, off the Rockville Bridge into Enola Yard—wide open and down in the corner, up-grade. There was (so they said) a little thunder when she went by.

June 1949, the "big show" was on a week-end jump from Baltimore to Pittsburgh. This (27 cars of animals) is the third of four trains and is "hittin it" through Marysville, Pa.

above, 6874 *makes a little smoke as it passes under one of the tracks that leads to the bridge across the Susquehanna River. right, A "thousand to one" shot. Eastbound coal drag at Mifflin, Pa. with M1b 6724, caught just as the engineer again "opens her wide". Trains with 111 loads is bound for Harrisburg from Altoona.*

below, There is little doubt that the 20 car "Duquesne" will have much trouble with the Horseshoe Curve this day. Assisting the pair of Baldwin diesels out of Altoona, are an M1 Mountain and a K4s Pacific.

211

This was just about the last of Pennsy's finest. 6888 on Northumberland's Turntable, June 22, 1957.

As the years went by, the trend was to install larger and larger tenders on steam locomotives. 6914 poses at Altoona with her 16 wheeler.

The M1a mountains sported dual air pumps, Worthington feedwater heaters (behind stack), but no trailing truck booster engine. This seemed to be just about all the gadgets they needed.

From any angle, "Pennsy's Best" really had it!

above, leaving Enola Yards with the "Buffalo Boxcar".

left, 6717 and 6921 pull under the mainline coal-water plant at Denholm, Pa. Towards the end of their careers they were hauling tonnage that the original designers would have thought impossible.

A lucky shot! Mainline "meet" 10 miles west of Harrisburg has M1a 6747 lugging eastbound coal and 6921 "hotshotting" westbound merchandise freight. Some roundhouse comedian has left a very undignified "Hot Cat" on 6747's air tank.

3 degrees below zero, makes tough work for M1b 6750 at Sunbury, Pa. as she strains mightily on stiff journals to m o v e 87 c a r s of merchandise freight.

Staufer Collection

above, 6815 is approaching Harrisburg with No. 500-54 in from Williamsport. There must have been a down wind, because the throttle man looks like he's ready to step onto a minstrel stage.

below, Rolling through Duncannon bound for Enola, on a brisk December day. The string of hoppers can be seen trailing out far behind on the S curve.

n Wood

CLASS 4-4-4-4 DUPLEX

Radical design and diesel replacements worked against them.

5505 *heads the "Duquesne" along the Susquehanna River at Duncannon, Pa. August 1948.*

".... the locomotives performed satisfactorily under all operating conditions .... we believe their performance in actual service stamps them as notable examples of railroad motive power." Editor Malcolm K. Wright was making an optimistic prognostication about the initial pair of T1 class duplex-drivers, engines 6110 and 6111; in his "Baldwin Locomotives Magazine" for December of 1942. Little more than five years later, and with a fifty-two-unit fleet of T1's that had passed Altoona test plant instruments with flying colors, President Martin W. Clement announced, early in 1948: "By May of this year, we expect all our important east-west through passenger trains will be diesel-powered west of Harrisburg."

What had happened to the long-awaited K4s replacement locomotive, and, was it possible that test plant findings could be inaccurate? Or, were other factors present to compound a design situation that needed revision? Many Belpaire followers are convinced Pennsy would have been far less susceptible to late 1940's dieselization decisions if its duplex-drives were more successful, or if 4-8-4's had been built instead. Unfortunately, a combination of mechanical and operating problems plagued them; in fact, there were implications suggesting that rigid frame duplexes might not be practical. At any rate, there was no time to experiment and find out, for serious economic pressures quickly swung the balance weight from steam to diesels.

convinging advantages; some of these principal selling points are listed below:

★ LIGHTER MACHINERY. Total weight of all rods and reciprocating parts of a rigid framed 4-4-4-4, 4576 pounds. Three representative 4-8-4's compared as follows—5344 pounds, 6167 pounds, 5426 pounds. Weights were for one side only, including front and rear drives of the Duplex.

★ SHORTER CYLINDER STROKE. Lower piston speed for any given locomotive speed.

★ LESS WEAR AND TEAR. Smaller and lighter moving parts.

★ LOWER PISTON THRUST. 4-4-4-4 carrying 300 pounds boiler pressure registered a thrust of 90,000 pounds. This compared to 160,000 pounds thrust on a 4-8-4 with 275 pounds boiler pressure.

★ SMALLER CYLINDERS. Increased efficiency at high speeds, as large cylinders were handicapped by piston valve's inability to deliver enough steam rapidly.

★ RIGID FRAME. Far more stability at high speeds than articulated underframes. Also, no hinged connection to maintain.

Baldwin delivered the first two (experimental) T1 engines, 6110 and 6111, in the year 1942. Beneath their dramatic, Loewy-styled exterior shrouds was the builder's advanced theory of the 4-8-4's successor. This brainchild of Eddystone's Chief Engineer, Ralph P. Johnson, had been developed in blueprint form several years earlier, but there were no takers until Pennsy signed on the dotted line (in 1940) just as Baldwin was about to build a demonstrator itself. PRR took the duplexes exactly as blueprinted, with but two major reservations. (1) They must haul 880 trailing tons at one hundred miles per hour on level tangent track (2) Franklin steam distribution with oscillating cams and poppet valves were to replace Walschaert valve gear, because of the poppet's outstanding success on K4s 5399. Pennsy wanted to establish a Harrisburg-Chicago through engine run of 713 miles, allowing one coal stop enroute, Millbrook, Ohio, 385 miles west of Harrisburg.

Through the years, many unusual locomotives have been twirled on PRR turntables, but none ever compared to a T1 in glamour, appearance and public appeal. Their complete departure from previous and spartan locomotive planning principles was as revolutionary as the class of motive power it produced. T1 was to be a dream passenger engine, a truly superlative machine.

Modified Belpaire boilers had a maximum outside diameter of one hundred inches, and grate area of ninety-two square feet. General Steel Castings Company supplied one piece, nickel steel locomotive beds with cylinders cast integral, tender beds, front truck frames, and Delta type trailing trucks. Baldwin cross-counter-balanced disc drivers were used. Timken roller bearings were on all engine and tender axles, driving rod crank pins and all reciprocating parts. Timken also supplied lightweight, high-dynamic alloy steel rods and other machinery parts. Four Nathan force-feed lubricators delivered oil to eighty-eight points; this, plus roller bearings, chalked up an overall machine efficiency rating of 93%-plus during tests. Hancock type TA-2 turbo feedwater heaters were used to save space, while stokers were Standard HT type. To save weight, 8500 pounds of aluminum went into streamlining jackets, hip castings, sand boxes, cab, decks, steps, skirting and running boards. This lightened the total weight by 17,000 pounds.

Class 180-P-84 tenders, wrapped in bulky and rounded skirting, rolled on sixteen wheels. Their capacity was 19,200 gallons and 42½ tons, for a total loaded weight of 221 tons. An exceptionally long trough and stoker screw were designed for tenders in lieu of mechanical coal pushers. 6111 got a Franklin booster in its trailing truck; this added 13,500 pounds tractive effort. No other T1's had boosters. Total length of engine and tender was 122 feet, requiring installation of a new 125-foot turntable at the Harrisburg enginehouse.

Bert Pennypacker

Available money (and credit) were most necessarily placed upon rounded noses of new internal combustion units, rather than upon further, and unpredictable experimentation.

In essence, rigid framed 4-4-4-4 type locomotives simply represented advanced mechanical engineering concepts of the highly popular 4-8-4. Both wheel arrangements were approximately equal in size and capacity, but progressive technology showed that doubling up on cylinders and machinery offered many operating bonuses. Top motive power department echelons were split into two groups regarding acquisition of conventional Northerns versus radical Duplexes.

Duplexes won out because they promised some mighty

Locomotive 6110 made the first through run from Harrisburg to Chicago with a train of fourteen coaches (possibly the "Trail Blazer") weighing one thousand tons. From Crestline to Fort Wayne, scheduled time was bettered by twenty minutes, while the final lap into Chicago saw thirteen minutes chopped from normal running time. Speed was consistently in the neighborhood of one hundred miles per hour. Engine 6111 did even better with a heavier train of sixteen cars. She streaked along the Fort Wayne Division speedway at an average of 102 miles per hour for sixty-nine continuous miles.

In April 1944, the 6110 was sent to Altoona test plant for a thorough instrument check after compiling 120,000 miles of road service. Generally speaking, test plant findings bore out her known road success and pointed to fleet production. For example, 2,980 drawbar horsepower was needed to meet stipulated requirements; 6110 topped this by a whopping 38%, producing 4100 indicated drawbar horsepower at the one hundred m.p.h. mark. Fuel and water consumption were moderate. Compared with the best preceding engine tested, an M1a, the T1 produced 46% more drawbar horsepower with but 11% more steam usage per hour. Both engines had eight drivers, with approximately identical weights on drivers. A T1 would also out-perform a four-unit, 5400 horsepower diesel at all speeds above twenty-six miles per hour. Some other test plant data follows:

Maximum Drawbar Horsepower	6,110
Maximum Indicated Horsepower	6,552
Test Run at Speed of	85.5
Cut off	25%
Boiler Pressure	295
Steam Chest Pressure	287

Indicated horsepower was 4838 at 38 miles per hour, and it was usually above six thousand at all speeds over 55 m.p.h.

With glowing T1 test plant reports piled high on their desks, PRR motive power men were elated as they placed orders for fifty engines. They were built during 1945 and 1946. Altoona got the nod for locomotives 5500-5524, plus all fifty tenders, while Baldwin built 5525-5549. Very slight modifications appeared in design; running board skirts were raised to expose tops of drivers, and prow noses seemed somewhat less pointed, while weight was up slightly. Later, completely enclosed front ends were radically modified to facilitate easier maintenance.

Then it happened; the proud and distinctive T1 fleet began to disprove its widely circulated merits. Poppet valve maintenance costs rose sharply, and they were notoriously slippery. Arguments and theories raged back and forth; everyone seemed to have a sure cure. To a railroad that found four cylinders unsatisfactory on an HC1s back in 1919, its T1 problems in 1946 were paradoxical indeed. Continuous contour rotary cams were tried on 5500, while 5547 was fitted with Walschaert valve gear to become class T1a. Two duplexes, a T1 and a Q2, were sent to Norfolk & Western for trials and possible sale, but Roanoke men preferred their own articulateds.

Early demise of T1's wasn't based entirely upon their unsatisfactory performance. Had steam operations continued, answers would probably have been found to remedy duplex shortcomings. A start in the right direction had already been made with elimination of expensive-to-maintain poppet valves on 5547. However, like all railroads, Pennsy found dieselization absolutely necessary in the face of sharply rising costs and falling revenues that followed World War II. Brief T1 years proved exceptionally interesting to trackside watchers, even though these same years were a nightmare for mechanical and operating men. West of Harrisburg, prow nosed T1's were exceptionally well liked by all who saw them, and by about half the enginemen who pulled their multiple throttles. A varied parade of duplexes, K4s Pacifics and diesels fronted tuscan red Limiteds for several years. Plans for long-distance through runs with T1's didn't last; they very seldom ran through Pittsburgh. In 1948, one was sent east as an exhibit at Reading, Pa. fair, where it shared the limelight with a new Reading Company Pacific.

A fairly common sight was doubleheading T1's with diesels, especially over the Pittsburgh Division. The duplex was usually first, and what a thrilling sight to see what appeared to be the T1 pulling diesel and train! T1's became grimy and covered with gray dust, leading to misunderstandings about their true color, which was regulation Brunswick green locomotive enamel. They were soon downgraded to lesser runs, semi-locals, mail and express trains. Finally, several ended up on Pittsburgh-Greensburg locals, of all places. The gallant T1 image was just about a memory by mid-1950's.

How could Altoona test plant write a 1944 report card listing spectacular marks, for a locomotive that proved the exact opposite in actual road service, just two years later? First, the plant had no way or foretelling maintenance costs which would show up after a given amount of road time. Franklin poppet valves and valve gear proved costly to maintain as did other complicated machinery. Secondly, test plant operation was conducted under ideal adhesive conditions, which varied considerably from all manner of poor rail factors encountered out on the road. Most experts agreed a definite adhesion problem existed, although railroad motive power officials said a T1 could be kept from slipping with "great skill," and that was putting it mildly.

T1's were so slippery as to be almost uncontrollible (and this was at speed) caused by weight transfer from front to rear engines. Possible improvements in T1 spring rigging might have helped, since other factors were OK. Although no plans were made to try articulation, some experts thought jointed frames might remove the rigidity and allow each set of drivers to find footing on rails.

An Association of American Railroads mechanical committee advised that duplex drivers should be designed with a higher factor of adhesion than conventional power. Standard formula of sound design principles was employed throughout T1 planning, with a factor of adhesion exceed-

Pennsylvania Railroad

ing four. Carrying this a bit farther, could there possibly have been a weight-to-horsepower relationship that had been exceeded? Modern weight-reducing construction methods, coupled with unparalleled efficiency of steam distribution and high horsepower were probably just too potent a combination. Interestingly enough, Q2 class duplex freighters, with considerably more weight per driving axle, dug in with good adhesive qualities. And, as a contrast, New York Central's conventional 4-8-4's, having comparable capacity and dimensions to T1's, except for cylinders, were quite successful.

Since no workable solution(s) were found to the T1 quandary, the foregoing ideas can serve only as a layman's conjectures in retrospect. However, there was never any doubt regarding T1's popularity as a highly unusual engine and mechanic's wonderland of moving parts. Their memory will remain strong for many years to come, but we're sorry to report that none were saved.

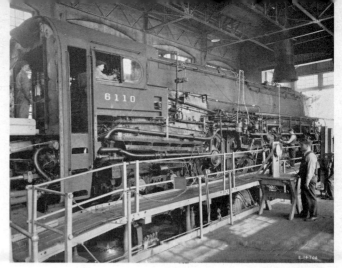

April 1944, 6110 digs in on the Altoona Test Plant.

T1, BALDWIN, APRIL, 1942, DUPLEX

Cylinders (4)	19¾"x26"	Grate Area	92 sq. ft.
Drivers	80"	Engine Weight	497,200 lbs.
Steam Pressure	300 lbs.	Tractive Force*	65,000 lbs.

*Sister engine 6111 equipped with booster developing 13,500 lbs. T.F.

T1, BALDWIN, MAY 1946, DUPLEX

Cylinders	19¾"x26"	Grate Area	92 sq. ft.
Drivers	80"	Engine Weight	502,200 lbs.
Steam Pressure	300 lbs.	Tractive Force	65,000 lbs.

T1, ALTOONA, AUGUST, 1946, DUPLEX

Cylinders	19¾"x26"	Grate Area	92 sq. ft.
Drivers	80"	Engine Weight	502,200 lbs.
Steam Pressure	300 lbs.	Tractive Force	64,650 lbs.

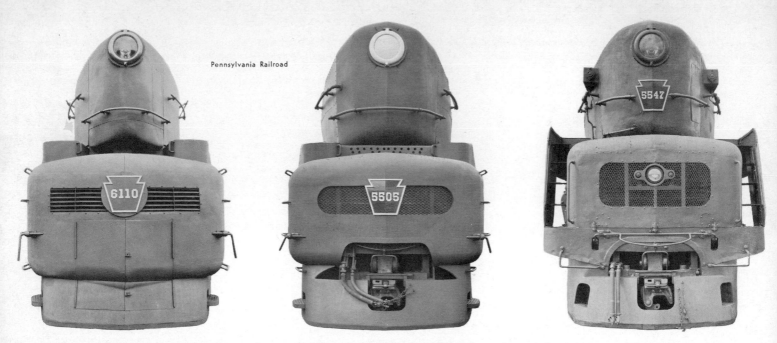

above, left, Sharp face of one of the two Baldwin built experimentals.

above middle, Later Altoona version had a flatter prow.

above·right, Face of the only T1a showing the influence of maintenance men over designers. The little headlight is an emergency unit, but was used by enginemen as fog lights or—both were used for extreme illumination.

below, The customer is always right. Baldwin wanted to build at least part of the T1 fleet with Walschaert valve gear. Pennsy, impressed with its fantastic performing K4s 5399, insisted that they be equipped with Poppet valves. So it was!

above, Altoona T1 with cowl swung open revealing the boiler front.

above right, April 1942 has Baldwin built 6110 under steam for the first time. Not all the shrouding has been applied.

right, A thing of beauty from any angle, 5519 is pulled onto the turn table at Altoona in 1946.

elow, New at Altoona, Pennsy built all 50 tenders and 25 of the ocomotives (5500-5524).

5547 had her Poppets replaced with the conventional Walschaert accuated piston valves, and re-classified T1a. It was probably a step in the right direction, but time had run out on the T1's before they were built.

In theory, the T1's should have been absolute optimum of steam passenger power.

T1 5500 received alterations in the form of rotary continuous contour cams. Instead of the valve gear box being driven by a rod from the crosshead, these poppets were powered by the eccentric driven rotating cam.

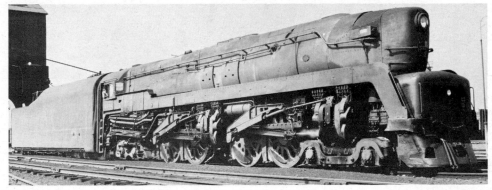

Engineman prepares to enter cab for the run over two divisions from Harrisburg to Pittsburgh.

Surprisingly enough, the crews rather liked the T1's, particularlly their greyhound speed. It took a real "throttle artist" to keep them from slipping, but they were comfortable riding and easy steamers.

Train No. 17, the Philadelphia-Pittsburgh local, pauses at Huntingdon for some "head end" mail and express business. To the rail fans delight, the T1's were very smoky (dirty), but the poor enginemen always looked like miners after a run.

The T1's operating shortcomings were compensated in part by their sheer beauty and speed. When new, they were a sight to behold, with beautiful gold striping and red key-stone on Pennsy's Brunswick green locomotive enamel (very, very dark green).

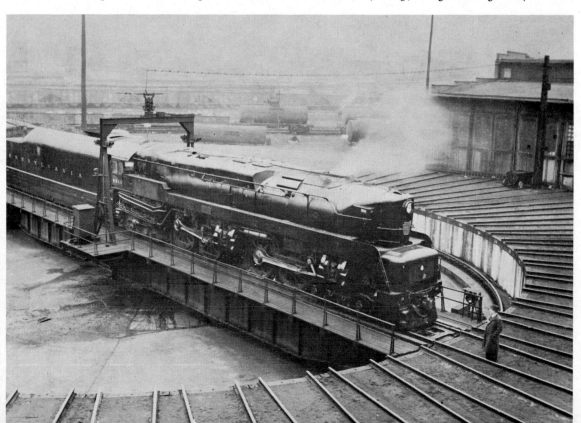

T

5535 *heads the "Admiral" out of Chicago, Jan. 18, 1948. The engineer is being unusually* Harold Stirton
careful as he "widens-on-her", lest one set of drivers begin to madly slip. Once underway
he can let his charger "fly like the wind" — and fly like wind she will.

T1 *roars under the signals near Cove, Pa. June 1948. One of the beauties of multiple-track*
mail lines is the necessity to span them with bridges for proper signaling.

Milton A. Davis

The T1 locomotives went through gradual changes or evolutions when built. There was a general utilitarian trend with less and less shrouding. Compare this later built 5511 (Altoona 8, 1946) with Baldwins 6110 or 6111. Raymond Loewy's (the designer) shark nose, deep skirting and portholes are missing.

The T1 was everything: beautiful, unusual, fast, slippery, success and failure. Pennsy's chunk of "too much experimentation" was born too late and died too soon.

They were always a beautiful sight in their short, controversial career. Here, a 24 car mail and express extra gets a fast ride on the Pittsburgh Division.

S1 CLASS DUPLEX

Aside from 125 Texas Types and 52 sharknosed 4-4-4-4's, Pennsylvania's final steam locomotive development years were punctuated by an eye-catching fllurry of new and unusual wheel arrangements that were never repeated elsewhere. Late-dated unorthodoxy included the following locomotives:

6100	6-4-4-6	S1	Altoona, 1939	Duplex passenger
6130	4-6-4-4	Q1	Altoona, 1942	Duplex freight
6131				
6175-6199	4-4-6-4	Q2	Altoona, 1944-45	Duplex frt.
6200	6-8-6	S2	Baldwin, 1944	Turbine pass. and frt.

Long-time followers of PRR motive power design were visibly shaken by this radical about-face from deeply rooted conventionalism. Careful mechanical department forethought however was aimed at procuring ultra-modern, super steam power with high speed and horsepower potentials. Toward that end, locomotives 6100, 6130, 6131 and 6200 were, admittedly, experimentals, and subject to the high mortality rates usual with such trial types. They also represented unswerving faith in steam propulsion at a time when diesels were getting their foothold. Indeed, these experimentals were actually planned toward bettering diesel performance records. At this late date, there's no point in lamenting what happened, but, it would have been extremely interesting to observe what might have transpired, had steam power been victorious.

Altoona's initial Duplex spent its first two summers (1939 and 1940) as an action exhibit at trylon and perisphere —trademarked New York Worlds Fair. Fairgoers gathered about a fenced-in enclosure to watch the monstrous No. 6100 steaming away, her 84-inch drivers revolved on the rollers installed beneath the driving wheels. Although built and owned by Pennsy, the S1's tender was graciously lettered AMERICAN RAILROADS. This unusual engine came into being through combined design talents of mechanical engineers at Altoona, Eddystone, Lima and Schenectady. This was Broad Street's first move toward a K4s replacement.

Railroad men called 6100 "the big engine," and rightly so, Raymond Loewy's aero-dynamically styled locomotive possessed a Commonwealth cast steel engine bed that set a record for length—77 feet 9½ inches, while total length of engine and tender was 140 feet. Average driving axle loadings were seventy thousand pounds and total weight was 304 tons — considerably above the largest Northern. This explains the use of six-wheeled trucks fore and aft, to carry excess weight. Her sixteen wheeled 250-P-84 tender carried 24,230 gallons and 26 tons, and was equipped with a Berkley stoker. The total weight of more than one million pounds (for engine and tender) was a magic figure, usually attained only by large freight articulateds.

Getting 6100 from Altoona to Flushing Meadows on Long Island was a problem. Hudson River carfloats and tunnels were far from capable of handling her. She traveled east, dead in a short ten-car freight, pulled by an L1s Mikado. Most overhead bridges were cleared by easing underneath at a slow crawl. From Trenton, the S1 moved cautiously up the Belvidere Branch, then via Lehigh & Hudson River to Maybrook, then New Haven and Long Island to her fairgrounds exhibit site.

The 6-4-4-6 was clearly too large for system-wide main line work west of Harrisburg, but she did provide valuable development information. Later-dated T1 duplexes would fit through tight places where the S1 dared not trespass. 6100 worked between Chicago and Crestline because she was too large to negotiate the west end curve approach to Pittsburgh's station. Her record was impressive; very slippery, but very powerful once she got going. The monster could easily haul 1200 tons at one hundred miles per hour, and she often whisked the "Trail Blazer" over the Fort Wayne Division at these incredible speeds. Skirting was removed to expose cylinders, machinery and drivers. As a youthful ten-year-old, the popular big speedster was scrapped in 1949.

S1, ALTOONA, 1939

Cylinders (4)	22"x26"	Grate Area	132 sq. ft.
Drivers	84"	Engine Weight	608,170 lbs.
Steam Pressure	300 lbs.	Tractive Force	71,900 lbs.

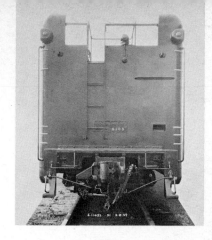

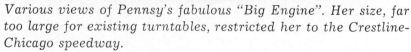

Various views of Pennsy's fabulous "Big Engine". Her size, far too large for existing turntables, restricted her to the Crestline-Chicago speedway.

She was the most publicized locomotive on the Lines, being featured on three (1939-41) calendars. Once in service, however, she was kept under close wraps.

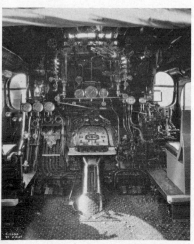

above, The 77' 9½" frame and cylinders after most of the sand was removed from casting. This was the largest one piece steel-locomotive frame ever cast.

left, Boiler, before lagging and jacket were applied. Note GG1 trucks in the background.

Altoona, 1938. The "Big Engine" begins to take shape. The boiler and frame are being lowered onto the wheels. Note that she has three hopper ashpans for cleaning the huge (132 sq. ft.) grate. The duplex was, in theory, superb in that steam distribution was easily accomplished with four cylinders—trouble was though—there were twice as many parts to wear out and maintain.

She was designed by Baldwin and built by Pennsy.

The mighty S1 pounds out of Chicago with No. 70. She has just completed a year and a half stint at the New York World's Fair. She suffered from the Duplex's usual shortcoming, slippery starts, but once under way she could handle 1,200 ton trains at 100 m.p.h.

For an engine that had basked in the limelight, her road records were unusually secretive.

Two views showing what happens to streamlining when the Railroad faces the facts of maintenance. The Big Engine was scrapped on her 10th birthday, 1949.

Q1&2 CLASS DUPLEX

Tremendous in size, revolutionary in design, but too costly to operate in the face of diesel competition.

Q1, ALTOONA, 1942

Pennsylvania Railroad

Cylinders—Front	23"x2 "	Grate Area	98.3 sq. ft.
" —rear	19½"x26"	Engine Weight	593,500 lbs.
Drivers	77"	Tractive Force	81,793 lbs.
Steam Pressure	300 lbs.	With Booster	90,043 lbs.

6130, JULY 23, 1945, AFTER PARTIAL DE-SHROUDING

Pennsylvania Railroad

Ultra-modern, ten-drivered freight locomotives shared two widely differing concepts during World War II years. First, Pennsy urgently needed a proven design and selected Lima's blueprints for a Chesapeake & Ohio 2-10-4. Altoona shopmen built 125, and they were fabulously successful. Secondly, untouched fields of ten-drivered Duplex development were necessarily slower. A single class Q1 engine, having opposed cylinders driving a 4-6-4-4 wheel arrangement, exited Altoona Shops in 1942. Two years later, a completely revised Duplex with normal cylinder locations and 4-4-6-4 wheel designation, was classed Q2. It proved unusually powerful during test plant trials, leading to hasty cancellation of a Lima order for twenty-five additional 2-10-4's. A like number of Q2's were outshopped by Altoona instead.

Correction of Q1's shortcomings produced some interesting changes. These were to be fast freight engines so the 77-inch driver was replaced by 69-inch size on the Q2. Most importantly, those opposed cylinders on Q1 6130 proved most unsatisfactory for a number of reasons. In addition to dirty location, cramped space and limiting firebox size, they had to run backwards in forward motion, increasing downward rod thrust. 6130 was sheathed in a homemade, streamlined shroud which was later removed. Q2's huge, 106-inch diameter boiler was immediately predominant, and disliked by engine crews because they had difficulty seeing around curves. This was a normal complaint whenever boilers grew in size, and it was similarly quite normal for the men to chew the fat about it.

A notable Q class idiosyncrasy, not usually found on simple engines, was front and rear sets of cylinders having different dimensions, to power differing numbers of drivers. No poppets here, but the piston valves also varied, with 12-inch forward and 14-inch size in rear cylinders.

Locomotives of the 1940's were certainly beautiful machines; Pennsy spared no expense to give them every possible mechanical advantage. All Q2 engine and tender axles were equipped with Timken roller bearings, while driving

Pennsylvania Railroad

rods had floating bushings on all pins. Valve gear was Walschaert, there were three Detroit lubricators per engine. Q2's had Worthington 6½ SA feedwater heaters, Standard HT stokers, and there were nine circulators in fireboxes and combustion chambers. Franklin type E boosters were installed in trailing trucks.

A most interesting new device was the American Brake Shoe wheel slip controller applied to all Q2's. When either set of drivers slipped more than one-half revolution, the controller automatically shut off steam supply by actuating a butterfly valve in the supply line. When slippage was arrested, steam was returned; all this with no action from the engineman. In actual practice, the device didn't work too well. It required more attention than busy mechanics could give, so they just didn't fool with the gadget. Class 180 F 84 tenders held 19,200 gallons and 42½ tons.

Q2's wrote a brilliant record for tremendous power and speed that was a final tribute to her designers. Unlike the other Duplexes, 4-4-6-4's dug in and galloped off with more tonnage than any other PRR engine had ever lugged. Perhaps the smaller drivers and average weight of 77,000 pounds per driving axle were the determining factors. During test plant operation, locomotive number 6175 whipped up 7,987 maximum indicated horsepower at 57.4 miles per hour. This was the highest such figure ever recorded for any steam locomotive, anywhere. Maximum evaporation was 137,479 pounds of water per hour.

The mighty Duplex freighters worked main lines west of Conway, particularly on runs to Crestline and Chicago. Crews loved their power, speed, and good steaming qualities. Unfortunately, the newest steam freight power was the first to go, so they had extremely short careers. By August of 1949, all but a very few were laying dead at Crestline while 4-8-2's, 2-10-4's and 2-10-0's remained to pull trains until 1957. Early Q2 inactivity resulted from a cost-conscious operating department's records, which showed increased maintenance, plus huge coal and water appetites.

Q1 as built.

after 1945 de-shrouding

backhead showing booster engine.

Q1

left, view of boiler front showing main steam pipes coming from the superheater header. This also affords an excellent view of the heavy heating pipes to the feedwater heater. The boiler feedwater is preheated here before being fed into the boiler.

right, The complex backhead of the Q1.

Right side view of the almost completed Q1, 6130. This engine was most unusual in many ways. Not only did the rear engine run backwards but each set of cylinders and valves had different length stroke and diameter.

The placement of the rear cylinders had two disadvantages; first, it was a very dirty location and second it limited the firebox size and design.

The designers put it on and the maintenance men take it off. It's the same old story on all shrouding applied to steam locomotives.

The iron horse was a tough utilitarian machine and by nature was not very condusive to "dressing up".

Although streamlined and radical in design there was no publicity given this engine, for it would have been taboo to "balyhoo" anything during the War (except the War itself).

We have no actual reports on how this huge freighter ran, but we suspect that her large (77") drivers were a little too much for her relatively small grate area (98.3 sq. ft.). The Q2 class (next page) had 69" drivers and a grate area of 121.71 sq. ft. 6130 is shown here at Chicago's 59th St. Enginehouse.

Q2, ALTOONA, APRIL, 1945

Cylinders—Front .... 19¾"x28"		Grate Area .... 121.71 sq ft.	
" —Rear .... 23¾"x29"		Engine Weight .... 619,100 lbs.	
Drivers .... 69"		Tractive Force .... 100,800 lbs.	
Steam Pressure .... 300 lbs.		With Booster .... 115,800 lbs.	

Pennsylvania Railroad

Q2

The Q2 was the largest and most powerful 10 drivered engine ever built. Size and power can be figured in many ways, but no matter how you figured it, the Q2 was one of the most powerful steam locomotives of all times. When tested on the Altoona Plant, Q2, 6175 broke all existing records for indicated horsepower—almost 8,000.

Pennsylvania Railroad

Front and rear view of new Q2 at Altoona, April 4, 1945.

6131 *was the first Q2. Shown here new at Altoona August 1944, she was the prototype for* 25 *additional units, No's 6175-6199.*

    Pennsylvania Railroad's Q2 *class represents the ultimate in steam freight locomotive development in America. Their life was short but brilliant. Pennsy's long fling with duplex's was about to pay off—then the diesel arrived en-mass.*

Q2

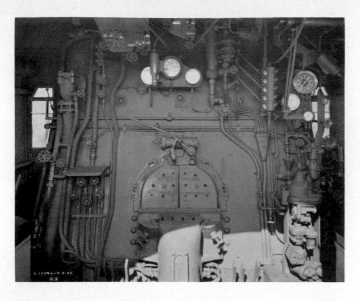

You ran a steam locomotive! They were certainly more complex, than either straight electric or diesel electric. Cab of a Q2.

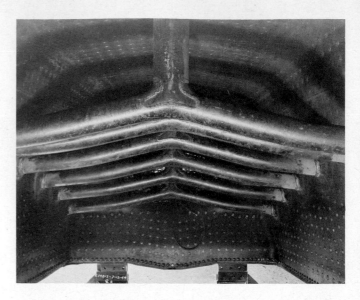

Interior of a Q2 firebox showing the Circulators. Their function was two-fold. They supported the fire brick arch, but more importantly they increased total heating surface and allowed better circulation in the side water legs of the firebox.

Two views of Pennsy's best performing duplex. Had it not been for steam's retirement they would have gone on to write brilliant performance records. They were strong and fast, each unit capable of almost 8,000 horsepower.

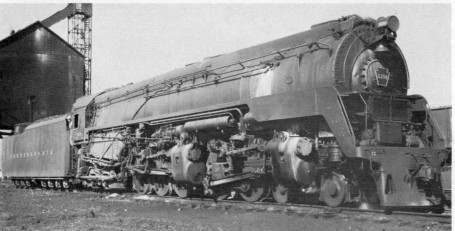

Crews were usually reluctant to wholeheartedly accept something new and radical, but the Q2 proved to be the exception. They were a pleasure to fire, free steaming and good on coal. In addition to riding like Pullmans, they practically doubled existing tonnage ratings on the Western Divisions where they were king. Their water consumption however, was another story, for they could drain their huge tank in an hour and a half when working "full" throttle. The anti-slip butterflys didn't always function, so when one set of drivers began to slip, the train had to be almost stopped before moving again.

Lima, Ohio Station gets a good rattling as Q2 6199 rips through an eastbound freight, Feb. 27, 1951.

When the 8,000 horsepower Q2 went by—you knew it! In fact the whole town knew it. Almost dwarfing the interlocking tower (Pennsy, Nickel Plate and B&O) at Lima is 6192 as she thunders towards Chicago.

POWER

Nine year old infant giants wait dead at Crestline, Ohio, Oct. 30, 1954. Though superb, they were complex and required much maintenance; too much for the cost conscious operating department. The last chapter of Pennsy Power was to be written by Consolidations, Decapods, Mountains and Santa Fe's,—all simple two cylinder power.

 ...

$\boxed{S}$2 CLASS 6-8-6 TURBINE

Roy Wake—Railroad Products

S2, TURBINE DRIVE BALDWIN, SEPTEMBER 1944

Cylinders .... Steam Turbine		Grate Area .... 120 sq. ft.
Drivers .... 68"		Engine Weight .... 589,920 lbs.
Steam Pressure .... 310 lbs.		Tractive Force .... 70,500 lbs.

Roy Wake—Railroad Products

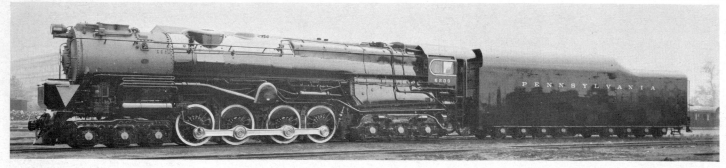

Most coal or gas turbine locomotives have employed their turbines to produce an electric drive. Pennsy's was a direct-drive steam turbine that represented something halfway between a normal reciprocating steamer and a diesel or electric. Although a boiler and many other components were present, there were no cylinders, pistons, or valve motion. Turbine drive produced a smooth power flow—that was uniform torque at all speeds, with no rail pounding (dynamic augment). This allowed relatively small (68-inch) drivers on a highspeed locomotive. Instead of being counterbalanced, drivers were perfectly balanced.

The Westinghouse 6900 horsepower turbine drove on the two middle axles through double reduction gears and a flexible-cup drive which was interposed between each of the final gears and the corresponding driving axle. Steam flowed into the turbine unit through dozens of steel nozzles, striking chromium turbine blades at a speed of two thousand miles per hour. There were more than one thousand blades of varying sizes and they imparted motion to produce drive as they turned on a spindle.

Number 6200 was equipped with all types of modern appliances, with roller bearings everywhere. Her class 180-P-85 tender held 19,500 gallons and 42½ tons. The tender was especially interesting, since it was originally applied to an I1s in the early 1930's as class 180-F-82. Later, it went onto streamlined K4s number 3768 as class 180-P-75. Needless to say, each engine change required rebuilding. Deck height changed each time, as did general outside appearance, and the S2 application included new eight-wheeled trucks.

When 6200 ran, there was no puffing; a loud swoosh-swoosh-swoosh sound had replaced stack music. PRR later installed a set of large smoke deflectors. Tractive effort at all speeds exceeded that of conventional steamers of comparable size, weight, and boiler capacity. It also exceeded the performance of a 6000 horsepower diesel above forty miles per hour. Below thirty miles per hour, steam consumption was high; above that speed, it was far less than normal steam engines.

As might be expected, the S2 operated over Pennsy's Crestline-Chicago proving ground. It ran well on fast passenger and freight trains, but was susceptible to diesel competition, cost-wise. Turbine maintenance was a big item, plus the normal expenses connected with owning steam power. The author saw number 6200 inside Crestline enginehouse in August of 1949. Her turbine assembly was torn out and it's doubtful that she ever ran again. Pennsy tried to retain steam power to the threshold of economically-forced dieselization, and the unorthodox S2 was just one of several unusual machines that evolved in the process.

The Westinghouse built turbine and reduction gear unit. This is a rail adaptation of a marine power plant. Steam enters the forward turbine (left) at over 300 lbs. pressure and is exhausted at a mere 15 lbs. The reverse turbine (right) is disengaged when the locomotive is in forward motion.

Two views of 6200 taken at Altoona after large smoke lifters were added. Dec. 10, 1946.

6200 *at Chicago, 1945. The 15 lbs. exhaust steam forces smoke through the four barreled stack.*

The big "Swoosh" churns up a bit of smoke on the Crestline Turntable, The Crestline-Chicago run was the stomping ground for the large Pennsy experimentals.

Under construction at Baldwin, 1944. The crank pins have heavy wood packing to prevent them from being damaged before the side rods are applied. Insulation is covering the boiler and steam pipes. Even the firebox sides get a layer of lagging.

The beautiful 6200 was the last "steam hope". She was a radical package with two strikes against her from the start. The turbine theory looked good and had it been developed a decade sooner—who knows?

She's shiny and new for a posed shot on the Horseshoe Curve. We note with surprise that there is only one vertical spring for each wheel of the leading truck. We won't even attempt an explanation on this one.

Pennsy's finest the "Broadway Limited" eases out of Chicago. The S2's fuel consumption was high on starts but once under way, she was very economical. Notice the shroud covering over the feedwater heater.

August 10, 1945, west of Warsaw, Indiana. First, a speck in the distance. As she looms larger he notices a steady roll of light gray smoke from the stack—and then at exactly 5:16 P.M., Ira H. Eigisti snapped the shutter. He captured this moment for all of us. The train is Pennsy's crack eastbound No. 28—the BROADWAY LIMITED.

The engineer is getting impatient as the last passenger boards at Englewood Station. His 250 ton steed is boiling and waiting to charge eastward.

C. W. Burns

Jim Shaughnessy

NUMBERING SYSTEM

For those accustomed to orderly methods of assigning locomotive road numbers in consecutive, blocked series, to identical groups, the Pennsylvania motive power roster probably looks like a haphazard mess. For example, a random pin-pointed glance might show consecutively-numbered engines running as follows: Consolidation, Decapod, Atlantic, Decapod, Pacific, and so forth. There have been a few exceptions to the so-called mixed-up sequence, such as 475 Decapods, 301 Mountains, 139 GG1 electrics, and a few others. There was method to this numbering madness, which dates back to the 1870's. Since PRR's far-flung railroad system was assembled from a large number of smaller roads, it was necessary, for many years, to keep each segment-railroad's locomotives separated. Toward this end, each section had its assigned block of numbers, into which road numbers were listed promiscuously. When engines were re-assigned from one area to another, their numbers were usually changed to coincide with the given series of the new area.

When locomotives were retired, their vacated numbers were very often filled immediately with whatever new engines were under construction at the time. Over a period of years, any given road number might have been applied to three or four engines of various types. All this serves to illustrate a second, and compelling reason for indiscriminate numbering, the reason being one of absolute necessity in order to keep numbers below 9999. Five digits were used at times to clear series, when a class was being replaced, but these were temporary measures. With a roster numbering anywhere from five, to over seven thousand units, and with this roster in a continual state of flux, there simply would be insufficient numbers to go around if consecutively-blocked series were allocated and held for each class grouping.

Other than making individual locomotive identification easier, orderly, blocked rosters have no value whatsoever in the business of running a railroad. Regardless of how the motive power is numbered, they are scattered around over many divisions, with each separate piece of equipment's mechanical records kept individually.

Pennsy road numbering methods had their good points for the purposes they served, even if the whole roster document was enough to confuse the precise-minded. Segment-railroad numbering was eliminated after the 1920 abolition of Lines East and West, when the Regional operating set-up was begun. Although given numbering series no longer indicated specific operating areas, many engines did remain in the general locality where they were always assigned. Many high-numbered former Lines West engines got into the Eastern or New York Regions only because of World War II traffic demands, and, later, because of dieselization-forced re-assignments. These two factors during the 1940's probably caused more mass re-assignments than ever before; shopped engines being sent immediately to points of need rather than back to points of former service. Through the years, on a railroad the size of Pennsy, there was bound to be considerable motive power re-assignment from area to area. Many engines carried small initials on them for years to show the former assigned section. Following is a list of principal segment-railroads, showing road numbering series of each, as used about 1920. This will assist in placing assignment locations of various engines:

LINES EAST:
No.   1-3999 Pennsylvania Railroad
No. 4001-4224 Northern Central
No. 5001-5228 Philadelphia Baltimore & Washington
No. 6001-6085 West Jersey & Seashore
No. 6201-6340 Western New York & Pennsylvania
No. 6501-6543 New York Philadelphia & Norfolk

LINES WEST:
No. 7001-7570 Pittsburgh Fort Wayne & Chicago
No. 7601-7800 Cleveland & Pittsburgh
No. 7901-7977 Little Miami
No. 8001-8950 Pittsburgh Cincinnati Chicago & St. Louis
    (No. 8701-8950 Vandalia)
No. 8977-8999 Terre Haute & Peoria
No. 9001-9106 Pittsburgh Youngstown & Akron
No. 9111-9134 Cincinnati Lebanon & Northern
No. 9200-9264 Erie & Pittsburgh
No. 9350-9455 Pennsylvania Company (fill ins)
No. 9530-9633 Grand Rapids & Indiana
No. 9650-9657 Wheeling Terminal
No. 9660-9687 Ohio River & Western (narrow gage)
    Waynesburg & Washington (narrow gage)
No. 9700-9796 Toledo Columbus & Ohio River
No. 9812-9895 Cleveland Akron & Cincinnati
No. 9900-9999 Pennsylvania Company (fill ins)

Because of the great size and complexity of PRR's locomotive roster, the authors felt it would be unwise to devote many pages to purely statistical material of this type, since the book's real values lie in descriptive word and picture.

Number of Steam Locomotives, Yearly Comparisons P.R.R. only—does not include Long Island, Washington terminal etc.

	7/1/1924	12/1/1929	7/1/1947
Class A—0-4-0	140	68	46
Class B—0-6-0	790	619	455
Class C—0-8-0	2	90	90
Class D—4-4-0	309	143	3
Class E—4-4-2	521	311	86
Class F—2-6-0	232	0	0
Class G—4-6-0	168	90	90
Class H—2-8-0	3335	2359	1060
Class I—2-10-0	598	598	598
Class J—2-6-2	1	0	0
Class J—2-10-4	0	0	125
Class K—4-6-2	584	692	450
Class L—2-8-2	579	579	566
Class M—4-8-2	1	201	301
Class N—2-10-2	190	190	190
Class Q—Duplex	0	0	27
Class S—Experimental	0	0	2
Class T—4-4-4-4	0	0	52
Articulateds	13	11	16
Odd Types	23	7	0
TOTALS	7486	5969	4157

Pennsylvania's famed 674 route miles of overhead catenary electrification has proved conclusively that no other type of train propulsion (not even diesels) can equal its economies in handling high-density traffic. Between New York, Washington and Harrisburg, 267 electric locomotives and over 500 multi-unit cars traverse 2200 miles of wired trackage. As might be expected, they pile up fantastic mileage figures: 125 million passenger car miles a year, 7.3 million freight locomotive unit miles each year, and fifteen million M-U car miles per year are representative totals for 1940.

Single-phase, 25-cycle alternating current is delivered through overhead trolley wires at 11,000 volts. This system was adopted in 1915 when the first Philadelphia suburban line (to Paoli) was electrified for M-U car operation. However, the original electrification of any consequence (through tunnels and into New York's Penn Station) used 650-volt direct current and third rails. That courageous, foresighted project included two single tracked tunnels under the main Hudson and four beneath the East River. It took seven years (1903-1910) and cost $112.9 million for all tunnels, Penn Station, and other facilities. This was probably the most costly 13.4 miles that any railroad ever built.

The line extends from Manhattan Transfer (Harrison), near Newark, through New York and to Sunnyside, Long Island, where large coach yards are located. Long Island R.R. M-U trains were also given access to Penn Station through two of the East River tubes. Third rail operation was chosen to match L1's identical system, and from 1910 to 1933, DD1 side-rodders hummed their way back and forth through the tunnels. Overhead a.c. catenary was installed in the latter year.

Long distance catenary reached Washington and Harrisburg during the 1930's. This monumental project included far more than the erection of steel poles, stringing of wires, and the building of sub-stations. The entire railroad plant was upgraded to achieve top efficiency. Many grade crossings were abolished, new electric interlocking plants were installed, as was new signaling, many miles of 152-pound rail and stone ballast. Several major passenger stations were replaced, including those at Newark, 30th Street (Philadelphia), and Lancaster. (The latter included a new route skirting the city).

World-famous GG1 and P5a motors cut running times of all trains. For example, the New York-Washington mileage of 226 was covered in 255 minutes with six intermediate stops by the DD1/K4s combination. GG1's cut this to 215 minutes hauling much heavier trains. In all fairness, there was no twenty-minute engine change stop at Manhattan Transfer with GG1 power. Two hours of freight running time was cut from Jersey City to Enola or Potomac Yard.

It's impossible to estimate the value of electrification to the Pennsy. The costly Penn Terminal work of 1910 has proved its worth many times over, and without the catenary during World War II, the railroad might well have collapsed. Comprehensive studies, conducted in 1950 and 1958, have proved the values of catenary retention during years when other areas have seen electrification mileage shrinking. Pennsy's electric locomotive roster included 70 units in 1924, in 1942 there were 284, the year 1947 saw 272, and at this writing, there are 267.

CATENARY TIMETABLE

1895—first experimental electrification, Burlington to Mt. Holly, N. J., 7 miles. Returned to steam operation after power plant burned down in 1901.

1905—first Long Island RR electrification using third rail, 650-volt d.c. current. For M-U car operation.

1906—Camden to Atlantic City via Newfield, using third rail and d.c. current, also some overhead wire, M-U car operation. Changed back to steam operation east of Newfield in 1931, then cut to Millville, and all-steam by 1948.

1910—Manhattan Transfer to Sunnyside, Long Island, 13.4 miles. 650-volt d.c. current and third rail. First main line electrification for heavy-duty service.

1915—Philadelphia to Paoli, 20 miles. Main line route, but only for M-U cars. First overhead catenary, 11,000 volts, a.c. current.

1918—Chestnut Hill Branch located in Philadelphia. 9 miles. For M-U car operation.

1918—New York Connecting Railroad (Hell Gate Bridge Route), owned by PRR and New Haven, (operated by NH). Permitted through train service from Boston.

1924—Fort Washington Branch, 6.2 miles. A branch off the Chestnut Hill Branch. For M-U car operation. Present status: out of service, wires removed, much of branch abandoned.

1928—Main line, Philadelphia to Wilmington and West Chester Branch. For M-U car operation at this time.

1930—Philadelphia to Norristown. Presently operated only as far as Manayunk, 7.8 miles, with M-U's. This is part of the Schuylkill Branch.

1930—Main line, Philadelphia to Trenton. For M-U cars at this time.

1933—Manhattan Transfer to Trenton. This closed the gap, allowing through main line trains to run between New York and Paoli or Wilmington with electric locomotives. First Philly-NY train left Broad Street Station on 1/16/1933.

1933—third rail replaced by catenary from Manhattan Transfer to Penn Terminal, 8.8 miles.

1935—Wilmington to Washington and Potomac Yard. NY-Washington through electric service started on 2/10/1935 with the first train being the CONGRESSIONAL.

1937—Manhattan Transfer abandoned, H & M electric trains provided with across-platform connections at new station in Newark.

1938—Paoli to Harrisburg and Enola, including all low-grade freight lines. First train, Philly to Harrisburg was No. 25, the METROPOLITAN, run on 1/15/1938 with GG1 number 4863.

Pennsylvania Railro

EARLY EXPERIMENTALS

Soon after work began on the New York Terminal project, President A. J. Cassatt appointed an electric locomotive committee and issued a blank check for development of a design that would haul passenger trains over 1.93 percent grades in the Hudson and East River tubes under construction. The committee included George Gibbs, Long Island's Chief Electrical Engineer; Alfred W. Gibbs,, Lines East Motive Power Chief; David Crawford, Lines West Motive Power Chief; and Axel S. Vogt, Mechanical Engineer. They soon had the following three small Westinghouse-equipped experimentals ready for testing:

LOCOMOTIVE 10001 B-B AA1 Juniata Shops, 1905 later re-numbered 3950 (EZN 8), then LI 323. Driven by four 350-HP motors, one per axle, direct geared. D.C. current.

LOCOMOTIVE 10002 B-B AA1 Juniata Shops, 1905 later re-numbered 3951 (EZN 9). One truck driven by two 320-HP gearless motors supported from main journals, the other truck propelled with two 300-HP motors attached to truck frames. D.C. current.

LOCOMOTIVE 10003 2B (4-4-0) Odd D Baldwin, 1907. Driven by two 375-HP motors and gearless quills. A.C. current.

In a quill drive, the traction motor turns a hollow shaft, or quill, which surrounds the axle without touching it. At the driving wheel end is a metal plate, or "spider," with projections that fit between driver spokes.. Actual quill-to-spoke hook-up is via spring cups and wearing plates. A quarter century later, quill drives of advanced design played no small part in making GG1 and P5a class so successful.

Strange as it may seem, electrical and mechanical problems were negligible but tests on Long Island revealed nosing, sideway motions and other poor riding qualities at high speeds. Accordingly, the three little motors were sent to a specially prepared test site on the WJ&S near Franklinville, N.J. Eighty special recording ties were used to register lateral thrusts. This was done by employing a hardened steel ball in each tie, to transmit wheel impact pressures onto a piece of boilerplate. Depths of impressions determined intensity of lateral thrusts.

The experimental trio was joined by a New Haven electric and PRR steam engines, D16b and an E2. All locomotives except the 10001 and 10002 chalked up good riding scorecards. This was an eye-opener to the esteemed testing team, and they nominated the 10003, with its 4-4-0 wheel arrangement and high center of gravity, as the best choice. It only proved what had been learned years before about high center of gravity contributing to smooth tracking of steam engines. Electrics having power trucks were discarded as unwanted track punishers. The standard, heavy-duty tunnel electrics were planned around a tall dimensioned 4-4-0 unit.

Both AA1's remained for many years as switchers, but 10003 was never re-numbered and soon disappeared.

Pennsylvania Railroad

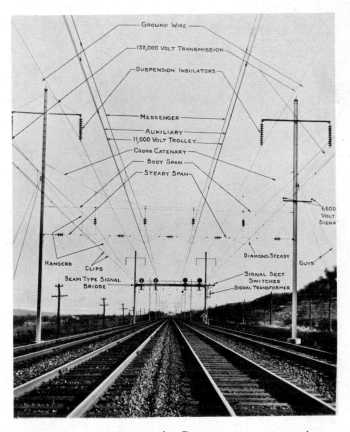

Diagram of Pennsy's Catenary construction.

DD1   2-B+B-2 (4-4-0+0-4-4)

The E class steam locomotive has turned its consist over to the DD1 electrics. Shortly, the steel car express will burrow under the Hudson River and arrive at midtown Manhattan.

Juniata's 1910 version of a Hudson Tunnel electric passenger locomotive was a two unit, box cab double 4-4-0, coupled back-to-back. These "twin American type electrics" were propelled by jackshaft and side-rod monkey-motion. Each DD unit carried a 2000 horsepower Westinghouse 315-A D.C. commutating pole type series motor. This was coupled through parallel rods and cranks to a jackshaft, which in turn was rod connected to 72-inch drivers. Side-rodded electrics are a monstrosity by todays standards, but half a century ago, it was the best practical way to harness a high-powered electric motor to four drivers. After all, those 315-A motors were large enough to have come directly from a powerhouse. Getting them low enough for direct gearing, and actually gearing them

Pennsylvania Railroad

was 80 miles per hour. The continuous rating (at 58 MPH) was 1,580 HP and 10,200 lbs. T.E. One hour rating (at 38 MPH) was 2,130 HP and 16,600 lbs. T.E. Although normal starting tractive effort was 66,000 lbs., a high of 79,200 lbs. has been recorded under excellent adhesive conditions. All the foregoing figures refer to a two-unit locomotive; they were never operated singly, and seldom were two, two-unit locomotives ever doubleheaded.

Tunnel operation by side-rod was accomplished with a fleet of thirty-three DD-class locomotives (66 units) as follows:

0990 to 0999 (EZN 02 and 00) odd-DD Juniata, 1909-10
3952 to 3995 (EZN 10 to 31) DD1 Juniata, 1910
3932 to 3949 (EZN 34 to 42) DD1 Juniata, 1911

EZN numbers refer to Electrified Zone Numbers, one EZN number being assigned to each two-unit locomotive for simplification of train dispatching. Each individual unit also carried its original four-digit number, which was used for mechanical records. Class odd-DD consisted of the first four trial units built, which differed slightly from the DD1's that followed.

The first regular passenger train left Penn Station on November 27, 1910, with a DD1 whirring smoothly on the head end. In its day, the DD1 proved just as spectacular a performer as present-day GG1's. Fourteen car trains weighing 1,000 tons were often handled, while 850-ton trains could be started on 1.93 percent tunnel grades. It seems almost unbelievable, but here was a 4,000 horsepower locomotive in 1910. Its weight equaled those of the steam K4's, which was still four years in the future (a DD1 could start far heavier trains). In essence, the mighty side-rodders were operated on mountain grades underground, for the Hudson tubes boasted grades that equaled those found on the Altoona to Gallitzin climb.

DD1's ran far more quietly and smoothly than their appearance suggested, with no appreciable rod clanking. They chalked up an enviable performance and maintenance cost record. During their first four years of operation, 3.9 million miles were run off with but 45 road failures and 271 total minutes detention. The first four years also saw maintenance costs at a low, low 7.2 cents per locomotive mile. However, this was but a prelude to the phenominal figure of only 3.5 cents, achieved from May of 1915 until April of the following year.

Pennsy figured the hourly capacity of its double-tracked 8.8-mile route from Penn Station to Manhattan Transfer as 144 trains. To this day, and including World War II traffic, this two-lane throat across the Jersey meadows and under the river has been able to handle all traffic adequately. By 1924, new L5 class electrics started coming in from Juniata, and many DD1's were gradually shifted to the Long Island, where 23 of them were numbered 338 to 360.

Although third rail was removed west of Penn Station, it remained in place east of there for several reasons. First, the LI needed it, as the two PRR and two LI East River tubes are often used interchangeably by both railroads. PRR catenary also extended eastward to Sunnyside Yards. Some DD1's remaining on Pennsy rails were used to haul empty passenger trains between Sunnyside and Penn Station. At this writing, four DD1 units remain stored at Sunnyside, with two reported to be destined for permanent historical preservation. The four DD1's are 3936, 3937, 3966 and 3967. Long Island sold most of theirs for scrap back in 1949-1951.

The rugged yet simple DD1's were one of the most successful bits of power to roll on Pennsy's rails.

the axles, was impossible. Furthermore, a high center of gravity was required.

One-piece cab unit construction allowed complete removal for shopping, a notable feature that was incorporated into all succeeding electric classes. Westinghouse electrical equipment was used throughout all DD1's, with all mechanical construction by Juniata Shops. Maximum speed

DD1 motors and running gear. A look at these huge 21 ton motors explains why the jack shaft was necessary. Smaller truck mounted motors were used on two of the experimentals, but they had poor adhesion and pounded the rails severely. Anyway—"the proof of the puddin' is in the eatin' " and the DD1's were real gems. In addition to unbelievable power, they were cheap to maintain.

The DD1's specifications were as follows—Drivers 72", Weight on drivers 199,000 lbs., total weight 313,000 lbs., tractive force 66,000 lbs. Each motor could develop 2,000 horsepower (4,000 total). All figures are for 2 semi-permanently coupled units.

below, New DD1, 3977 poses with train and company officials.

DD1

Motor No. 39 with the "Trail Blazer" on her first eastbound trip, at the New York World's Fair, July 29, 1939.

3983, new at Sunnyside Yards. The man at the controls looks like, and probably is, our old photographer friend, C. B. Chaney. The small pantograph was used to pick up current when the locomotive was passing over complex track work.

DD1, No. 11, races across the Jersey Meadows. Soon, she will plunge into the dark tubes at the Bergen Hill portals. After descending the grade she will climb the stiff 1.9% grade and be resting beneath the concourse of Penn Station.

The DD1's secret of success can be attributed to two factors—careful planning and simplicity.

Artist's sketch showing a DD1 bursting into brilliant daylight as it emerges from the 13,685 ft. twin bores that plunge beneath the broad Hudson's choppy waves. Several ventilating shafts, plus the "push and pull" of rushing trains, keep tunnel innards fresh and clean.

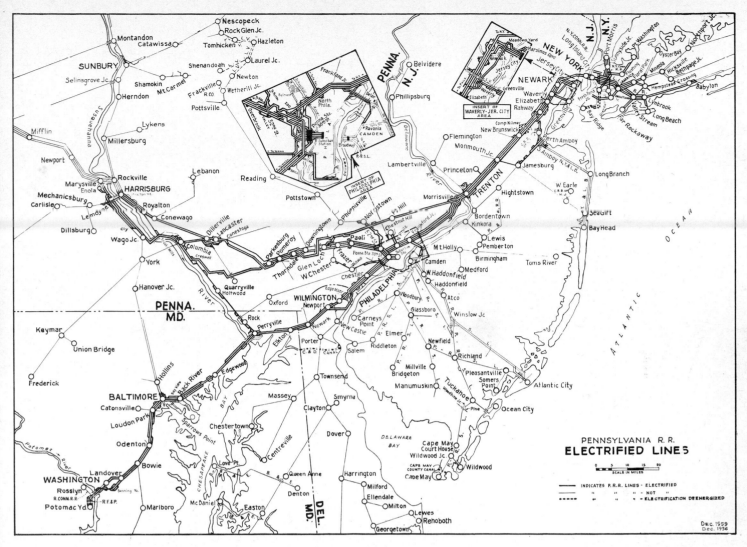

An updated (1959) map of Pennsy's 674 route-miles under catenary. Keystone electrification is far more than high-voltage wires and sub-stations. Plans were laid early in this Century and carried forth with care and foresight. A few superior advantages include few grade crossings, cab signaling, remote-controlled interlocking plants, 152 lb. rail and easy gradients.

Night at Sunnyside Yards in Queens (New York City). The once proud DD1 has long since given up her spot at the head of "Limiteds" and is now used on work trains. A B1 switcher is at the right.

Jim Shaughnessy

FF1 1-C+C-1 (2-6-6-2)

FF1, JUNIATA, 1917

Pennsylvania Railroad

Motors (4) .... Westinghouse		Total Weight .... 516,000 lbs.	
Drivers .... 72"		Tractive Force .... 87,200 lbs.	
Wt. on Drivers .... 439,500 lbs.		Starting Tractive Force ... 140,000 lbs.	

Pennsylvania's first heavy duty main line A.C. electric locomotive was a monstrous, jack-shafted experimental "double Mogul." No. 3931 was out-shopped by Juniata in 1917 and destined for trial use along the pioneer (1915) 11,000-volt A.C. catenary installation erected from Philadelphia to Paoli for multiple-unit passenger service. The lumbering 76½-foot long side-rodder was aptly dubbed "Big Liz" by PRR men.

Each FF1 jackshaft carried two flexible gears which meshed with pinions on the shafts of two motors. There were four Westinghouse 451 squirrelcage traction motors in all, totaling 7640 horsepower. These were of the three-phase induction type (without commutators) and ran at one or the other of two continuous speeds—10.3 or 20.6 MPH. Speed was maintained regardless of grade conditions, drawing power on the upgrade and returning it on the downgrade. Single-phase trolley wire current was changed to three-phase by a rotary converter driven by a synchronous motor. Acceleration was controlled by a liquid rheostat.

Big Liz's continuous output was 4,000 horsepower at the rail and 87,200 lbs. tractive effort. The starting drag-power, however, hit a fantastic 140,000 lbs. TE and maximum h.p. of 4,800. Looking toward a dream that has yet to be realized, PRR people figured that two engines of this type could, theoretically, help level out Pittsburgh Division's heavy grades. They could take 3900 tons out of Altoona and up the eastern slope, while easier western slope gradients could allow 6300-ton trains—all this at a steady 20.6 drag-freight crawl speed.

Close-up showing the twin motors geared to the flexible spring driving wheel.

The difference between continuous tractive force and starting tractive force is great because the motors will take a tremendous overload for a short period of time.

Overbrook, Pa., August 24, 1917. Big Liz is about to drag her first train from Overbrook to Paoli. She hauled 68 loads plus an L1s steamer (with throttle closed) over the one percent ruling grade with ease. Liz was never duplicated—she ran well but she was just too darned big and powerful for 1917 equipment. After pulling out too many couplers, she was assigned pusher duty. Her destructive capacities were even greater here, for one day on Barmouth Hill she pushed with such "Heave Ho" that box cars began to pop out of the middle of the train like toothpicks. Liz kept pushing and cars kept crunching. She was simply too much power in a single electric unit.

1924 L5 1-B-B-1 (2-4-4-2)

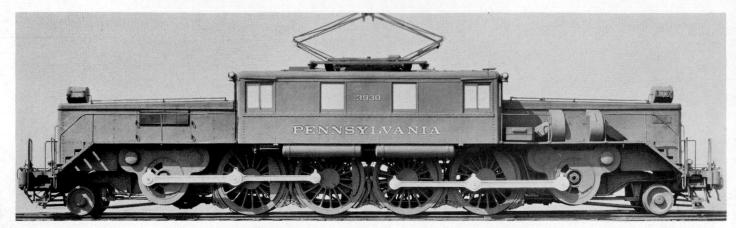

L5paw (PASSENGER, D.C., WESTINGHOUSE) ALTOONA, 1924

Pennsylvania Railroad

Motors (4) .... Westinghouse	Total Weight .... 408,600 lbs.
Drivers .... 80"	Tractive Force .... 59,000 lbs.
Wt. on Drivers .... 308,600 lbs.	Starting Tractive Force .... 100,000 lbs.

Pennsy's final jackshaft design was just about the weirdest-looking electric that ever turned a side rod or slid a contact shoe along a third rail. Looking toward the future of expanded electrification mileage, class L5 was tagged a universal concept, suitable for easy change-over between passenger-freight work and/or A.C.-D.C. current operation. Also, it seemed to combine DD1's two-unit power into a single unit. The first L5's carried Westinghouse equipment; then the railroad broke their monopoly by trying other manufacturers when more were built.

L5 LISTING

3922 to 3929 L5pdw Altoona, 1924-26 (pass., D.C., Westinghouse)

3930 L5paw Altoona, 1924 (pass., A.C., Westinghouse)

7801 to 7807 L5pbd Juniata, 1927-28 (pass., D.C., Boveri)

7801 to 7807 L5pdg Juniata, 1928 (pass., D.C., Gen. El.)

7812 to 7815 L5pdw Juniata, 1927 (pass., D.C., Westinghouse)

Locomotive 3930 was originally class L5, and locomotives 3922-3929, 7812-7815 were built originally as class L5a. When other makes of electrical equipment were adopted for later L5's, the unusual sub-letters were added to classes showing type of service, type of current, and type of equipment. Nevertheless, all L5's were closely similar throughout. Most were used at New York, as shown by the D.C. current notation, however, several of these might have been changed over for A.C. operation. 3930 carried a pantograph (later, two pantographs) and was used in both passenger and freight work in the Philadelphia area. As a freighter, it was known as L5faw.

Four single-phase, A.C.-D.C. electric motors (two at each end) produced a total maximum horsepower of 3,340, with 3,070 continuous horsepower output. It seems almost unbelieveable, but the L5's rolled on 80-inch drivers. This was probably the largest ever applied to any electric engine, and created a top speed of 70 miles per hour. Comparative pulling power of freight and passenger adaptions is shown below:

	Freight	Passenger
Gear Ratio	30 to 118	50 to 98
Starting Tractive Effort	100,000 lbs.	82,500 lbs.

One Hour Rating	59,000 lbs.	43,500 lbs.
	(21 MPH)	(35.9 MPH)
Continuous Rating	50,000 lbs.	37,000 lbs.
	(23 MPH)	(37.8 MPH)

Passenger gearing was changed to 53:95 on all L5's except 3922-3929 and 7812. Length between couplers was 68 feet 2½ inches. Big things were expected of the 24 peculiar siderodders. They were expected to set standards for all motive power during future expansion of electrification. Most L5's joined the DD1's for New York Terminal service. It became apparent that they weren't living up to expectations. The older DD1's were far better. Something else would have to be found before the voltage could flow in long-distance concepts. Looking back, it's plain to see that side-rodders had seen their day. Although excellent for short tunnel operations, enlarged versions weren't adaptable to heavy, long distance work. This was due in part to their long wheelbase which failed to give them the DD1's tracking qualities.

Progressive electric locomotive development depended upon smaller motors of high horsepower, and they weren't long in coming. The L5 was a very interesting experiment along the way toward bigger and better things. All L5's are, of course, long gone.

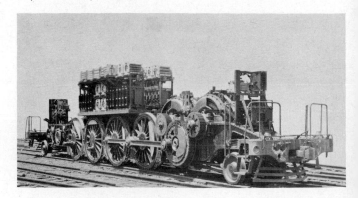

Running gear, motors and machinery.

256

3929 shown new at Altoona, Jan. 1925. She is equipped with pick-up shoes for tunnel operation. The successful DD1 was the spirit and thinking behind the L5 class, but they lacked one vital ingredient of their predecessors. The DD1's were, in a sense, articulated, giving them far superior tracking qualities.

3930 was first fitted with one pantograph (see pg. 256) then two after being assigned to Philadelphia area freight service. These 80" drivered monsters were to be the Pennsy's main line electric power, but they never lived up to expectations.

Pennsylvania Railroad

left, Head-on view of the first L5 when new. She was built to operate from overhead trolley wires.

below, A Juniata shop foreman poses beside the huge motors and drive wheel. The L5 was not nearly as flexible as the old DD1 class. Huge 80" drivers gave it a long (22'3") rigid wheel base. The heavy motor weight was not over the drivers either.

L5

Pennsylvania Railroad

This affords a good view of the pick-up shoes that slide along under the wood covered third rail. In areas of complex track work, where the third rail could not be used, juice was picked up from overhead lines by the small pantograph.

The first L5, 3930, churns it up on the Altoona Test plant. It's somewhat surprising to note that even though they never lived up to expectations, they were built over a period of 4½ years (1924-28).

The advent of the P5 class, in the early thirties, spelled doom for these side-rodders.

These "steeple cabbed" side rodders were a most unusual looking bit of American railroad power. The circular protrousions on the running boards are air ducts for traction motor blowers.

B1   0-C-0 (0-6-0)

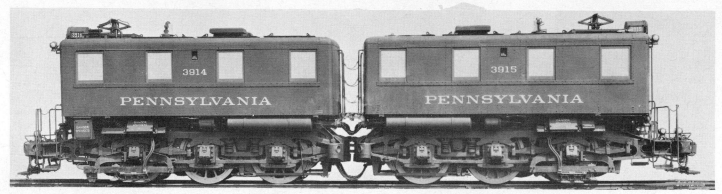

B1 (BB2 WHEN BUILT) ALTOONA, 1926

Pennsylvania Railroad

Motors (3) ....
Drivers .... 62"
Tractive Force at 25% Adhesion . 39,250 lbs.

Weight per Unit (With
Westinghouse Equipment) 157,045 lbs.
(With Allis-Chalmers Equipment) 157,700 lbs.

B3 (BB3 WHEN BUILT) ALTOONA, 1926

Only a few electrified railroads could afford the luxury of owning "juice" switchers, since prohibitive costs are associated with electrifying many miles of light usage sidings and yard tracks. However, Pennsylvania's high-voltage operations are extensive enough to warrant the use of 28 switchers, particularly in congested terminal areas around New York and Philadelphia, where they've been used principally on passenger equipment.

Beginning in 1926, Altoona Shops built a total of 42 little box-cab six-wheelers. Two thirds were for Pennsy, the rest for Long Island. Some were A.C. and some were D.C. They originally operated in semi-permanently coupled pairs.

PRR 3900, 3901 BB1 Altoona, 1926 A.C. Philadelphia area

PRR 3910 to 3921 BB2 Altoona, 1926 D.C. New York area

LI 324 to 337 BB3 Altoona, 1926 A.C.

PRR 5684 to 5697 B1 Altoona, 1934-35 A.C.

Between the years 1933 and 1935, class BB2 was rebuilt with A.C. electrical equipment. This class and BB1 were also split to operate as single units; all became class B1. Fourteen additional B1's were also constructed. These changes and additions were made to fit into expanded needs generated by New York-Washington electrification. Long Island's 0-6-0's also became single units, class B3.

Each B1 unit is propelled by three resistance lead, single-phase series traction motors, direct-geared to the axles with a 16:87 ratio. Electrical equipment is Allis-Chalmers or Westinghouse. Continuous ratings include 570 horsepower and 13,500 lbs. tractive effort at 15.9 MPH. Top speed is 25 MPH, while coupled length of a tiny B1 is just 31½ feet. Most of those operating in the New York-Sunnyside Yard area are equipped with high-frequency radio (PRR's main line low frequency trainphone system is subject to great static interference from high-voltage power lines).

A diminutive B1 with its single pantograph fully raised has the appearance of stretching mightily to reach its trolley wire power supply far overhead. Seems like they were continually buzzing back and forth through the upper level of Philly's 30th Street Station with mail cars and passenger equipment being herded between the general post office, Penn Coach Yards and Broad Street Station. Although possessing a mere fraction of the great GG1's strength, they make ten times as much noise with motor blowers and gears loudly whining and buzzing.

Several B1's saw service at Harrisburg, which was just about the only exception to their gregarious, clustered usage at Philly and New York. At this writing, seven have been scrapped, leaving 21 in existence. All Long Island B3's are gone. Passenger train curtailments have eliminated B1 use around Philadelphia; diesels now perform the required work under catenary.

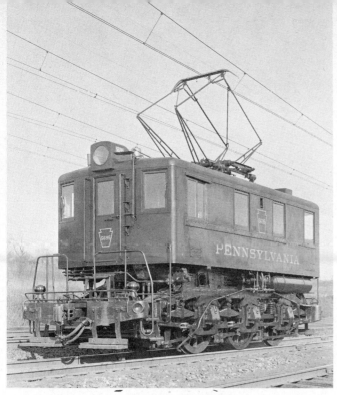

Looking more like a Lionel toy model than the real thing, a little B1 reaches for the wires.

They looked as big as a GG1—head on, that is. A ¾ view revealed her short (31'6") length. Electric switchers were real rarities on American Railroads.

Under construction at Altoona, 1934, showing frame, drivers and equipment deck. The three low-slung motors were direct-geared to the driving axles.

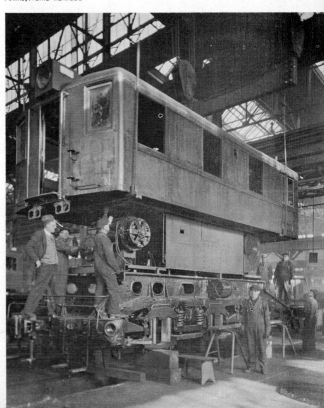

Lowering the cab structure over the equipment deck. All Pennsy electric locomotive cabs were removable for easy maintenance.

November 1926. A pair of Consolidations (H8sb and H6sa) head a string of 14 new BB3 units from Juniata to Long Island. When built, the B class switchers were semi-permanently coupled, but were later separated and used individually.

above, The special stops for water at Lewistown.

below, A pause for a portrait on the Middle Division.

Pennsylvania Railroad

Four B1's ready for service at Sunnyside Yards. Electric engines usually strike the novice as "spooky" because of the silent way they glide past with their trains. There's nothing very mysterious about the B1 switchers though, as they churn up more noise than something 10 times their size.

below, The B1 is most at home amidst a sea of passenger cars, usually in Philadelphia or New York. This is Penn Coach Yard, located behind Philly's 30th St. Station.

Pennsylvania Railroad

1930 O1 2-B-2 (4-4-4)

O1c, ALTOONA, NOV., 1931

Pennsylvania Railroad

*Motors (4) .... 625 H.P.		Total Weight .... 300,000 lbs.	
Drivers .... 72"		Tractive Force (Starting) .. 33,500 lbs.	
Weight on Drivers .... 150,000 lbs.		Tractive Force (Continuous) 14,900 lbs.	

*All specifications for one O1c unit—only.

Pennsylvania continued to advocate jackshaft-driven electrics through the 1920's, even though more-or-less conventional direct-geared types (that were large and powerful) had been built for use elsewhere since 1918. These other electrics simply lacked the sustained, highspeed capacity required for an anticipated New York to Washington electrification. PRR's L5 engines proved limitations of a jackshaft and showed that smaller, more powerful, electric motors were a basic need.

The technological break-through came in 1927, when the first single-phase twin motor capable of delivering 1,000 horsepower per axle (or 500 HP per armature) was developed by major electrical manufacturers. This motor also had sufficient capacity to achieve 25 percent adhesion at start and attain speeds up to 100 miles an hour, yet was small enough to go between driving wheels, a radical improvement never before achieved in a single-phase, A.C. commutator type motor.

This was, of course, just what Pennsy wanted, and by early 1930's, electrification plans were in full swing. Three basic locomotive types were designed in collaboration with electric equipment manufacturers. The railroad's Electrical Engineer, J. V. B. Duer, made certain that innumerable parts were standardized and made interchangeable between various classes, regardless of what company produced them. Class O1 was planned for light passenger work, with P5 for heavy passenger duties, and L6 was the freight puller.

The initial group of locomotives included eight 4-4-4's classified O1 (and various sub-letters) and were built by Altoona Shops in 1930 and 1931. There were clearly experimentals. Three had General Electric equipment, three had Westinghouse, and two were fitted with Brown-Boveri. Even though each locomotive had two, twin motors driving through geared quills and spring cups, motors were of varying horsepowers, and gear ratios differed as follows:

Numbers	Class	Con. HP	HP per Motor	Gear Ratio	Con. Speed	Con. T.E.
7850 7851	O1	2000	500	31:91	56.0	13,200 lbs.
7852 7853	O1a	2500	625	36:103	63.0	14,900 lbs.
7854 7855	O1b	2200	550	49:114	46.0	17,800 lbs.
7856 7857	O1c	2500	625	31:91	63.0	14,900 lbs.

The O1's represented the beginning of a master plan that was soon to produce the finest highspeed electric railroad in the world. No corners were cut here. The 4-4-4's had roller bearings on all axles and top speed was 90 MPH. Front trucks were free, while the rear trucks were equalized with drivers. All weighed 150 tons, with half their total weight on the 72-inch drivers, the same size as used on the DD1's (apparently that 80-inch L5 driver was too large). An O1 was 52 feet 8 inches in length. Like all PRR electrics, they had two cabs, cab signals and oil-fired steam heat boilers for passenger service.

Pioneering box cab O1's proved two important points. First, the basic design was extremely successful, electrically and mechanically speaking. This laid a firm foundation for other designs, using similar techniques and single-phase A.C. twin motors. Secondly, a 4-4-4 proved too light for general use, or, putting it another way, if an engine isn't universal enough to handle ALL trains, it's sure to handicap the operating department. That line of thinking toward electric locomotive development has paid uncountable operating dividends. Just ask any Pennsy man who works east of Harrisburg.

All classes of PRR box cab electrics carried fat aluminum handrails across each end—a unique trademark. O1 engines always ran in pairs, and sub-letter classes were never mixed. Thus, the two O1's were always M-U'd together, as were the two O1a's, and so forth. They were somewhat slippery in starting a train, but once the transformer relay switches stopped popping and they'd get rolling, a pair of O1's would run like greased lightening. Engines 7850-7851 hauled trains 633-632, "The Susquehannock," between Philadelphia and Harrisburg all during World War II. With an extra stop not usually made by through trains, the O1's handled this train on an extremely fast schedule.

The O1's were occasionally used in freight work, even though they couldn't pull much tonnage. All classes of early box cab motors carried very small road numbers, painted within the borders of a red keystone. Interlocking tower operators had trouble seeing the small numbers, so regulation locomotive numbers of large size were applied to each end.

A long-time O1 occupation was hauling relatively light Lehigh Valley passenger trains between Penn Station and Hunter Tower in Newark. Final O1 years were spent around Sunnyside Yard and the New York area as utility engines, handling empty passenger equipment. The last two, 7853 (O1a) and 7857 (O1c), were scrapped recently.

The O-class 4-4-4's usually operated in pairs, but here on a test train, 7851 is running alone. They were good little locomotives but not quite large enough to warrant fleet production. right, Head-on view of O1b 7855.

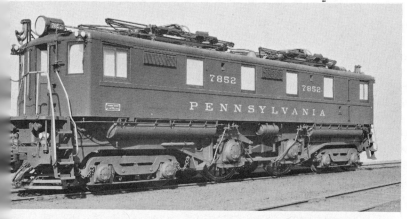

O1 locomotive sub-classes varied chiefly in traction motor horsepowers, with small differences in weights. O1a was the heaviest, weighing 309,400 lbs., while continuous horsepower ranged from 2000 to 2500. 4-4-4 electrics were designed to replace 4-4-2 E6s steam engines.

P5 2-C-2 (4-6-4)

Some were square, some were streamlined, but all were rugged.

Pennsylvania's many-faceted P5a fleet has proved to be a noteworthy phenomenon under the singing catenary. Although it is frequently overlooked in favor of the famed GG1's, hard-working P5a has established an equally enviable record east of Harrisburg and north of Potomac Yard. Simultaneous design made the first P5 class experimentals an enlarged version of the O1. The principal exterior appearances being ten foot differences in length and one more driving axle. They were planned and built through the composite efforts of an engineering trio: General Electric, Westinghouse and PRR's electrical staff headed by J. V. B. Duer. Components and parts were standardized throughout, regardless of what manufacturer produced them.

In box cab form, 64 heavy passenger P5a's protected schedules of the railroad's first long-distance catenary hookup. K4s steam power was pushed out of Manhattan Transfer (Meadows Enginehouse, Kearny) and moved to Wilmington and Paoli when P5a's began running into New York in 1933. Then came the famous GG1, and the P5a was immediately a second-choice passenger hauler. True, two P5a's might be M-U'd together to haul the heavier trains, but this was wasteful over-powering.

Meanwhile, on another front, more things were happening to make P5a's into freight haulers. Construction was halted on the L6 class electric freighters for a number of reasons. They proved somewhat too light for intended use, and their frontal box cabs were extremely dangerous in event of collisions. P5a box cabs were already being re-designed (for future construction) with steeple cabs, after one hit a truckload of apples at a grade crossing on the New York Division, killing the crew. Regeared P5a's were perfectly adaptible freight substitutes and soon became the backbone of voltage-propelled tonnage work.

Even as the first batch of GG1's was under construction, a final order for 28 re-designed (streamlined body) P5a's was built as dual service power. All P5a's eventually went into the freight pool, but streamlined ones hauled passenger trains when needed. In freight work, one box cab and one streamlined engine were paired together as much as possible, affording the safest operating cab location in at least one direction of travel, since they were never turned. By the late 1940's, all steam heat boilers were removed and replaced by blocks of cement.

Occasional misguided opinions have sometimes labeled the P5a's as "passenger engines forcibly misplaced into freight work." Truth of the matter is that they've been equally successful in both services. Regearing from 90 to 70 MPH gears simply adapted them to heavier work.

The P5a engineering formula specified weights of 75,000 pounds upon each driving axle and each four-wheeled truck. Its 3,750 continuous horsepower rating is produced by three twin motors of 1,250 horsepower each. This means a total of six, 625 horsepower motors, which are either Westinghouse 425-A or General Electric 625-A. Single-end, geared quills drive 72-inch wheels. A short-time rating of 6500 maximum horsepower is possible. All axles are roller bearing equipped, while the center pair of driving wheels has no flanges. Length over couplers is 62 feet 8 inches.

The first two (box cab) locomotives were experimentals and classified P5. The design was a whopping success from its inception and after some minor changes, the rest were classed P5a. One of the differences between the P5 and P5a was that the latter class got much larger traction motor blowers. Streamlined bodies were adopted for P5a's built after May 1, 1934. These were also called "modifieds" and were similar, mechanically and electrically, to box cab models. Below is a listing of road numbers and construction dates:

        4700 and 4791 P5 box cab Altoona, 1931
        4701 to 4732 P5a box cab Westinghouse, 1932
        4733 to 4742 P5a box cab Westinghouse, 1933
        4743 to 4754 P5a modified Westinghouse, 1935
       *4755 to 4774 P5a box cab General Electric, 1932
        4775 to 4779 P5a modified General Electric, 1935
                4780 P5a modified Altoona, 1934
        4781 to 4790 P5a modified Altoona, 1935
    *except 4770 which is modified.

Altoona-built engines have General Electric and Westinghouse equipment. Westinghouse-built engines were actually constructed at Baldwin Locomotive Works. Locomotives 4700 and 4791 carried road numbers 7898 and 7899 when built. In 1937, the 4702 was given motorized trucks and re-classified P5b. Four 375 horsepower motors were put into the trucks, one per axle. This gave the P5b a total horsepower of 5350, adding 26 tons to total weight. No other P5a's got motorized trucks; apparently 4702's booster motors didn't produce enough added hauling power to justify its existence.

Below is an interesting comparison of operating capacities between P5a's geared for passenger and freight service:

	Top Speed	Gear Ratio	Con. Speed	Con. T.E.
Passenger	90 MPH	31.91	63 MPH	22,350 lbs.
Freight	70 MPH	25:97	49 MPH	28,700 lbs.

The first P5a-powered regular passenger train left Broad Street Station, Philadelphia, for New York on January 16, 1933. Pennsy's long-distance electrification dream was coming true. Engine crews liked the P5a's immediately. They were smooth, powerful and certainly clean when compared to K4s steamers. About the only complaint was their cold and drafty cabs in wintertime. One operating problem developed involving the old bugaboo of lateral forces, or rail pounding at high speeds. When designed and built, mechanical engineers from one electric equipment manufacturer actually turned down a sub-contract for P5a components. They figured high running gear would cause unsteady balance and even possible broken axles. These predictions proved unfounded and the lateral force difficulty was ferreted out by running road tests with strain gages and other recording instruments. The truck equalization was changed and everything checked satisfactorily.

With the completion of the New York to Washington catenary in 1935, electricity was soon powering 686 daily passenger and freight trains operating 29,000 train miles under 1405 miles of trolley wires. There were 191 electric locomotives and 431 M-U cars on the roster. Bear in mind the foregoing figures do not include anything west of Paoli, or low-grade freight lines, all of which didn't get "juice" until 1938. P5a's made excellent runs with New York to Philly, hourly "clockers" with 8 to 10 car consists. But they had trouble maintaining fast schedules with heavy passenger trains. That was the principal reason for developing

GG1's. After all, no other electric railroad ever demanded so much sustained highspeed running capacity from its engines.

A few other interesting changes occurred to P5a's through the years. As originally built, modified types were 9½ tons heavier than box cabs. After removal of all steam heat boilers and weight adjustments, the difference in weight was narrowed to just one ton. Many P5a's had small trolley car type whistles, which were considered sufficient for passenger service. However, in freight work, flagmen couldn't hear them and for better grade crossing protection as well, loud air horns were installed. Box cabs had heavy, reinforcing steel girders installed on each cab end for better crew protection in event of collisions.

Along low-grade lines and other electrified freight routes, P5a's became a way of life and a tradition with PRR men. They were dependable and faithful servants, handling the bulk of fast symbol trains, heavy tonnage drags and division locals. An indication of this traffic volume is shown by daily average freight train density figures for 1942, for main line division routes: Philadelphia Division—54 eastbound and 45 westbound; New York Division—47 eastbound and 40 westbound; Maryland Division—24 northbound and 23 southbound.

P5a's usually swarmed in thickest groups at Enola, where an average of 125 electric units are serviced every 24 hours. Enola also handles monthly inspections for a majority of juice freighters. The 1942 average daily figures for eastbound freight train power dispatched from Enola was 73 trains. Westbound, engines were received from 64 trains. This could be one, two or three units per train, and included both Philadelphia Division routes and the Maryland Division low-grade line to Perryville.

Today the sturdy P5a is living on borrowed time. As of April 1962, there were still 52 in existence, only four of these being modified type. They are being replaced by new E44 class rectifiers, and GG1's. As things stand at this writing, Pennsy plans to retain about 20-25 P5a's indefinitely, so it's quite possible a few will be around for some time to come, even if they wind up as idle, emergency power.

Pennsylvania Railroad

The automobile practice of "sub-assembly" is also applied to locomotives. Above is a P5a with the complete equipment deck being lowered onto the chassis. Below, the interior of G-E's Erie Works with 15 P5a units in various stages of construction.

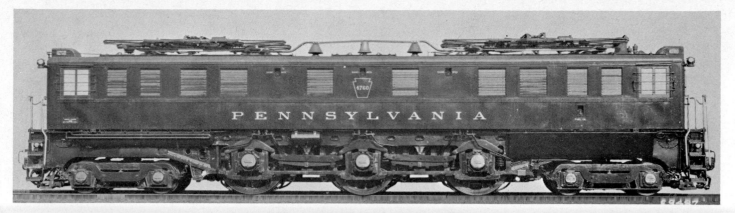

P5a, GENERAL ELECTRIC, 1932

Motors (6)		Total Weight	392,000 lbs.
Drivers	72"	Tractive Force (Starting)	55,000 lbs.
Weight on Drivers	220,000 lbs.	Horsepower Per Motor	625

P5a (MODIFIED) GENERAL ELECTRIC, 1935

Motors	6	Total Weight	394,000 lbs.
Drivers	72"	Tractive Force (Starting)	57,250 lbs.
Weight on Drivers	229,000 lbs.	Tractive Force (Continuous)	28,700 lbs.

P5b, REBUILT BY ALTOONA, OCT., 1937

*Motors	10	Total Weight	444,700 lbs.
Drivers	72"	Tractive Force (Starting)	80,000 lbs.
Weight on Drivers	233,400 lbs.	Total Horsepower	5,310

*Each of the four guiding axles is equipped with a 375 h.p. motor.

The heavy rivet construction is prominent in this head-on view. right, June 15, 1932, shows five brand new P5a "motors" ready for delivery.

It's interesting to note that most of Pennsy's problems, when developing new electric power, revolved about riding qualities and track punishment, to a higher degree than propulsion equipment.

"Juice jack" experimentation didn't stop, even though GG1's proved to be a motive power jackpot. P5a No. 4702 was upgraded to a 5,350-horsepower machine by installation of four 375 HP traction motors on the truck axles. This proved to be a one-shot trial, since the truck design made motor cooling difficult.

Manhattan Transfer, the steam and electric interchange, became just another station stop after 1933.

P5

above, One of the first electric trains in regular service is about to leave Broad St. Station enroute to New York.

left—P5 "Box Cab" 4739 at South Amboy, N. J. ready to head symbol freight train ET-1. Note the exterior sand pipes.

A common sight along multiple-tracked main lines is trains speeding along side-by-side. P5a 4773 on a freight drag is overtaken by Atlantic City-bound K4s 1339. Philadelphia, Sept. 1955.

Bert Pennypacker

Box Cab whisks along near Frankford Junction, Philadelphia. Normal Pennsy operations call for the usage of rear pantographs only. During snow and ice storms a "double pantograph order" will be in effect to help keep the trolley wires clean.

Pennsylvania Railroad

P5a with N/B freight is entering Philadelphia after run from Edge Moor Yards in Wilmington.

Pennsylvania Railroad

P5a with test train in Philadelphia. The K4s Pacific is in the consist to offer controlled resistance.

"White Flag Extra" test train between Philadelphia and Harrisburg, 1937.

right, You name it, and three P5a's could haul it. Train has just crossed the Potomac River, Washington, D. C.

273

Mountain grade—underground. A 1.3% grade is a tough climb in anyone's book. The portals at Bergen Hill are just three miles from Penn Station.

The gigantic statue of William Penn looks down upon his city from atop the City Hall. The Pennsylvania Railroad and Philadelphia are permanently entwined. They are, historically, a part of each other.

Bert Pennypacker

A caboose hop on its way to Coalport Yards, Trenton, to pick up a westbound freight. This is near the western end of the Trenton Cut-Off low-grade freight line. The two P5a's are just about to cross over No. 1 and 2 tracks of the E/B main.

Train No. 526 "The Susquehannock" (Williamsport to Philly) races by a freight that is waiting for a pusher engine at Thorndale, Pa. The GG1 is 4826.

Two P5a's head a freight over the Maryland Division. Make no mistake about it, the P5a's are big engines, 62' long and weighing almost 200 tons each.

L6 1-D-1 (2-8-2)

Truly brilliant engineering work produced mechanical and electrical successes in all three trial classes of panto-graphed locomotives developed during the early 1930's. But there were other hurdles to clear. Complications involving satisfactory adaption to operating requirements kept the L6 class "Mikado type juice freighter" plans from getting off the ground. First of all, they proved somewhat too light for the job. A number of partially-built L6a's were shelved because of their unsafe box cabs. A list of L-class motors follows:

5938 to 5939 L6   Altoona, 1932 1 West. and 1 GE equipped
     5940 L6a Lima, 1933 Westinghouse equipped
5941 to 5969 L6a Lima, 1933 bodies built, never completed

Locomotives 5938 and 5939 were originally numbered 7825 and 7826. Incidentally, it seems rather unusual to note that Lima built very few electric locomotives in its day. The L6 weighs only about 150 tons (same as O1), yet carries the same weight on eight drivers that the P5a has on six. The 2-8-2's starting tractive effort is much higher, but it loses out on horsepower, having only four single motors of 625 horsepower each, making a total continuous horsepower of 2500. Had L6's been planned with four double motors, it's possible 5000 horsepower would have produced an inter-

esting contender for P5a/GG1 freight pulling honors.

These 2-8-2's were roller bearing equipped on all axles, while driver size was smaller, 62 inches. They are not driven by quills, but have direct axle gearing with a ratio of 20 to 86 for 5938 and 5940, and a ratio of 23 to 98 on 5939. Top speed is 54 MPH, with a continuous speed of 37.5 miles per hour and 25,000 lbs. tractive effort. L6 classes are 51 feet 10 inches in length and their appearance is somewhat different from other box cab electrics, particularly in the running gear. L6 and L6a are generally similar, except for larger traction motor blowers on the latter class.

The uncompleted lot of L6a's consisted of entire locomotives minus electrical equipment. From a photograph standpoint, they looked able and ready to pull trains. These empty shells on wheels were stored at Altoona for several years and finally cut up. The three L engines that were built originally saw road freight work for a few years and have since become New York area passenger equipment haulers. Locomotive 5938 has been scrapped, but her two sisters remain in existence. It's a bit surprising that even though not very successful, they survived the time test quite well.

L6, ALTOONA, DECEMBER, 1931

Pennsylvania Railroad

Motors 4	Total Weight . . . . 300,000 lbs.	
Drivers . . . . 62"	Tractive Force (Starting) . . 55,000 lbs.	
Weight on Drivers . . . . 220,000 lbs.	Horsepower Per Motor 625	

L6a, LIMA LOCOMOTIVE WORKS, AUGUST 1933

Pennsylvania Railroad

Motors 4	Total Weight . . . . 305,110 lbs.	
Drivers . . . . 62"	Tractive Force (Starting) . . 55,250 lbs.	
Weight on Drivers 221,000	Horsepower Per Motor 625	

¾ and front view of Pennsy's "Electric Mikado".

Electric locomotives are really power converters, that is, they do not create power, they merely transform 11,000 volt A.C. juice into propulsion energy at rail level. This "stepping down" takes much equipment as can be seen in the photo, left.

L6, 5938 helps a H9s with a S/B freight by North Ave. Baltimore. Sept. 26, 1936. The H9s crew is being particularly careful about smoke because of the tunnels in the area.

GG1 2-C+C-2 (4-6-0+0-6-4)

They roll on in the dimming shadows of the great steam fleet.

No one has ever put together a single-unit locomotive that can match the all-powerful GG1's get-up-and-go capacities. These fabulous twelve-motored streamliners pack a short-time maximum of 8,500 horsepower which is available in starting. Highspeed prowess includes 4,620 continuous horsepower at 100 miles per hour. It's a routine performance for them to effortlessly whisk 18-car limiteds between New York and Washington at ninety-miles-an-hour top cruising speeds. Many trains gobble up the 226 catenary-hung miles in 215 minutes, including five intermediate station stops. Harrisburg-bound runs travel at a "moderate" 75 MPH.

The 139-unit GG1 fleet was built during a ten-year period commencing in 1934. Their availability and mileage records are fantastic. Total fleet mileage as of 1959 added up to 337 million locomotive miles. This is reflected in daily average passenger train density figures for the year 1942: New York Division—236 trains; Philadelphia Division—73 trains; Maryland Division—107 trains. These are division-length runs in both directions, excluding short-haul commuter traffic and 29 additional trains south of Baltimore.

Of course the foregoing refers to times when GG1's were principally haulers of tuscan red passenger trains. During the 1950's passenger train mileage reductions have transformed the engines into a prime dual service class with 57 assigned to freight work. However,, all except No. 4800 are also available for passenger assignments if and when needed.

The fantastic GG1 powerhouse of energy is almost unbelieveable. Consider for a moment the testing of locomotive 4899 (now 4800) at Claymont, Delaware, back in 1934. Pulling one car of test equipment, this original GG1 was repeatedly accelerated under full power from stop to 100 MPH in just 64.5 seconds. This performance required a peak output of 9,300 horsepower at the rail, equivalent to 11,000 diesel locomotive horsepower. During these tests and others held in the late 1940's to study braking power, GG1's with short trains easily hit 128 MPH. Without considering other basic advantages of electric traction, it's plain that diesel-versus-catenary survey data of the 1950's was influenced in no small part by the GG1 abilities. Let's now go back to 1933 and see how GG1's were developed.

The composite efforts of a small engineering army were pooled from various corporations to design and perfect the GG1 locomotive. First of all, PRR's man-in-charge was J. V. B. Duer, Electrical Engineer. Other members of the "electrical brain trust" came from Baldwin, General Electric, Westinghouse and Gibbs & Hill Consulting Engineers. In the year 1933, these men faced a variety of problems. On the good side, single-phase twin-armature motors were a reality and successfully propelled O1 and P5a locomotives. Problematical was P5a's inability to meet schedules with heavy trains on an individual basis, and its poor tracking qualities with exceptionally high lateral stresses.

A highspeed testing set-up was inaugurated near Claymont, Delaware, to check upon P5a's riding qualities while simultaneously laying groundwork for blueprinting a larger electric locomotive. Three hundred special impact recording steel ties were installed in a track test section. Locomotive-mounted weigh bars and strain gages were used to measure lateral forces against axles and wheel flanges. Multi-element oscillographs and sensitized rolls of paper were located in a test equipment car to make accurate records. This data soon provided a solution to the P5a stress problem, which was corrected with changes in the truck equalization.

Then PRR borrowed a New Haven class EP3 juice passenger engine which was built by Baldwin-Westinghouse in 1931. The 2,740 horsepower machine had a 2-C+C-2 wheel arrangement and was regeared from a top speed of 80 MPH to 120 for testing. The NH job proved to be an eye-opener; it recorded substantial reductions in lateral forces. P5a and EP 3 trials brought forth two differing theories about basic designs. One idea gave EP3's low axle weights the credit for good riding qualities; the second opinion stated that certain wheel arrangements (regardless of axle weights) fostered good tracking characteristics.

Two sample locomotives were ordered built with design emphasis being placed upon different wheel arrangements and axle loadings. Already perfected twin traction motors were no problem, however they were improved to give the same power in half the size. Baldwin-Westinghouse built a 2-D-2 (4-8-4) rigid frame engine which was, in essence, an enlarged P 5a with one more driving axle and lower axle weights. General Electric was given the job of constructing a 2-C+C-2 (4-6-6-4) with higher axle loadings than NH's EP3, but lower than the 2-D-2's. Horsepowers were increased in both engines, both had new style streamlined bodies, and they were ready for testing in 1934. Below is a comparison listing:

Wheel Arrangement	2-D-2	2-C+C-2
Builder	B-West.	G.E.
Engine Number	4800	4899
Class	R 1	GG 1
Horsepower	5000	4620
No. Twin Motors	Four	Six
Total Motors	Eight	Twelve
HP Per Motor	625	385
Wt. Per Axle	57,500 lbs.	50,500 lbs.
Con. Speed	100 MPH	100 MPH
Gear Ratio	27:74	24:77
Con. T. E.	18,750 lbs.	17,300 lbs.
Length	64' 8"	79' 6"'

Both engines were equipped with roller bearings on all axles and were driven via geared quills. R1's traction motors were duplicates of those used in P5a's, horsepower-wise, while the GG1 employed a principle of many small motors which has probably been the secret of its success. Interestingly enough, General Electric Also originated the 2-C+C-2 wheel arrangement in 1929 with Cleveland Union Terminal (NYC System) 3000-volt d.c. catenary passenger haulers. These 2465 horsepower locomotives are sometimes credited with being the GG1 prototype, but this relationship is very slight, extending only to generalities of wheel arrangement and concepts of light axle weights.

Pennsy's traditional thoroughness in testing new experimental locomotives was never so carefully handled as it was with R1 and GG1. Sizeable complements of engineers and other testing personnel took their two noteworthy pantographed proteges down to Claymont for the

...he author's opinion, the picture, left, is one of the most striking he has even seen. Taken by Robert Dudley ...th, it is presented here through the courtesy of the Pennsylvania Railroad Company.

full-scale treatment. After that, they ran the engines at 100 MPH between New York and Philadelphia. Oscillographs wrote continuous paper-imprinted score cards on tracking qualities. Both units proved to be extremely powerful and produced minimum lateral forces. Close analysis of the overall tracking characteristics disclosed that GG1 possessed a slight edge over R1, but the difference was not great. This result nominated GG1 for the fleet production and standard heavy electric class of the railroad. GG1's two-section, jointed underframes were conducive to excellent tracking characteristics.

GG1's were built as follows:
4800 General Electric, 1934
4801 to 4814 General Electric, 1935
4815 to 4857 Altoona, 1935
4858 to 4862 Altoona, 1937
4863 to 4871 Altoona, 1938
4872 to 4888 Altoona, 1939
4889 to 4908 Altoona, 1940
4909 4910 Altoona, 1941
4911 to 4928 Altoona, 1942
4929 to 4938 Altoona, 1943

The R1 and GG1 traded road numbers, then, in 1940, when GG1 numbers reached 4899, the R1 was again renumbered to 4999. R1 continued in service for many years and was scraped about 1958. It hauled the westbound "Broadway Limited" regularly, returning east on a heavy mail-express run. R1's rigid frame caused some difficulties in traversing sharp curves in yard switches , causing occasional derailments around Sunnyside Coach Yards.

Raymond Loewy probably did his best locomotive styling job of all time on the GG1. PRR wanted operating cabs removed from the vulnerable frontal location, and Loewy achieved this with unparalleled esthetics in a streamlined form. The body of GG1 4899 (later 4800) was fashioned from riveted sheets by GE; all others got smoothly welded outer skins. General Electric and Westinghouse supplied identical sets of electrical equipment for GG1's, while Baldwin and its subsidiary, General Steel Castings Corp., made many structural parts such as underframes, lower cab decks and inner cab frames. All except the initial fifteen were assembled at Altoona. The first 58 engines were built with flat, steel pilots and normal couplers. Those built after January of 1937 got rounded pilots and drop couplers. Each GG1 carried a price tag of approximately $250,000.

GG1 operation soon became routine; no train was too long or heavy for them. Needless to say, sound planning for the future had established eastern lines electrification and GG1's in time to do a tremendous World War II job. This task could not have been handled by three times as many steam or diesel units. Engine 4823 had a jinxed career plaguing its first few months of operation. The locomotive was the first to be involved in a fatal accident, later it was struck by lightening and lost the main transformer, then her engineer suffered a heart attack at the controller. However, after these occurrences, 4823 was pictured on the 1936 wall calendar and met no further bad luck.

In the year 1945, locomotive 4840 struck a huge bulldozer at a grade crossing near Stanton, Delaware, while traveling 80 MPH. It threw the 'dozer across four tracks, but only dented the GG1's nose and derailed the front truck. Unlike most electrics and diesels, GG1's have practically indestructible inner body frames. The frames are shaped like a girder truss bridge built with heavy steel I-beams anchored in concrete bases, and braced crosswise by cast steel beams.

A morning "Clocker" lea

Engine 4876 figured in what was probably the most sensational accident of recent years. Approaching Washington Union Station with the "Federal" from Boston in January, 1952, train brakes failed and the 4876 roared past the end of the station stub track and plunged through the concourse floor into a baggage room underneath. This occurred just a few days prior to President Eisenhower's inauguration, so the concourse floor was boarded over temporarily and thousands of inauguration-goers tramped over the GG1 laying below. After inauguration traffic subsided, the engine was cut into six-foot sections and sent to Altoona for re-assembly. Ten months later,, it was back hauling trains in tuscan red livery. Its inaccessible position in the baggage room had created problems. Since cranes couldn't reach the 4876, perhaps it should be scrapped; but the cut-up and re-assembly plan was dictated by the insurance company (GG1's are insured by Lloyds of London) as cheaper than replacement by a brand new engine.

Bad weather has had little effect upon GG1 operation until the day they stopped running in February, 1958. A freak snowstrom produced unusually small snow par-

Philadelphia for New York, 1941, She looks more like a new toy than a 200 ton giant.

ticles very seldom encountered in the Mid-Atlantic States. This Diamond snow, as it is called, actually penetrated fine meshed Japanese silk snow screens applied over GG1 air inlet louvers. As snow got to traction motors, they shorted out immediately. Passenger service was soon badly crippled with dozens of GG1's stalled on the road or in shops being repaired. Trains were annulled, repaired GG1's went out on the road and immediately lost more traction motors; diesels rescued many stalled trains and ran east under catenary to Newark. Until the storm and its lingering snow particles subsided, Pennsy east of Harrisburg and north of Washington was a crippled railroad, struggling in vain to overcome an impossible obstacle.

A solution was found and it won't happen again. An epoxy resin of special formula was devised to coat on traction motors and other electrical equipment. This proved far superior to former methods of protection, and an epoxy-coated motor was actually operated while fully submerged in a tank of water as a demonstration. All electric and diesel traction motors will eventually get epoxy resin protection.

Engine 4888 was exhibited at the New York World's Fair of 1939-1940. All 139 GG1's remain in service. Originally only a few were used in fast freight work, but 57 are now so employed. However, passenger demands require the GG1 freight pool to be interchangeable for dual service. Pulling freights with 90 or 100 MPH gearing works a slight disadvantage, and maybe a few GG1's with 70 MPH gears will appear someday. Change-over from passenger to freight operation requires a few simple valve adjustments to change trainline brakepipe pressure. Also, in freight work, GG1 controllers are operated only to notch 17 instead of full power (notch 22).

GG1's have shown the wear and tear of hard work. Most of their original steam heat boilers have been replaced by new ones. Some of the inner structural steel girders have rusted badly on the oldest engines and are being replaced. Likewise, various early GG1's have shown metal fatigue fissures in underframes, particularly near the ends. Entire new sections have been welded in place to correct this trouble.

Without a doubt the GG1's are the most famous and successful fleet of electric motive power in the world.

R1, BALWIN-WESTINGHOUSE, 1934

Motors	8	Total Weight	402,000 lbs.
Drivers	62"	Tractive Force at 100 M.P.H.	18,750 lbs.
Weight on Drivers	**230,000 lbs.**	Length (Over Couplers)	64'8"
Horsepower—Each Motor	625	Rigid Wheel Base	23'0"

R1

"Battle Of The Titans". The GG1 didn't inherit the throne. She had to fight for it. Her worthy opponent was this 5,000 horsepower giant—the R1. Both the GG1 and R1 performed superbly, but GG1's slightly superior tracking qualities gave her the nod that meant fleet production.

GG1

The rugged monster R1 at Wilmington Shops just before her retirement.

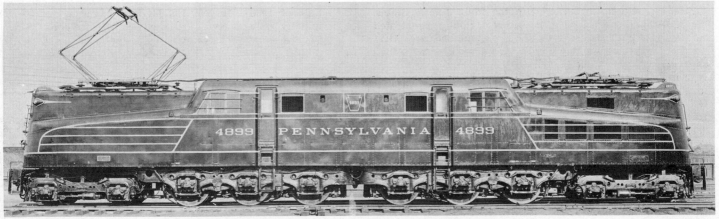

GG1, GENERAL ELECTRIC, 1934 (FIRST GG1 AS BUILT)

Motors	12	Total Weight	475,000 lbs.
Drivers	57"	Tractive Force (Maximum)	65,500 lbs.
Weight on Drivers	303,000 lbs.	Length	79'6"
Horsepower—Each Motor	385	Rigid Wheel Base	13'8"

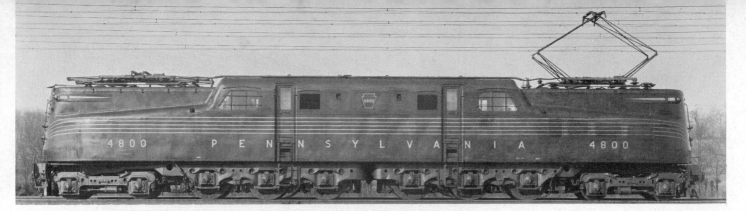

GG1, THE FIRST GG1 RE-NUMBERED AND RE-STRIPED

GG1, ALTOONA, JUNE 1935

Motors	12	Total Weight	460,000 lbs.
Drivers	57"	Tractive Force (Maximum)	75,000 lbs.
Weight on Drivers	300,000 lbs.	Horsepower—Each Motor	385

GG1, ALTOONA, JUNE 1942

Motors	12	Total Weight	477,000 lbs.
Drivers	57"	Tractive Force (Maximum)	70,700 lbs.
Weight on Drivers	303,000 lbs.	Horsepower—Each Motor	385

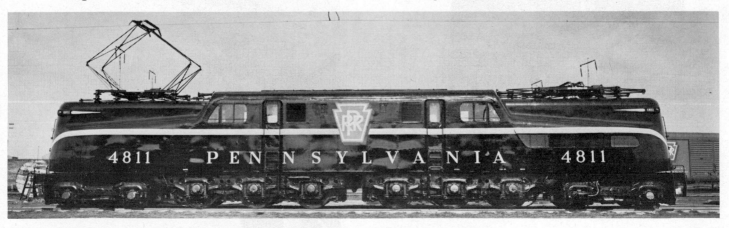

GG1, WITH NEW BRUNSWICK GREEN PAINT SCHEME

The GG1 had a variety of lettering styles and stripes, but the combination shown here is by far the best. Tuscan Red color, CrawClarendon letters and stripes in buff-gold all say "Pennsylvania Railroad".

Head-on view of 4856. One of the severest tests of art is longevity. The GG1's design passed this one superbly, for she seems to improve with the passing years.

Pennsylvania Railroad

Right—two views of pantographs. The height of most Pennsy Electrics is 15' with pans locked down (ex G.N. FF2 is 15,11").

Except for the first GG1 (4800), 4876 received the most publicity. It was January 1952 and she was slipping into Washington Station for the 3,000th time and her Brakes Failed! She rolled right into the huge concourse and crashed through the floor into the baggage room below. She was cut up in 6-foot sections and rebuilt at Altoona. Here is 4876 after being rebuilt.

left, Cab interior showing indicator lights. Compared to a steam locomotive, these controls are ridiculously simple. below, Head-on view of 4800 when new. Her rivet constructed "skin" (she still has it) gives her more of a locomotive look. Today (1962) she is the only GG1 permanently assigned to freight duty.

At left is the team of 385 horsepower motors, middle is the Quill Drive assembly and right is the complete quill and driving wheels. The wheel axle rolls independently inside the large hollow "quill" shaft. The Spring—Cup Drive (middle) absorbs the motors' thrust or torque.

The construction start of a GG1 showing body truss assembly. With framework like this, is it any wonder they are indestructible?

Pennsylvania Railroad

The heavy skin supports are welded to the truss frame and we begin to see the GG1 take shape.

Sub-assembly of the locomotive cab. The general procedure is much the same as automobile construction.

    The gauge of the metal, needless to say, is about 5 times as heavy.

Pennsylvania Railroad

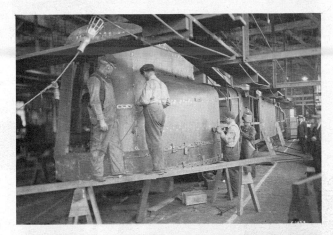

Drilling, welding and grinding. The sheet metal would be bolted in place and then welded between the holes in temporary bands (right). After these were removed and the welding completed, the grinders finished the surface to a smooth-skin effect. GG1 4800 was the only one with exterior riveted skin

The finished cab being lowered onto the wheels and side frame.

Pennsylvania Railroad

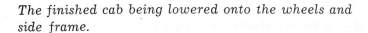

May 17, 1935—GG1's at various stages of building at the Railroads Altoona Shops.

A new type of locomotive usually gets treated to a bit of splash and publicity. GG1 really got the works, for it declared the advent of not just a new engine, but a whole new electric plant.

above, The oddly-striped 4800 gets a comparison shot with her steam counterpart, the K4s Pacific. W. Philadelphia.

If you want to really "impress," Park your new creation next to a pint-sized A5s 0-4-0 steam switcher.

4800, new in 1934. On her 25th birthday (1959) the first GG1 had piled up an impressive record. She had run a total of 2,795,577 miles and used up 122,219,240 kwh of electric energy costing $1,582,296 (more than six times the cost of the locomotive when new).

"Good-bye Steam, Hello Electric!" Harrisburg is jubilant as the first regularly scheduled passenger train rolls in, to fulfill a long-awaited dream. Shiny 4863 heads the Pittsburgh-bound "Metropolitan" on a cold and icy January 15, 1938.

It's our wish to see this scene repeated, eventually, at Pittsburgh.

March 1950, a New York express prepares to leave old Broad St. Station, Philadelphia. The station and tracks are gone; in fact, Pennsy's new main office building is just about where GG1 4896 is standing.

Pennsy's crack "Congressional" rumbles over the Susquehanna River at Perryville, Md. This run, New York-Washington, is considered the choicest "plum" in America by locomotive engineers. The track is fast, grade crossings few and the locomotive is the renowned GG1—Could there be more?

Westbound through Paoli. Each GG1 carries 2,755 gallons of water and 390 gallons of fuel oil for use in the steam heat boiler.

GG1 "motor" (Pennsy Men call all electrics motors) emerges from Bergen Hill Portals enroute from New York to Philadelphia. The trolley voltage of 11,000 (single phase 25-cycle alternating current) is stepped down to 340 for the traction motors.

291

Jan. 28, 1935. The famous 4800 emerges from Hoffman St. Tunnel, Baltimore, during a severe East Coast snow storm. Her train heating boiler is spouting steam in the bitter cold.

Hotshot MD-6 (known as the "Medical Doctor") with 4805 and 4807 hit it eastward through Colonia, N. J. at a flat 65 m.p.h.

This is private enterprise in Action! No government subsidies here. The railroad owns the right of way, catenary, locomotives, cars and track. They also maintain and pay heavy real estate taxes on same.

No steam and smoke, but we have the graceful arc of track and wire as 4829 heads 14 coaches through the Philadelphia suburb of Wynnewood. It's a thrilling sight, particularly for those accustomed to roaring steam and growling diesels, to watch these giant GG1's slip by like silent ghosts.

Why electric? If you have the traffic density, it can't be beat. One advantage is the factor of overload. A GG1 has a rated horsepower of about 4,600; but with the 11,000 volts over head, you can overload to 9,000 horsepower for a short time.

above, Semi-automatic "Locomotive Laundry" at Sunnyside Yds. can wash a GG1 in 15 minutes.

above left, Conductor and Engineer talk things over before departing for New York City.

left, Dust and sand tell a story of speed as the "Pennsylvania Limited" roars through Coatesville, Pa.

below, The position lights are vertical for the "Afternoon Congressional" as she streaks through Frankford Junction.

below, One of the three that were painted silver gray with red stripe, black lettering, in 1955.

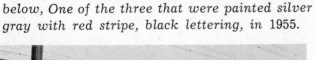

above, Looming in the darkness with a "painting" quality are 4904 and 4887 at Washington's Ivy City Engine Facilities.

above left, The "motors" don't spend much "down time" for repairs. This is the railroads Wilmington Shops.

left, Resplendent in its newest livery, GG1 motor makes a North Philadelphia Station stop with a Florida to New York streamliner. The forward raised pantograph suggests that the rear one is not functioning properly.

below, GG1's at Washington. Only five (4876 and 4908-4911) GG1's are painted the traditional Tuscan Red. All the rest are Brunswick Green (practically black).

295

Two locomotive designs shared modern day laurels for greatness and tremendous personal love of all PRR men. GG1's and 4-8-2 steamers proved unbeatable. Ageless GG1's have neither slowed or weakened—139 of them roll on in dimming shadows of their Great Steam Fleet brothers.

Pennsylvania Railroad

ALEXANDER·JOHNSTON·CASSATT
PRESIDENT·PENNSYLVANIA·RAILROAD·COMPANY
1899–1906

WHOSE·FORESIGHT·COURAGE·AND·ABILITY·ACHIEVED
THE·EXTENSION·OF·THE·PENNSYLVANIA·RAILROAD·SYSTEM
INTO·NEW·YORK·CITY

No book on Pennsy Power would be complete without this man's picture, Alexander Johnston Cassatt. His reign, though short (1899-1906), was the era of great improvement. His untimely death in 1906 prevented him from seeing his fondest dream completed: entering of the Pennsylvania Railroad into mid-town Manhattan.

DD2   2-B+B-2 (4-4-4-4)

The idea of a universal passenger-freight electric locomotive didn't die with the mediocre performance of L5 siderodder classes during the 1920's. By the year 1938, a universal concept was back under catenary. Its form was the Altoona-built experimental number 5800, a husky looking streamliner packing 5000 horses within a 4-4-4-4, jointed underframe wheel arrangement. Two alternative gear ratios were planned for the DD2; for passenger or freight work.

5800 represented a homogeneous hybrid with various good features of other electric classes. Its high horsepower was borrowed from the GG1 and R1 engines, and the jointed frame allowed better tracking qualities than R1. DD2's also possessed high axle loadings, similar to P5a's, while the total weight of 5,800 was midway between that of R1 and GG1. This supposedly lethal package of advanced ideas, might have conceivably replaced both P5a and GG1 fleets in time, but this of course, didn't happen. Like many an experimental, DD2 served its intended development function, but never fulfilled expectations sufficiently for duplication. 5800 was equipped with freight gearing and the class was never tried in tuscan red passenger work.

The experimental was powered by four Westinghouse 428-A twin armature motors of 1,250 horsepower each. This breaks down into eight, 625 horsepower motors, two per driving axle. Drive was via geared quills. Number 5800 was equipped with roller bearings on all axles, and was 72 feet 6¼ inches long over couplers. Her top speed was pegged at 70 MPH with a gear ratio of 21 to 83. Continuous ratings included 5,000 horsepower, 49 miles per hour, with 38,300 lbs. tractive effort.

The foregoing figures are, of course, for freight work. Proposed passenger service gearing would have been 28:76 with a top speed of 100 miles per hour. Incidentally, notice that PRR practice states gear ratios in opposite sequence from the normal and universally-used method. Engine 5800 remains in service; at this writing she is assigned to the Philadelphia Region and is hauling a short turn-around job between Wilmington (Edgemoor) and South Philly.

DD2, ALTOONA, FEB. 1938

Motors 8		Total Weight .... 450,000 lbs.	
Drivers .... 62"		Tractive Force (Maximum) 71,500 lbs.	
Weight on Drivers 286,000		Horsepower—Each Motor 625	

1957 FF2 1-C+C-1 (2-6-6-2)

In August of 1956, Great Northern Railway shut down its 72-mile electrified district, between Wenatchee and Skykomish in Washington State, and substituted diesel operation. By the following Spring, eight of GN's mammoth box cab 2-6-6-2 electrics were being sent eastward to assist in moving PRR's growing import iron ore traffic. Big G locomotives 5010 to 5017, class Y1 and Y1a, were built by Alco-General Electric between 1926 and 1929. Their journey between western and eastern catenaries was interrupted at Altoona Shops, where 48 separate structural, mechanical and electrical changes were made to adapt them to Pennsy practice. One engine was reserved for extra parts supply, while seven went into service carrying the unusual road numbers 1 to 7, with keystone class FF2.

. These 73 foot 9 inch-long giants were so large their territory was limited to Philadelphia, Enola and Enola plus Baltimore (via Perryville) runs. When major repairs were needed, components had to be removed at Enola and shipped in boxcars to the main electric shops at Wilmington, since a whole FF2 was too large to run there on its own

wheels. They occasionally saw road freight work out of Philly, but were used principally as pushers westbound from the Quaker City to Paoli. They also did helper work out of Thorndale and Columbia. Most recently, they hauled Baltimore freights from Enola. Their service expectancy wasn't more than a few years, and as of April, 1962, locomotives 1, 3 and 5 remained.

FF2's were motor- generator electrics, whereby alternating current from the trolly wire ran a motor that turned two direct current generators. These powered six 550 horsepower General Electric 290-A D.C. traction motors; one motor geared to each axle with a ratio of 21 to 82. In essence, this set-up paralleled the theory behind rectifiers, but many moving parts in motor-generator sets were more costly to maintain.

One hour horsepower rating was 3,300, while the continuous rating was 3000 horses at 18 miles per hour and tractive effort of 60,000 lbs. Top speed was 55 MPH. Plain journals limited them to slower trains. Their tremendous weight and power made them excellent helpers—forty years after the gargantuan (Big Liz) FF1 was conceived.

FF2, ALCO-GE, 1926-1929

Motors	6	Total Weight	527,600 lbs.
Drivers	55"	Tractive Force (Maximum)	102,900 lbs.
Weight on Drivers	411,600 lbs.	Horsepower—Each Motor	550

From the Cascade Mountains to Philadelphia. These displaced giants are now doing freight and pusher service in the Philadelphia Region. They are the only Pennsy electrics that must operate with both pantographs raised.

Pennsylvania Railroad

E2 and E3 EXPERIMENTALS

Two new kinds of experimental freight electrics, aimed at a P5a replacement, hummed onto PRR rails in 1951. "Popular Science Magazine" editorialized the occurrence as a "Battle of the Electrics," and that's just about what it amounted to. General Electric's entry was an advanced design, heavy-duty straight alternating current engine. Baldwin-Lima-Hamilton-Westinghouse's contribution was the much-desired ignitron, mercury-arc rectifier. This type combined advantages of high voltage A.C. transmission in trolley wires with the very efficient pulling power of D.C. traction motors. Rectifier tubes on the locomotive make this current change.

Below is a run-down of road numbers, wheel arrangements, and classes:

4939 to 4944 2(B-B) E 2b GE, A.C. (3 locomotives)
4995 to 4996 2(B-B-B) E 3b BLHW, A.C.-D.C. rectifier
4997 to 4998 2(C-C) E3c BLHW, A.C.-D.C. rectifier

They roll on motorized trucks and look like diesels with pantographs, representing a new look in PRR electrics. Class numbers and sub-letters refer to truck arrangement per unit. All are "A" units, having one operating cab, and normal operations sees two units per locomotive. E2b will M-U with P5a's. Units 4943 and 4944 were GE demonstra-

tors which ran tests for a time on Great Northern as road numbers 5020 and 5021. Rectifier D.C. traction motors are completely interchangeable with diesels.

Major operating data for each two-unit hook-up is shown below:

Con.	Total HP	HP Per Motors	Gear Ratio	Top Speed	Con. Speed	Con. T.E.
E2b	5000	Eight 625	21:83	65	26.5	70,800 lbs.
E3b E3c	6000	Twelve 500	15:68	63	17	132,000 lbs.

Drive is by axle-hung, direct-geared motors. All units roll on SKF roller bearings, and all have dynamic brakes. Each GE single unit is 54 feet 3 inches in length, while the comparative figure for BLHW units is 62 feet. Except for differing truck styles, the two rectifier classes are identical.

All three classes were quite successful, but rectifiers proved to be slow speed, incredible tonnage movers, unsuited to fast symbol train assignments. As of April, 1962, all ten units were in service on the Chesapeake Region. "Battle of the Electrics" is now recorded history, and rectifiers (not built by BLHW, but by GE) have won out over straight A.C. types.

E2b, GENERAL ELECTRIC, 1951   Pennsylvania Railroad

Drivers .... 48"   Total Weight .... 491,000 lbs.
Weight on Drivers .... 491,000 lbs.   Tractive Force (Maximum) 122,750 lbs.

These specifications are for two units.

E3c, BALDWIN, LIMA, WESTINGHOUSE, 1951   Pennsylvania Railroad

Drivers .... 44"   Total Weight .... 723,960 lbs.
Weight on Drivers .... 723,960 lbs.   Tractive Force (Maximum) 180,990 lbs.

These specifications are for two units.

E3b, BALDWIN, LIMA, WESTINGHOUSE, 1951

Drivers .... 44"		Total Weight .... 756,000 lbs.	
Weight on Drivers .... 756,000 lbs.		Tractive Force (Maximum) 189,000 lbs.	

These specifications are for two units.

4995 and 4996 are a two unit (one locomotive) hookup with a B-B-B wheel arrangement. The units develop 6000 horsepower, 11,000 volt A.C. trolley current is transformed into D.C. (by the ignition rectifier tubes) for the diesel like traction motors. They are running on the Trenton Cut-Off freight line.

Two of the six units built by G.E. move over the Philadelphia Division. These are straight A.C. electrics.

REGIONAL ASSIGNMENT—ELECTRIC LOCOMOTIVES— APRIL 1962

New York Region:
 B1: 3910 3912 3913 3918 3919 5685 5690 5693 5694 5695
 DD1: 3936 3937 3966 3967
 L6 and L6a: 5939 5940
 GG1: 4827 to 4938
 P5: 4700
Philadelphia Region:
 B1: 3900 3914 to 3917 5684 5687 5688 5689 5692 5695
 E44: 4400 to 4434
 DD2: 5800
 FF2: 1 3 5 6 7
 GG1: 4800 to 4826
 P5a: 4703 4704 4705 4707 4708 4710 4711 4712 4714 4716
  to 4724 4726 to 4734
Chesapeake Region:
 E2b: 4939 to 4944
 E2c: 4997 4998
 E3b: 4995 4996
 P5a: 4735 to 4742 4746 4749 4750 4754 4755 4756 4757
  4759 4760 4762 4763 4768 to 4772

E44 C-C

E44, GENERAL ELECTRIC, 1960

Drivers	40"	Tractive Force (Maximum)	89,000 lbs.
Weight on Drivers	386,000 lbs.	Tractive Force (Continuous)	55,500 lbs.
Motors	(GE) 6	Maximum Speed	70 m.p.h.
Horsepower—Per Motor	733	Rigid Wheel Base	13'0"

Pennsylvania's 1951 outbreak of experimental juice freighters was clearly suggestive of imminent decisions favoring mass construction of P5a replacements, but such was not the case. Timeworn, but capable, P5a's whined along with tonnage during the 1950's while PRR concentrated upon two other important matters. These were dieselization of unelectrified lines and three separate and comprehensive surveys by private researchers to determine economic advantages of catenary retention—or discard.

Needless to say, survey statistics became self-explanatory in a $32 million order for 66 General Electric-built ignitron rectifier locomotives of 4,400 horsepower each. To produce the PRR model without costly custom designing, GE simply upgraded specifications of its 1956-vintage 3300 horsepower rectifiers built for Virginian Railway. Delivery of the new PRR E44's began in October of 1960 with locomotive number 4,400, and it'll probably be sometime in 1963 before the final unit—4465—hums into service.

Each E44 unit has twelve ignitron type rectifier tubes which convert alternating current to direct current for use in six GE 752-E5 D.C. traction motors. One 733 horsepower motor is geared to each axle with a ratio of 20 to 63. Continuous horsepower rating of 4,400, and 55,500 lbs. tractive effort are available at all speeds between 33 and 55 miles per hour. Top speed is 70 MPH. The 69½-foot long road-switcher style electrics have dynamic brakes, roller bearings on all axles, and, like all PRR pantographed power, are equipped with dual operating controls and M-U jumpers at both ends.

Rectifier type locomotives with diesel-interchangeable traction motors represent a major technological achievement, but the ignitron tubes don't seem to be the ultimate answer. These tubes must be water cooled, placing the liquid very close to high voltage areas. This involves some difficulties aboard moving locomotives with attendant vibrations. An electrical manufacturer is currently working to perfect a new tubeless type of rectifier which requires no cooling water. This would revolutionize the rectifier.

It's an accepted fact that electrification is the cheapest method for any railroad to handle high density traffic, but initial construction costs have seemed to balk catenary expansion. John W. Barriger, President of P&LE, has suggested that electric utility companies might be interested in erecting the overhead wire systems and selling power to railroads through meters on locomotives. Looking into the future and making a completely unofficial prognostication, it would seem that this might be PRR's answer toward realization of a long-proposed dream to push catenary westward across the Alleghenies to Pittsburgh.

Such a project might have other benefits. If and when the new tubeless rectifier becomes available, such equipment could be dropped into existing diesel bodies, in place of the diesel engines and generators. Diesel traction motors would remain intact. And, a further improvement can be made in trolley wire power distribution and low efficiency by changing to 60-cycle current in place of today's (less satisfactory) 25-cycle type. With interesting possibilities like these, who can tell what might develop someday in the future?

We quote from an official Company announcement, "In May, 1958, The Pennsylvania R.R. initiated three independent studies to evaluate the economic advantages and disadvantages of diesel-electric vs. electric locomotives in the electric territory. Completed in 1959, they unequivocally proclaimed the superiority of the electrification."

This independent endorsement of electric meant the purchase of P5a replacement equipment. We see it here in the E44, the latest bit of Pennsy Power.

Pennsylvania Railroad

Pennsylvania Railroad

CALENDAR PAINTINGS

The Pennsylvania issued its first large picture calendar in 1925. The same painting was used in 1926, but thereafter we had an unbroken line of drama extending to 1958.

All the originals were oil paintings, some as large as 7' wide. They portray not just the motive power, but the spirit of the railroad as well.

Some contain specific Pennsy scenes, some general; in either case we have resisted the temptation to include explanatory captions. Appreciate each as a work of art that reflects its era.

We thank the Pennsylvania Railroad for their permission to reproduce them here.

SPEED AND SECURITY

1925

AND

1926

Harold Brett

THE BROADWAY LIMITED OPERATING THROUGH THE STEEL DISTRICT

1927

Harold Brett

WHEN THE BROADWAY MEETS THE DAWN

1928

Grif Teller

HARNESSING THE PLANE TO THE IRON HORSE

1929

Grif Teller

1930

SERVANT TO THE NATION'S INDUSTRY

Grif Teller

GIANT CONQUERORS OF SPACE AND TIME

1931

1932

ON TIME

Grif Teller

SPIRIT OF AMERICA

1933

1934

THE NEW DAY

Grif Teller

HORSESHOE CURVE

1935

1936

SPEED—SAFETY—COMFORT

Grif Teller

READY TO GO!

1937

1938

Grif Teller

MAIN LINE OF AMERICAN COMMERCE

LEADERS OF THE FLEET OF MODERNISM

1939

Grif Teller

1940

Grif Teller

SERVING THE NATION

THE STEEL KING

1941

Grif Teller

1942

Grif Teller

PARTNERS IN NATIONAL DEFENSE

SERVING THE NATION

1943

Dean Cornwell

312

1944

Dean Cornwell

FORWARD

POWER

1945

A. Leydenfrost

313

1946

Frank Reilly

1846–1946

Grif Teller **WORKING PARTNERS**

1947

1948

PROGRESSIVE POWER

Grif Teller

MAIN LINE, FREIGHT AND PASSENGER

1949

1950

CROSSROADS OF COMMERCE

Grif Teller

1951

MAIN LINE OF COMMERCE

Grif Teller

1952

HORSESHOE CURVE

Grif Teller

1953

CROSSROADS OF COMMERCE

Grif Teller

1954

PITTSBURGH PROMOTES PROGRESS

Grif Teller

1955

MASS TRANSPORTATION

Grif Teller

1956

DYNAMIC PROGRESS

Grif Teller

1957

VITAL LINK TO WORLD TRADE

Grif Teller

1958

CONWAY YARD

Grif Teller

In the preparation of this Volume, I am beholden to many; so many that I can at best, call myself co-author. Bert Pennypacker (text writer) and Martin Flattley (research) each gave a year of their lives. Both lived and were raised in the heart of "Pennsy Country" — Greater Philadelphia. Stated honestly, without them, PENNSY POWER could not have been.

The Pennsylvania Railroad gave me their whole-hearted support and cooperation. A glance at the picture credit lines reveals the depth and completeness of this help. In addition to the loan of thousands of irreplacable photographs, they responded immediately with any historical or technical data available. Those whom I met and worked with personally were: L.E. Gingerich, Chief Mechanical Officer; J. K. Murphy, Director of Public Relations; Ralph Timbers and Randy Dunlap of the Public Relations Dept.; and, the man who received the blunt of my onslaught, Hugh Devlin of the Motive Power Dept. There were others that I could not meet or ever know, but to all from the Pennsy, I offer a sincere and humble — THANK YOU!

We are also privileged in seeing the Pennsy through the eyes of the fans. Some entrusted me with their entire negative collections. I'd like to extend a personal thanks to: Milton A. Davis, C. W. Burns, Jim Saughnessy, Bert Pennypacker, Martin Flattley, Dr. Philip Hastings, Don Wood, A. W. Johnson, Si Herring, Bob Lorenz, Bill Jernstrom, Ed May, Bud Rothaar, H. Reid, John M. Prophet III and Jack Pearson

A very special word must go to Bud Rothaar and Bob Lorenz; Bud for his days collecting personal antidotes from train crews and Bob for handling the mound of photographic work involved in a volume of this size.

Loren D. Butts did a superb job with the complex Belpaire Boiler plans.

John H. White Jr., Curator of Land Transportation, Smithsonian Institution was most cooperative and congenial.

Behind the project, waiting with financial assistance when needed, was my lifelong friend, James Kroupa.

I have traveled extensively and met many people and I must say that this has been the most pleasant labor of my life. I am thankful to the powers to be, that we were able to produce PENNSY POWER when we did, for the shadow is dimming on "THE GREAT STEAM FLEET."

Yours truly handled all layout, production, organization, picture selection, caption writing and art work.

Sincerely,

Alvin F. Stauffer

Smithsonian Institute

Pennsylvania Railroad

Al. Staufer